19631

Peace with Honor?

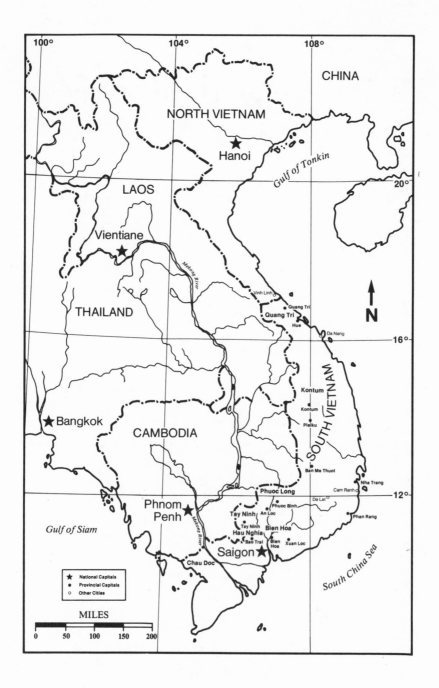

100°   104°   108°

CHINA

NORTH VIETNAM

★ Hanoi

Gulf of Tonkin

LAOS

20°

★ Vientiane

Mekong River

THAILAND

Vinh Linh

Quang Tri
Quang Tri

Hue

16°

Da Nang

Kontum

Kontum

★ Bangkok

CAMBODIA

Pleiku

SOUTH VIETNAM

Ban Me Thuot

Nha Trang

Phuoc Long

Cam Ranh

Da Lat

12°

Phnom
Penh ★

Mekong River

Phuoc Binh

Tay Ninh

An Loc

Phan Rang

Tay Ninh

Bien Hoa

Hau Nghia

Bao Trai

Bien
Hoa

Xuan Loc

Gulf of Siam

Saigon ★

Chau Doc

South China Sea

★ National Capitals
● Provincial Capitals
○ Other Cities

MILES

0   50   100   150   200

N

Peace with Honor?

An American Reports on Vietnam
1973–1975

LTC Stuart A. Herrington

PRESIDIO

TO THUAN, KIM, LYNN,
AND THOMAS

Library of Congress Cataloging in Publication Data

Herrington, Stuart A., 1941–
  Peace with honor?

  Sequel to: Silence was a weapon.
  Includes index.
  1. Vietnamese Conflict, 1961–1975, Personal narra-
tives, American.   2. Vietnamese Conflict, 1961–1975 —
Vietnam — Saigon.   3. Herrington, Stuart A., 1941–
I. Title
DS559.5.H48   1983   959.704'3   83-10908
ISBN 0-89141-182-8

Jacket design by Jill Losson
Book design by Lyn Cordell
Composition by Helen Epperson
Production by Lynn Dwyer
Printed in the United States of America

Contents

PREFACE

In an earlier work, *Silence Was a Weapon,* * I recounted my experiences as an intelligence advisor to the South Vietnamese territorial forces during 1971 and 1972. This is the sequel to that book. It is a highly personalized account of life in Saigon during South Vietnam's so-called decent interval from 1973 to 1975. The story is not pleasant, ending as it does when a North Vietnamese tank crashed through the wrought-iron gates of Independence Palace and Saigon became officially known as "Ho Chi Minh City." Taken together, the two volumes should contribute to an understanding of why our well-intentioned efforts in Vietnam ended with Ambassador Graham Martin's ignominious departure from Saigon in an evacuation helicopter. *Silence Was a Weapon* dealt with the difficulties we encountered in attempting to comprehend our Communist adversary. This volume addresses that problem as well as another, perhaps more serious, shortcoming: the overall failure of Americans to understand our South Vietnamese ally.

I am indebted to MG Edward G. Lansdale for his support; to Col. Harry G. Summers, Jr., of the U.S. Army War College; to Col. Thomas Fabyanic (Ret.), formerly of the Air War College; and to Col. Tom Jones, U.S. Army (Ret.), all of whom read the

---

Silence Was a Weapon: The Vietnam War in the Villages (Novato, CA: Presidio Press, 1982).

manuscript and offered sound advice. MG John E. Murray
(Ret.) and MG Homer D. Smith (Ret.) also patiently reviewed a
ponderous draft of the manuscript and provided invaluable
feedback on both style and content.

I would also like to acknowledge the assistance of Jerry
Jablonski, Ron Radda, Louise Le Tendre, Tony Lawson, Bill
Laurie, and Mr. J. C. Smith. Finally, no work can be its best
without an objective editor, and I was fortunate to have two:
Adele Horwitz at Presidio Press, and my wife, Thuan.

Heidelberg, Germany   Stuart A. Herrington
                                           March 1983

Part I

RETURN TO VIETNAM

THE RICE OF THE U.S. NAVY

April 30, 1975, on board the U.S.S. *Okinawa* in the South China Sea:

It couldn't possibly happen, but it did. The "Unthinkable." The North Vietnamese Army had just kicked us out of South Vietnam. Repeatedly bloodied and defeated by American fighting men from 1965 to 1972, Hanoi's divisions had just swept aside the South Vietnamese Army in a seven-week blitzkrieg. In a humiliation far greater than that suffered by the French, the members of the American diplomatic and military community had been forced to flee Saigon aboard carrier-based helicopters. The American Ambassador had escaped from his Embassy's rooftop in a marine helicopter, scant hours before a column of Communist tanks clanked by on their way to raise their banner over "liberated Saigon."

After a panic-filled night spent pumping refugees out of the U.S. Embassy onto the lumbering helicopters of "Task Force 75," I sat exhausted among the human debris of my country's bankrupt policy. The belly of the carrier *Okinawa* was pregnant with hundreds of stunned Vietnamese, many of whom shared the vessel's sick bay with me. The navy had billeted us there until arrangements could be made to transfer the Vietnamese to

1

transport vessels that would ferry them to Guam. I recognized some of the Vietnamese, people whom only hours earlier we had rushed onto evacuation helicopters in the crowded Embassy parking lot.

The cramped compartment afforded no privacy. On one side of me, a Vietnamese woman nursed her child. Across the bay sat a gaggle of Vietnamese adults and children, spellbound by their first look at color television on the ship's closed-circuit system.

The public address system crackled, "Ladies and gentlemen, this is Captain Moore speaking. I would like to welcome you aboard the U.S.S. *Okinawa* and assure you that my crew and I will do everything possible under the circumstances. I'm sorry for the cramped accommodations, but we will do our best to take care of you."

A hastily recruited interpreter assisted the captain, who continued, "Ladies and gentlemen, we have just received word that the North Vietnamese have entered Saigon. President Minh has broadcast an appeal to all Republic of Vietnam armed forces to lay down their arms. I am sorry to bring you this bad news, but I feel you want to keep track of events as they occur. We will keep you posted of any further developments." Few of the refugees understood the surrender bulletin. Then the interpreter spoke for a moment, telling everyone that the ordeal was finally over. Saigon had become Ho Chi Minh City.

The Vietnamese wept quietly. Some held one another, while others tearfully repeated the news to the elderly who hadn't comprehended the announcement. Almost all of them had lost immediate relatives in the panic and confusion of the last days. A middle-aged woman grabbed my arm. Her husband sat nearby on a bunk, sobbing uncontrollably.

"This is the second time the U.S. Navy has rescued us from the Communists," she began in a pronounced North Vietnamese accent. "In 1954, we were students in Hanoi. When the French withdrew and the Communists took over, an American ship took us from Haiphong to Saigon. We took nothing but the shirts on our backs. My husband and I worked as common laborers at first. We saved our money and put him through the university. He became a lawyer in Saigon. Now it's all lost. All we have is our clothes, and now we must again eat the rice of the U.S. Navy." She broke down as her husband held up an Air Vietnam shoulder bag—all that was left of twenty years of work. The sense of pathos and tragedy aboard the *Okinawa* that morning was overwhelming.

The ship's crew couldn't fathom the tension and chaos we had left behind in Saigon, yet they sensed the gravity of the events that had engulfed their floating home. All over the vessel, sailors performed their duties with subdued solemnity, as if they were intruders at a funeral.

I was in a bitter mood. A career army officer, I had just devoted nearly four years of my life to the South Vietnamese cause—four years that had ended abruptly on an Embassy roof as a participant in a humiliating retreat under fire. By 1975, I had learned to speak the language of the Vietnamese, to savor their unique cuisine, and to understand their dread of Ho Chi Minh's brand of Communism. As I tried to describe my departure from the Embassy to a persistent reporter, my mind was plagued with images of the Vietnamese we had left behind, of the years of suffering of the rural peasants, and of the American and Vietnamese lives that had been expended in vain pursuit of victory. As I spoke, tears of shame welled out of my eyes.

PEACE WAS AT HAND

San Francisco, August 1972:

Strange sensations swept over me after that first tour in Vietnam. Nothing seemed real as I rode along a California freeway in a plush, air-conditioned bus. To one accustomed to the sights and smells of crowded oriental cities, San Francisco seemed unusually clean and orderly. Its downtown streets appeared spacious and tranquil—the same streets that had seemed so alive and busy during a two-day fling I had enjoyed while awaiting the flight that would spirit me off to war. But that had been in January 1971, and I had spent the intervening months in a different world. Actually, San Francisco hadn't changed much; it just seemed that way. The asphalt and neon of urban

America was so different from the dust and dangers of rural
Vietnam or the chaotic clamor of Saigon that I was experiencing reentry problems. Thousands of GIs before me had
dubbed rotation to the States as a return to "the world." Now I
knew why.

As the bus neared the San Francisco airport, I watched the
California real estate flash by and marveled at how completely
the world could change in the space of a brief plane ride. In
Saigon, Americans lived a circumscribed existence. Life was a
montage of rationed gas, liquor, and tobacco; reconstituted
milk; frozen meats; a post exchange that specialized in out-of-
stocks; and the ever-present midnight curfew. Yet Saigon's hardships were luxuries compared to the conditions that confronted
Americans who served in rural Vietnam. In the "boondocks,"
hot water and air conditioning were virtually unknown, and the
forces of the revolution ruled the night. Curfew commenced at
dusk, and violations could be fatal. During that bus ride through
suburban San Francisco, it occurred to me that most of our
American poor lived better and enjoyed more creature comforts
than all but the wealthiest Vietnamese. Conditioned as I had
become to the uglier realities of life in wartime Vietnam, the
images of abundance and prosperity that flashed past as my bus
neared the airport caused me to reflect on how much Americans
take for granted. Vietnam had done wonders for my sense of
perspective. It was good to be home.

I had just served almost two years as an intelligence advisor
to the militia forces that were struggling against a deeply entrenched Communist insurgency in South Vietnam's Hau Nghia
province. Hau Nghia lay on the Cambodian border, directly
astride a traditional invasion corridor to Saigon and perilously
near a major enemy base area in the infamous "Parrot's Beak."
I had arrived in Vietnam in January 1971, fresh from Vietnamese language school, anxious to tackle the formidable task of
tracking down and eliminating the Vietcong "shadow government." Hau Nghia duty had exposed me to the subtleties of
guerrilla warfare during 1971, then to the stark reality of full-
scale conventional combat during the 1972 North Vietnamese
Easter Offensive. By the time I left Hau Nghia province in

August 1972, the Communist offensive had stalled, and the last American combat unit had departed Vietnam. Only forty thousand American advisors and technicians remained in the country, men who were serving as unwitting bargaining tools in the Paris peace talks then in progress between Henry Kissinger and North Vietnam's Le Duc Tho.

Readjusting to the comforts of American society was easy, but terminating my involvement with the Vietnamese cause proved more difficult. I struggled to keep abreast of developments in Vietnam, combing the newspapers for references to the war in Hau Nghia province. But the war had apparently ceased to be newsworthy. Coverage of the continuing struggle between General Giap's units and the South Vietnamese was sparse, as media attention shifted to the Paris talks and the impending presidential election. Presidential candidate George McGovern was accusing President Nixon of dragging his feet in the search for peace, claiming that the President was more concerned with South Vietnamese President Nguyen van Thieu's political survival than he was with the fate of American prisoners of war. Fresh from a controversial trip to Hanoi, former Attorney General Ramsey Clark echoed Hanoi's accusation that American bombing was killing innocent Vietnamese civilians. Clark was telling anyone who would listen that an election victory by Senator McGovern would induce Hanoi to release its American prisoners.

As a staunch believer in the rectitude of South Vietnam's struggle against Hanoi's Communism, I bristled at the lack of American concern for what had been the basis of my existence for so long. The Vietnam War had been suddenly reduced to a single issue—get our prisoners home. I was contemptuous of the Ramsey Clarks and Jane Fondas who could condemn and misrepresent the actions of our air force, yet conveniently ignore Hanoi's destructive attacks against South Vietnam's populated areas in 1968 and 1972. American disenchantment with the war in Vietnam seemed greater than the disenchantment of the Vietnamese themselves. Outside of the military, I found few Americans who felt that the United States owed anything to the South Vietnamese people. The war had simply dragged on too long and engendered too much bitterness and misunderstanding. "Vietnam" had become an ugly word.

I signed in at Fort Huachuca in the Arizona mountains for a nine-month course at the U.S. Army Intelligence Center and School. My class consisted of sixty officers, brought together to study the nuances of the intelligence profession in preparation for higher-level assignments. During the year, I found time to serve as an escort officer for a group of Vietnamese intelligence officers who were enrolled in the foreign officers' course. Like me, their attention was focused on decisive events that were unfolding in Paris and Saigon as 1972 drew to a close and Henry Kissinger strove to finalize the terms of a cease-fire settlement. When the Paris talks stalled on the threshold of agreement, President Nixon confounded the North Vietnamese by ordering B-52 raids against Hanoi and Haiphong, to the great satisfaction of Fort Huachuca's small Vietnamese community. North Vietnam, still recovering from the sacrifices of the Easter Offensive, was again learning the hard way that Richard Nixon was willing to strike where his predecessors had feared to tread.

By January 1973, Hanoi's shaken leaders sent their negotiators back to the conference table to conclude the agreement. At Fort Huachuca, we anxiously awaited details of the terms that President Nixon told the American people would bring "peace with honor" to Vietnam.* We knew that South Vietnamese President Thieu had stubbornly opposed the proposed settlement, for the American media had given ample coverage to Washington's determined efforts to persuade its independent ally to sign. When the terms of the agreement were finally made public, one could understand why Thieu had balked and why Hanoi could easily claim a diplomatic victory. In exchange for the repatriation of all American prisoners, the United States had agreed to a total military withdrawal within sixty days of a cease-fire. Despite the strenuous objections of President Thieu, the agreement tacitly permitted Hanoi's troops to remain in South Vietnam. This fact caused one Vietnamese officer at Fort

---

*From a televised report to the nation on 24 January 1973. See *New York Times*, 24 January 1973, p. 1.

Huachuca to state bluntly, "Dai Uy,* your country has just sacrificed a loyal ally. This treaty is the end of South Vietnam." Not all of the Vietnamese at Fort Huachuca were this skeptical, but all of them regarded the Paris Agreement to be deeply flawed since it did not require Hanoi to withdraw its forces to North Vietnam. As one Vietnamese officer told me, "Your president has forced South Vietnam to sign the Paris Agreement because he promised peace to the American people. America will soon have her soldiers and prisoners at home, but there will be no peace for South Vietnam as long as the North Vietnamese Army occupies our land."

I tried unsuccessfully to allay their fears. After all, had not President Nixon personally reaffirmed America's continued support for South Vietnam? And had the President not consistently demonstrated his readiness to employ American military power in South Vietnam's defense? Our air force in nearby Thailand and our naval forces in the South China Sea were ready to react if Hanoi failed to respect the terms of the agreement. Finally, in an effort to bolster South Vietnamese confidence, the United States had shipped large quantities of planes, tanks, and other weapons systems to Saigon before the signing of the agreement.*

Privately, I shared the fears of my Vietnamese colleagues. Americans were fed up with Vietnam, and it was becoming increasingly doubtful that President Nixon would be able to reintervene militarily anywhere in Southeast Asia once we had closed the door on this frustrating chapter of our military history. Still, the President was not one to shrink from difficult and unpopular decisions, and his recent reelection to a term that would extend until 1976 seemed to insure that Saigon had a

*Dai Uy: Pronounced "Die Wee." Vietnamese for "Captain."
*The best account of the pressure that Washington exerted on President Thieu to obtain his support of the Paris Agreement appears in Henry Kissinger's The White House Years (NY: Little, Brown & Co., 1979). Thieu agreed to sign only when faced with the prospect of a total cutoff of American aid. South Vietnam signed, but Thieu made certain that his people knew that he had done so under duress and that he regarded the terms of the treaty to be dangerously one-sided.

committed friend in the White House for some time. It was also true that the South Vietnamese Army had matured considerably on the battlefield by 1973, and that Saigon's air force boasted a formidable array of aircraft and American-trained pilots. Not only that, but Hanoi's army had been badly mauled during 1972 and the time required to rebuild would give Saigon a breather.

But these arguments were not convincing to the South Vietnamese, whose reservations were typified by the words of one officer who felt compelled to remind me of the history of the war:

Dai Uy, you know enough about the motivation and tactics of the Communists to know that they will use this agreement precisely as they used their own self-declared cease-fire in 1968 to mask preparations for the Tet Offensive. This agreement gives them a rest when they need it the most, and it puts an end to American involvement. Now the Communists can say that they tried the path of peace when they launch their next offensive. We understand why President Nixon desired an agreement. We just don't understand why he was in such a hurry. Now we must deal with thirteen North Vietnamese divisions that are occupying our territory, and they are backed by the Chinese and the Russians.

By the time I graduated from Fort Huachuca, Washington had declared me to be a Southeast Asian specialist, an honor that came with orders to report to the Defense Attaché Office in Saigon. I reassured my worried parents that this assignment would be safe and cushy compared to Hau Nghia province. After all, the war was over. What could possibly happen to me in cease-fire Saigon? At the time, I had no way of knowing that I would soon be forced to reappraise this optimistic view of life in Saigon, courtesy of the North Vietnamese Army.

SAIGON, 1973: "LONG TIME NO SEE, DAI UY"

"Could this really be Vietnam?" I thought as I surveyed my new home. Teakwood furniture, air conditioning, a private bath with hot water, and a swimming pool directly outside the door.

Drinks at the bamboo poolside bar, I soon discovered, were thirty cents. Across the courtyard was the billet's modern restaurant and nightclub, both staffed by a bevy of black-tressed hostesses. So this was life in Saigon! No wonder we had contemptuously dubbed the Saigon garrison "REMFs" during the war.*

I had just arrived on a sweltering August day aboard a commercial charter flight, complete with drinks and a movie—a definite change from the tension-filled flight I had shared with two hundred GIs during the war. Then, I was a career officer who had orders to 'Nam and no choice but to comply. This time around, I had volunteered to return to Vietnam, the result of my involvement with the Vietnamese and their cause in Hau Nghia province. I had convinced my assignments officer in Washington that I belonged in Southeast Asia after he had tried to convince me that I had already punched that ticket and should pursue a command position in the States. Anyone who would voluntarily return to Vietnam twelve months after leaving that hellhole must have been crazy. Crazy or not, my persistence had paid off, and there I was, sipping gin and tonic, poolside at Saigon's BOQ #1.

To get my first look at cease-fire Saigon, I hailed a cab. Two cruising blue and yellow heaps almost collided as they swerved recklessly to pick me up. An American fare in Saigon had become a rare and sought-after economic opportunity. Cabdrivers in the overcrowded city competed fiercely for the reduced number of American customers, who usually paid double or triple the normal fare.

My driver, a wrinkled old fellow with a mouthful of gold teeth, smiled broadly as he executed a harrowing U-turn and aimed his ancient Renault for Saigon. *"Dai Uy, lau qua khong gap Dai Uy,"* he beamed. ("Captain, long time no see, Captain.") *"Co phai nguoi My sap tro qua Vietnam khong?"* ("Is it true that the Americans are about to come back to Vietnam?")

The old man was a Saigonese with a heavy southern accent. In one of the colloquialisms of his language, he was telling me

*"Rear Echelon Mother Fuckers."

that he hadn't seen a uniformed American captain in a long time. His words and animated tone of voice told me that he regarded me as "a sight for sore eyes." As he negotiated the traffic on Cong Ly Street, I heard the first of many reports on the economic ills of cease-fire Saigon. "From the day the Americans left, Dai Uy," he complained, "the economic situation has gotten worse and worse. Business is dead, Dai Uy, and no one has the money to take the taxi anymore. The people say that the Americans are coming back, Dai Uy. Is this true?"

I tried gamely to reassure my anxious questioner. Some Americans would remain in Saigon, but South Vietnam no longer needed large American military forces. The old man's face betrayed no reaction when I refuted the latest rumor. He continued to smile, but I had long since learned that the Vietnamese smile often meant something other than happiness.*

Outside the Eden Arcade on Tu Do Street, I paid the standard Vietnamese fare of 150 piasters and extricated myself from the the cramped backseat of the tiny vehicle. I could have given him the 500 piasters customarily paid by Americans and thereby earned an obsequious expression of gratitude, the Asian smile, and his total disrespect. Such generosity would have permitted him to tell his friends how the rich and foolish American had paid 500 piasters for a 150-piaster ride, further proof of Vietnamese superiority over Americans. By paying him the Vietnamese fare, I would be remembered as "cheap," but I preferred this to being thought of as foolish. Most Americans didn't have to worry about such choices. Blissfully ignorant of the Vietnamese way, they paid their 500 piasters and basked in the conviction that the smiles of the Saigonese indicated appreciation of American generosity. The "Bwana Syndrome." All they needed to complete the image was the white pith helmet.

I shouldn't have worn my uniform on that foray into downtown Saigon. The sight of an American Army captain strolling

---

*The Military Assistance Command, Vietnam (MACV), closed its doors, and the last American military man departed Saigon in late March 1973. The Americans took with them a healthy chunk of the total cash flow of South Vietnam. The Vietnamese never recovered from the economic vacuum created by our abrupt departure.

down the street generated an electric response from the side-walk salesmen, the cyclo-drivers, and other peddlers who made the streets of the capital a teeming mass of humanity. The reaction was the same everywhere I walked.

"Dai Uy! Dai Uy! Long time no see, Dai Uy!"

"Hey, Captain, where you been?"

As I passed the stalls offering postcards, old coins (mostly fake), and cheap oil paintings for sale, I could understand the reactions of Saigon's sidewalk society as the people caught sight of me: *"Troi Oi! Lau qua khong gap ong nay!"* ("Dear God! Long time I haven't seen the likes of him!") And, after I responded to several of them in their language, a trio of street urchins, called *"Bui Doi"* ("Dust of Life") by the Saigonese, preceded me everywhere, trumpeting the news that the American captain could speak Vietnamese. Like the troubled old taxi driver, the downtown crowd wanted to hear the good news— the Americans were coming back!

Downtown Saigon hadn't changed much. The multicolored flower stalls of Nguyen Hue Boulevard were as stunning as ever, and the streets were still haunted by a squad of predatory Polaroid photographers who pestered passersby into having souvenir pictures taken. Scarlet government propaganda banners still festooned the walls of public buildings and monuments. Only the themes had changed. A year ago, the signs had extolled the "Heroes of An Loc" and the "Defenders of Quang Tri." Now, on a pedestrian barrier outside the Ben Thanh Market, a large banner proclaimed: "The entire Vietnamese people condemn the North Vietnamese Communist clique for sabotaging the peace." Farther down the street, a long red and white banner hanging outside the old Rex Theater warned: "If the native soil is still in the hands of the Republic, then we have everything. But allow the native soil to be lost into the hands of the Communists, and we have lost everything!"

Crowds of shoppers spilled off the sidewalks into the streets, and my veteran eyes observed that Saigon's women were still the most beautiful and graceful in all Asia. Clad in brightly colored *ao dai* dresses, they walked with a grace and self-assurance that no American could fail to notice. Perched in pairs on

Downtown Saigon: Signs reads "If native soil still belongs to the Republic, then we have everything; allow it to fall into Communist hands, and we have lost everything."

their small Honda motorcycles, the raven-haired girls of Saigon wound their way through traffic, their oversized sunglasses and trailing skirts a striking blend of East and West.

But something was missing from Saigon's bustling streets. It was the military traffic—the hundreds of jeeps and trucks that had clogged the streets, belching forth exhaust fumes and hogging the road as if Saigon were a military base where civilians were only tolerated. During the war, the olive drab fleet of the American and South Vietnamese military had been as much a part of Saigon as the cyclo-drivers and the dilapidated taxis. At least the cease-fire had wrought one improvement. The roar of the traffic and the omnipresent blue haze that had hung over Saigon seemed to have diminished in the twelve months since my last visit. Maybe there was hope for Saigon yet. The French had designed the city to accommodate six hundred thousand citizens, but it had swollen to almost six times that number by the end of the war. Now, with a cease-fire of sorts, there had been hope that some of the millions of peasants who had fled to Saigon to escape the war could return to their rural lands. So far, however, the cease-fire had not taken hold in the country-side, and Saigon remained a refuge for tens of thousands of dispossessed rice farmers and their families.

I sought shelter from the oppressive heat on the veranda of the Continental Palace Hotel, a venerable white stucco structure where Saigon's remaining French residents still congregated for a drink in the late afternoon. Sipping a "33" beer, I fended off the inevitable procession of hustlers and hucksters? Would the captain like to buy silk-screen Christmas cards? How about lacquerware, oil paintings, or perhaps some risqué photographs? Does the captain desire female companionship? The street urchins expressed this as "go boom-boom," while the more couth, miniskirted working girls merely suggested, "We go to my apartment and have fun, yes?"

Once the word got out that the captain was interested only in drinking his beer, the procession of commercial visitors ended. Next came the curious and the hopeful. People stopped at my sidewalk table to inquire if I was the vanguard of a new flow of Americans. Others paused merely to tell me of an American friend or a relative in California or Kentucky. As one South Vietnamese Air Force lieutenant told me of his training in Texas, others lingered by the table to eavesdrop. The Saigonese were entranced by the opportunity to talk to an American in their own language and clearly entertained by my American accent. It seemed that almost all of them had heard the rumor that the American military was about to return to Vietnam.

While serving in Hau Nghia province, I had become sensitive to a paradoxical feature of the Vietnamese psyche. On the one hand, the Vietnamese could never develop a genuine fondness for Americans, for we were Westerners, a fact that precluded a true communion of spirits. But, on the other hand, the Vietnamese in Hau Nghia exhibited a deep-seated psychological need for the physical presence of uniformed Americans. In Saigon, I sensed that this insecurity had escalated since my departure. It was as if the Saigonese needed to hear someone say, "You aren't alone in this thing. We are with you." American-built F-5

fighters or M-113 armored personnel carriers could not provide this reassurance, no matter how tangible and useful they
might be. The Vietnamese psyche demanded reassurance in the
familiar sight of the tall GI in jungle fatigues. Thus, while it was
true that we Americans belonged to that culturally deprived
group called *nguoi Tay* (Westerners), the pragmatic Vietnamese
knew that the military/political realities of 1973 demanded the
American presence. Since I symbolized what was needed at the
time, the Saigonese were according me a warm welcome. Knowing that my greeters expected reassurances from me that I simply couldn't provide, I soon became uncomfortable with my
celebrity status. It would not be the last time during the cease-
fire that I would feel uncomfortable around the Vietnamese.

PENTAGON EAST

I was assigned to the Defense Attaché Office (DAO), an organization spawned by the Paris Agreement that made its home in
the former "Pentagon East," the modern, sprawling complex
that had housed MACV Headquarters during the war. As I
passed through the main gate for my first day's work, nostalgia
beckoned. During the war, I had once conducted a uniformed
North Vietnamese prisoner unchallenged through this same gate
on our way to an interview with an American general officer.
That memorable day had taken place a mere fourteen months
earlier, but the events that had transpired in the interim had
fundamentally altered history. Now, with the MACV colors
furled and deposited in some stateside museum, I braced myself
for the arctic blast of air conditioning that I recalled from that
visit and strode through the thick glass doors.

The familiar display of the flags of the nations that had
assisted South Vietnam during the war remained in the foyer,
but the starched military policeman who manned the reception
desk was missing. In his place was an attractive Vietnamese
woman in an emerald green *ao dai*. In the building's labyrinth
complex of corridors, the khaki-clad legions of staff officers had
been replaced by hundreds of American and Vietnamese civilians. Hosts of graceful Vietnamese secretaries glided from office

Pentagon East.

to office as they moved the paperwork generated by all large headquarters. The DAO looked like a bachelor's paradise.

At an introductory briefing, I learned about the organization and functions of the Defense Attaché Office. The DAO was a creature of the U.S. Embassy, with responsibility for administering the American military assistance program to the South Vietnamese. For this reason, the entire operation was heavily staffed with supply and budgetary specialists. Our boss, the Defense Attaché, was MG John E. Murray, a logistician with a transportation corps background. The general's complement of fifty military men consisted of officers representing all services and was functionally organized into Army, Navy, and Air Force materiel divisions. These were the men and women who worked closely with the South Vietnamese general staff to coordinate American military aid programs in support of Saigon's hard-pressed armed forces. In the performance of this mission, General Murray was answerable to his military superiors in the chain of command. But, because the DAO had to function in the delicate political environment of cease-fire Saigon, the general also had to work closely with and for Ambassador Graham Martin, a silver-haired veteran diplomat and aristocrat who preferred to be introduced as "the personal representative of the President of the United States," lest anyone forget.

Because the cease-fire had not yet brought an end to the fight-

ing, the DAO organization chart also included a sizable Intelligence Branch. In addition to a number of civilians engaged in
liaison duties with Vietnamese intelligence, a small Current
Intelligence Section worked overtime to keep abreast of the fluid
military situation. During a regular morning ritual known as
the "walk-through," a team of civilian operations and intelligence analysts briefed General Murray on the continuing hostilities. As the Executive Officer of the DAO's Special Security
Office, I was a part of this intelligence organization. Among my
varied duties was the enforcement of a travel restriction that
prevented certain members of the DAO (myself included) from
leaving the Saigon area.

It was good to be back in Vietnam. A military intelligence
officer with an interest in Southeast Asian affairs could not have
been better placed to observe the give-and-take between the
Washington policymakers and the executors of that policy in
Saigon. But the revelation that I was not permitted to travel outside the city limits of Saigon was a big disappointment. The
basis for this restriction was security. Because the in-place
cease-fire had resulted in a patchwork juxtaposition of government and Communist-controlled areas (often called the "leop-
ard spot configuration"), anyone traveling the length and
breadth of the country risked an unexpected encounter with
hostile forces. This had already occurred shortly after the cease-
fire when an unlucky American civilian contractor drove his
pickup truck directly into a Communist roadblock on a highway in the Mekong Delta. Vietcong troops had riddled his
vehicle with automatic weapons fire and taken him into cus-
tody. My travel was restricted because I had access to sensitive
information and could not be allowed to fall into Communist
hands. I appreciated the sentiment, but how was I to visit
friends from my former tour in Hau Nghia province? I wasn't
even allowed to visit neighboring Bien Hoa province, which
would prevent me from contacting a number of acquaintances
at the Vietnamese Corps Interrogation Center. Unless I could
get it relaxed, the travel restriction would effectively cut me off
from the many contacts I had developed in the Vietnamese
intelligence community. I made my first entry on my "Things

to Do" list; the travel restriction was a prime candidate for
early attention.

I also learned during my introductory briefing that I was
about to lose my new job. Since his organization was limited to
only fifty military members, General Murray had decided to
convert the military positions in the Special Security Office to
civilian slots. This would permit him to assign several additional, badly needed logistics officers to his overworked staff.
The target date for the conversion was January 1974. Unless I
could locate another job in Saigon by then, I would be re-
assigned to another location in Asia for the remainder of my
tour.

I thus found myself scouting for a new job within a week of
my arrival in Saigon, for I had no desire to transfer to Thailand
or Korea. But the task seemed hopeless. There was no room in
Col. William LeGro's Intelligence Branch for me. Only three
intelligence officers worked for the colonel, all of whom were
lieutenant colonels. All others engaged in intelligence work were
civilians. There was simply no job in the rank-heavy Defense
Attaché Office for a junior intelligence officer, regardless of his
qualifications.

But luck was on my side. When a friend tipped me off that the
U.S. delegation of the Four-Party Joint Military Team (JMT)
was looking for an officer with a background in Southeast Asian
affairs, I jumped at what was undoubtedly my last opportunity
to stay in Vietnam. The Joint Military Team had been established by the Paris Agreement and charged with responsibility
for the conduct of negotiations on the missing-in-action (MIA)
question. My contact depicted duty with the JMT as frustrating,
but highlighted by the opportunity to make regular flights to
Hanoi. That was all I needed to hear. During my duty in Hau
Nghia province, I had only been able to see the Communist side
of the war through the eyes of prisoners and defectors. Service
with the JMT would enable me to meet our adversary on his
own turf.

A few days later, I sat across a desk from Col. Bill Tombaugh,
the square-jawed, crew-cutted infantry officer who was the
Chief of the U.S. delegation. In a brief interview during which I

said very little, the loquacious Colonel Tombaugh impressed
upon me the seriousness of America's obligation to the families
of the missing and the dead, as well as the need for dedicated
professionals to carry out this duty. Later, I learned that I had
passed muster and would be assigned as a liaison officer to the
Communist delegations that were living under diplomatic
immunity in Saigon as part of the cease-fire accords. I had
found a job, and a good one at that. I began to count the days
until my security position was civilianized.

Part II

LIFE UNDER THE PARIS AGREEMENT

NO WAR, NO PEACE

The broad-faced, smiling man who sat across the table from me wore the dark green fatigues of the South Vietnamese Army. A single gold bar and pip on his collar tabs proclaimed him to be a major. No insignia advertised the fact that Major Hoang Manh Sang was the Chief of the Military Security Service (MSS) in Hau Nghia province, or that he and his operatives were responsible for a myriad of intelligence operations against the Communists. Among Sang's responsibilities were the detection of Vietcong penetration agents in the South Vietnamese military and the recruitment of agents to infiltrate the Communist "shadow government" that ruled much of the countryside. In both areas, he was an unqualified success. During my tour in Hau Nghia, Sang's steady hand had guided his MSS office from one successful operation to another, earning for him a reputation as one of the most effective intelligence officers in Vietnam.

We were seated at a balcony table located discreetly in the rear of the Ngoc Huong Restaurant, a North Vietnamese establishment that Sang had always favored. My future in Saigon now assured, I had commenced my campaign to tap unofficial sources for an unvarnished view of military/political realities in

cease-fire Vietnam. A trusted friend, Sang would be as candid
with me as any Vietnamese could be with a Westerner. From
my experience in Hau Nghia province, I knew that the Americans frequently received incomplete information through official Vietnamese channels. In Hau Nghia, it had taken me
months to penetrate the smoke screen that surrounded the frail-
ties of our ally. Now, totally reliant on the press and on official
American/Vietnamese perceptions of reality, I was determined
to reestablish my own sources of information about life under
the terms of the Paris Agreement. As we shared a platter of suc-
culent *cha gio* and *com chien* (spring rolls and fried rice), Sang
filled me in on the military situation in Hau Nghia since my
departure twelve months earlier.

Because Hau Nghia was located astride the strategically
important western approach to Saigon, the North Vietnamese
had tried desperately to gain a foothold there just prior to the
anticipated cease-fire in October 1972. Determined to seize
territory astride Highway 1, a vital lifeline that linked Saigon to
the western provinces, North Vietnamese units had launched a
series of heavy attacks into government-controlled hamlets in
Trang Bang and Cu Chi districts. Regular North Vietnamese
units had conducted these attacks, but Hau Nghia's well-trained
militia forces had ejected the invaders at every point of intrusion. Sang shook his head as he recalled the high cost of these
operations. The thirty thousand civilian victims of the earlier
Spring Offensive had just been resettled when the new Communist attacks burst upon the province, creating fifteen thousand
new refugees virtually overnight. Still, the October fighting had
ended in a series of heavy setbacks for the Communists. According to Sang, enemy prisoners revealed that the North Vietnamese high command had expected the cease-fire to commence
at the end of October. Communist commanders had therefore
launched their bold, daylight assaults in the belief that the
cease-fire would protect them from South Vietnamese counter-
attacks. But it was not to be. When the negotiations unexpect-
edly stalled and the anticipated cease-fire failed to materialize,
the hapless Communist troops became victims of the politicians.
There had been no time for their commanders to get the word to

call off the last-minute land grab. The result, Sang gloated, had
been a catastrophe for the Communists. When the North Vietnamese abandoned their jungle sanctuaries and occupied the
hamlets along Highway 1, counterattacking South Vietnamese
forces decimated the exposed Communist light infantry. It was
a repetition of the disastrous Communist defeats during the
1972 Easter Offensive at the hands of Hau Nghia's militia
troops. In less than two weeks, more than five hundred North
Vietnamese regulars had died in Hau Nghia at the cost of less
than one hundred friendly lives.

But this setback had not deterred the determined Communists
from subsequent attempts to establish their presence in Hau
Nghia before the guns stilled. In November and again in December, Hanoi's rebuilt 271st Regiment had repeated its spring-
time incursions into the populated areas of Duc Hoa district,
only to be ejected once again by Hau Nghia's vaunted militia
troops. Sang recalled with obvious relish that frustrated local
Vietcong cadre had spent the last days before the cease-fire
obliterating the yellow and red government flags that were sten-
ciled on rural homes and destroying photographs of President
Thieu. When the cease-fire went into effect on 27 January 1973,
the outmaneuvered Communists were in control of no new territory in Hau Nghia province. With assistance from the diplomats
and only minimal help from the regular army, the Army of the
Republic of Vietnam (ARVN),* the Hau Nghia militia forces
had once again defeated the North Vietnamese.

Sang explained that Hau Nghia's war-weary soldiers and
civilians had initially welcomed the Paris Agreement, until
events dispelled the notion that the new political environment
would somehow cause the Communist soldiers to disappear.
Hau Nghia experienced only a brief lull in the fighting as the
battered Communist units withdrew to their base areas to

*ARVN refers to the thirteen divisions of the South Vietnamese Army, as dis-
tinct from the "Territorial Forces," or militia, which consisted of Regional
Forces (RF) companies and Popular Forces (PF) platoons. In general, the RF
and PF militia troops were more lightly armed than the regular ARVN, and
they operated in their native districts and provinces. American advisors
often referred to the RF/PF as the "Ruff-Puffs."

recover from the costly, last-minute jousting for position that had marked the final seventy-two hours of the war. The few who rallied and the prisoners who fell into South Vietnamese hands told of massive resupply efforts under way in the "liberated zones" and Cambodian sanctuaries. Convoys of Russian-supplied Molotova trucks were now transporting supplies and ammunition to the North Vietnamese Army, which was rebuilding with impunity under the protection of the cease-fire. As the Communists recovered, the level of hostilities in Hau Nghia escalated in spite of the cease-fire. Enemy units began to penetrate Hau Nghia's hamlets, their political officers exhorting the people to join the "political struggle" against the "puppet regime." Government troops reacted with spoiling operations and night ambushes. In Hau Nghia, it was clear, both sides were involved in wholesale violations of the cease-fire accords. Sang admitted that the morale of government forces had begun to drop as the "no war, no peace" bloodletting continued.

Strangely enough, Sang insisted that the decline in popular morale was caused primarily by the deteriorating economic situation. War and its incumbent violence was something that Hau Nghia's sturdy peasantry had long since learned to endure. But the sudden downturn of the economy was a more insidious enemy than the black-clad guerrillas and their North Vietnamese sponsors. Since the American withdrawal, the price of gasoline had jumped from 31 to 105 piasters a liter. The price of a bag of rice had also sharply risen. Everyone felt the squeeze, but the underpaid military suffered the greatest hardship. Sang confided that he received only twenty liters of gasoline a month for his government jeep. Anything he used above that inadequate ration had to come out of his own pocket.

To compound the problem, President Thieu had gone to elaborate lengths to blame conditions on the departed Americans. Thieu made no secret of the fact that he had resisted the terms of the Paris Agreement until Washington had all but forced him to sign it. Popular disillusionment in the face of the continued fighting and the sick economy was taking its toll. As belts were tightened, the underpaid military man's incentive to supplement his income by unethical practices increased. Corruption was on the ascent, illicit trade with the Communist-controlled "liberated zones" was flourishing, and an increasing number of people were laying the blame for the resulting mess at the feet of President Thieu.

On a brighter note, Sang announced that Hau Nghia had both a new province chief and a new national police commander. After a little more than a year as province chief, the contro- versial Colonel Hau had been transferred to another position under the shadow of suspicion involving missing provincial funds. His replacement, Colonel Soan, was a marine officer known for his honesty and aggressive leadership. Sang optimis- tically compared Soan with Colonel Thanh, a former Hau Nghia province chief who had been assassinated by the Com- munists in 1972. This was the highest praise. Hau Nghia's cor- rupt police chief, Colonel Ty, had finally been arrested after the American advisors exposed him for taking bribes to release Viet- cong suspects. Ty's replacement had already introduced long- overdue reforms in the national police organization and, in the process, had eliminated a major source of popular discontent with the government.

Sang conveyed greetings from Lanh, a North Vietnamese pris- oner whom he and I had convinced to cooperate with the gov- ernment in 1972. As a reward for his assistance in defeating the invading North Vietnamese, Lanh had been granted amnesty by the province chief. The former Communist infantryman had been drafted recently and was undergoing basic training, after which he would serve in the Hau Nghia militia forces. I felt a pang of guilt on hearing this news, recalling Lanh's determi- nation never to carry a weapon again. Perhaps he could accept his fate if the cease-fire could stop the fighting. But, if the con- flict continued to escalate, Do van Lanh would again find him- self stalking the mosquito-infested base areas along the Vam Co Dong River, his AK-47 assault rifle exchanged for an American- supplied M-16. Somehow, I felt responsible for whatever hap- pened to him.*

In Ho Nai, a suburb of Bien Hoa populated by North Vietna-

*Lanh's story is related in my book *Silence Was a Weapon.*

mese Catholics, I located Lieutenant Tuan, the former leader of
Hau Nghia's intelligence and reconnaissance platoon. As one of
my counterparts in 1972, Tuan had been a key actor in numerous intelligence operations that had helped repel an invasion by
three North Vietnamese regiments. Tuan had since been re-
assigned to Long Thanh district in Bien Hoa province. While his
round-faced, Hanoi-born wife served "33" beer and ice, we
reminisced about Hau Nghia briefly before Tuan turned to the
cease-fire.

Tuan's report was as pessimistic as Sang's. As in Hau Nghia,
there was no cease-fire in Long Thanh. Enemy military incursions into government-controlled areas were frequent; government and Communist casualties were exceeding pre-cease-fire
levels. Tuan was deeply discouraged as he lamented the poor
timing of the cease-fire accords. In his view, we had given the
Communists a badly needed rest, for which the South Vietnamese military would pay in blood eventually. President Thieu
would never agree to share political power with the Communists, and so another major Communist offensive was inevitable.

By now, this had become a familiar refrain. I eventually
spoke with dozens of Vietnamese officers, all of whom told the
same story, and all of whom were unanimous on one point—the
Paris Agreement contained the seeds of an inevitable return to a
major military confrontation on the scale of the 1972 offensive.
It was an article of faith that Hanoi would bide its time, rebuild
its forces, and strike when the time was ripe. Every knowledge-
able military man I met raised the same question: "Will the U.S.
Air Force intervene when (not 'if') the Communists launch their
next offensive?"

I was dismayed that the Vietnamese outlook could take such
a drastic downturn so quickly. A little more than a year earlier,
I had boarded a "freedom bird" to the States with memories of
an almost cocky South Vietnamese military flushed with confidence gained from its victories over the North Vietnamese. The
defense of An Loc and the repulse of Communist armored
assaults during the Easter Offensive had been therapeutic, and
one had the feeling that Vietnamization had jelled with the
defeat of the North Vietnamese. Now, in the place of smugness

and confidence, a disturbing edginess permeated South Vietnamese in all walks of life—an attitude that reflected an acute case of insecurity in the wake of our withdrawal.

One air force officer explained his feelings to me when I asked him why the South Vietnamese military was violating the ceasefire:

> You see, Dai Uy, we feel like the Frenchman who agreed to a duel of honor with pistols. Standing back-to-back with his opponent, he began to take fifteen paces without looking back. His opponent, who had no scruples, turned around, stalked him from behind, and shot him down before he could turn around. The man who played by the rules lost his life. That is how we feel. The North Vietnamese Communists have no scruples, and they are not playing by the rules. Like the honorable but naive Frenchman, we will lose at such a dangerous game if we blindly follow the rules.

PURVEYORS OF DOOM AND GLOOM

December 1973:

"Nha Be, Dai Uy, Nha Be! Vietcong dang danh Nha Be!" ("Nha Be, Captain, Nha Be! The Vietcong are attacking Nha Be!") the guard shouted as he pointed to a colossal pillar of black smoke churning its way high into the southeastern sky.

"Oh, Lord," I thought as I rushed past the excited guard and a growing crowd of gaping onlookers. Nha Be was the location of a sprawling gasoline and oil storage tank farm on the Saigon River, just downstream from the capital. Within minutes, the burgeoning black shroud had blotted out the morning sun and cast an eerie shadow over the city. Two frightened Vietnamese secretaries interrupted my dash down the long corridor that led to the Command Center. Was it true that the Communists were attacking the entire Saigon area, Dai Uy?

In the Command Center, all the phones were tied up as the civilian duty officer and his staff tried to find out what was happening. Was it a Communist ground attack? If so, was the target confined to Nha Be, or was there a widespread assault under way? The Vietnamese liaison officer was in earnest conversation with the Joint General Staff Headquarters. From his end of the conversation, I deduced that Nha Be was under a rocket attack.

As the picture came into focus, it appeared that a barrage of enemy rockets had slammed into the tank farm and detonated several of the massive storage tanks. These explosions and fires were now spreading unchecked throughout the complex. Available details were sketchy and conflicting, but the towering column of black smoke was convincing evidence that the Communists had struck where it would hurt the South Vietnamese. Our analysts were expecting a clearer picture of the drama soon, for the attack had occurred as an American civilian was visiting the facility. That lone American was now rushing from tank to tank, frantically turning valves in a vain and heroic effort to contain the damage.

Later in the day, the rocket attack version of the incident fell through. Long before the fires were extinguished, it became clear that a squad of Vietcong sappers had penetrated the lightly defended perimeter of the installation and triggered the conflagration with plastic explosives. No rockets had been fired from across the river as originally reported by the Nha Be garrison. The discovery of one sapper's body floating in the Saigon River was concrete proof that the tank farm had been the victim of a well-planned and well-executed sabotage operation.

The ever-alert Saigonese quickly divined the meaning of the black cloud that hovered over their city. Within hours of the attack, the city's filling stations were mobbed. Pandemonium reigned as hordes of anxious citizens panic-bought as much fuel as they could fit in their tanks and in every container they could lay their hands on quickly. Lines of cars, motorcycles, and three-wheeled lambrettas stretched for hundreds of meters in all directions around the Caltex station near the old Massachusetts BOQ. Each line ended in confusion and disorder as the Saigonese competed for shares of the precious fuel.

The government responded to the crisis by ordering all filling stations temporarily closed. Gray-shirted national police appeared at the filling stations to guard the pumps. When sales of gasoline resumed the following day, the price quickly skyrocketed from 105 to 240 piasters a liter—approximately $1.75 per

Nha Be, December 1973; 35 million liters of fuel go up in smoke.

gallon. What the recent Arab oil embargo had begun, a team of Hanoi's elite sappers had finished. Within days, the losses at Nha Be would be reflected in further restrictions on the use of vehicles in the South Vietnamese Army.

Considered in terms of its costs and results, the Nha Be attack must rank as one of the most successful sabotage operations of the Vietnam War. At a cost of one or two men killed, the Communists blew up thirty-five million liters of fuel and destroyed a significant percentage of South Vietnam's petroleum storage capacity. It was a military, economic, and psychological defeat of massive proportions. More than ever, the Saigonese realized their vulnerability to the growing North Vietnamese threat. Hanoi's army was once again beginning to take on the stature of a ten-foot-tall enemy.

The burden of tracking Hanoi's buildup in the South fell on the shoulders of a small group of civilian analysts who had been rushed to Vietnam from other positions in Washington at the time of our military withdrawal. The results of their efforts were communicated each month in an exhaustively researched and well-rehearsed manuscript briefing known as the MISTA (Monthly Intelligence Summary and Threat Analysis). Attended by General Murray, the Ambassador or his representative, and a host of other key military and civilian members of the mission, the MISTA soon became an ominous chronicling of the North Vietnamese logistical buildup. Since the in-boxes of our analysts overflowed with hard evidence of Hanoi's disregard for the provisions of the Paris Agreement, it was not difficult to document a convincing and bone-chilling indictment of Communist actions. In a darkened conference room with several screens at the front, the briefers would recite chapter and verse of the Communist preparations for military actions in the south as reconnaissance photos of snakelike truck convoys threading their way down jungle trails flashed across the screens. Each month, the briefers made the same point—Hanoi's actions clearly demonstrated that the North Vietnamese regarded the Paris Agreement as a green light for unrestricted military preparations.

Much has been written since 1975 on the scope of Hanoi's logistical buildup during the cease-fire, but no single work impressed me more than the recollections of Senior General Van Tien Dung, the North Vietnamese officer who commanded Hanoi's forces during the final drive to victory. In "Great Spring Victory," Dung boastfully describes how Hanoi used the cease-fire to prepare for the military undoing of Nguyen van Thieu's government. An excerpt from this testimonial:

> A rule of revolutionary war is to start with small units and proceed to large-scale corps and branches, and then attack the cities and the nerve centers of the enemy government. Only in this way could we defeat the enemy and liberate the fatherland. Thus, we had to have an ample number of wide roads and facilities for transportation of mechanized equipment to ensure enough grain, food, ammunition, and weapons for the front line. The strategic route east of the Truong Son Range, which was completed in early 1975, was the result of the labor of more than 30,000 troops and shock youths. The length of this route, added to that of the other old and new strategic routes used during the various campaigns during the last war, is more than 20,000 kms. The eight-meter-wide route of more than 1,000 kilometers, which we could see now, is our pride. With 5,000 miles of pipeline laid through deep rivers and streams and on mountains

more than 1,000 meters high, we were capable of providing enough food for various battlefronts. More than 10,000 transportation vehicles were put on the road.[1]

I first read this account in late 1977, after it had been translated and released in English by the U.S. government. As I read Dung's account, a sense of déjà vu flickered across my mind. Had I read these words before? Impossible, of course—the work had just become available in the States. Then it dawned on me. General Dung's vivid description of the events that were taking place in South Vietnam's "liberated zones" during the cease-fire was so close to the reporting I remembered in the DAO MISTA briefings that I was experiencing the sense of being transported back to our darkened conference room as the briefer clicked off the details of the Hanoi buildup. Dung's testimonial may have been intended as a tribute to the motivation and diligence of the North Vietnam Army, but it meant something else to me as an intelligence officer. Even though the American withdrawal had weakened our intelligence collection capabilities by 1973, the DAO civilian analysts had been able to piece together a detailed and accurate picture of Hanoi's preparations for renewed warfare. The morale of the Saigonese was low, but I wondered what might have been the effect had they known the full extent of North Vietnam's preparations for what Dung calls "the drive to final victory."

As it was, our Embassy and the South Vietnamese Ministry of Information had publicized many details of the military situation in an effort to turn world opinion against Hanoi. Even the Saigon taxi drivers began to ask me about the improvement of airfields by Communist forces in the "liberated zones." Horror stories about massive amounts of North Vietnamese tanks and artillery pouring down the modernized, all-weather Ho Chi Minh Trail circulated freely through the capital. Saigon's government television channel featured documentary programs that harped constantly on Hanoi's exploitation of the cease-fire. All over Saigon, new propaganda banners appeared that castigated Hanoi: "Don't listen to what the Communists say, but watch carefully what the Communists do."

But these attempts to mobilize the population against the Communists were not without their drawbacks. The more the Americans and the South Vietnamese government beat the drums about the perfidious North Vietnamese buildup, the more frightened and depressed the South Vietnamese people became, particularly the Saigonese, who received the brunt of the government's campaign on their television sets and radios.

In October 1973, a battalion of the ARVN 25th Division was ambushed and mauled during a sweep operation in northern Hau Nghia province. An unusually somber Major Sang described the action to me during one of our Saigon rendezvous at the Ngoc Huong Restaurant. The government unit had been sucked into the kill zone of a North Vietnamese ambush as it pursued a small group of enemy soldiers it had spotted—one of the NVA's oldest but most effective tricks. When the North Vietnamese sprang the trap, the command group of the government unit had been among the first casualties. The battalion commander died instantly, and his executive officer fell with his jaw shot away. After that, the unit lost all discipline and suffered heavy casualties as it attempted to disengage. Sang had seen a report that admitted losses of 46 men killed, 126 wounded, and more than 200 missing. Dozens of weapons had been lost to the Communists. The defeat was so bad that the South Vietnamese command had concealed it from President Thieu for two days. Shortly after the dimensions of the defeat became known, the division commander was relieved by the President.

Defeats of this magnitude were the exception rather than the rule during 1973, but many South Vietnamese seemed to regard them as portents of the future. South Vietnam was the victim of a progressive disease, the chief symptom of which was the erosion of the people's confidence in ultimate victory. As 1973 drew to a close, I shared this pessimism and wrote a troubled letter to my brother in California:

The situation over here is bad. The North Vietnamese are building up their forces in total disregard of the treaty, while we are scrupulously sticking to the one-for-one replacement of combat losses as permitted by the treaty. If there is a general offensive and the North Vietnamese begin to move close to Saigon, I look for South Vietnamese anger and frustration to take the form of openly hostile anti-Americanism. It could be that the streets of Saigon will be more dangerous than the swamps of Hau Nghia ever were, and that's no joke. Bitter anti-U.S. resentment is just below the surface now, since the Vietnamese view the Paris Agreement as having the effect of "legitimizing" the VC movement and lending tacit legitimacy to North Vietnamese presence in South Vietnam, closer than ever before to Saigon and other population centers. What a mess! In the absence of renewed U.S. Air Force support, the next general offensive, if launched, will result in Americans being evacuated from this country. I'm sure the only thing that will inhibit North Vietnam from launching the attack is Nixon's total unpredictability.[2]

Alarmed, I considered writing a report to General Murray to communicate my conviction that Vietnamese morale (and my own!) had dangerously deteriorated and that we faced a serious risk of an anti-American reaction in Saigon if the military situation should take a sudden turn for the worse. Twice I began to draft such a report, and twice I hesitated. Was I overreacting? And if this were possible, did I want to compromise my case of nerves by confronting General Murray with an alarmist report? After all, I was the junior man in the DAO, and I had been in Vietnam for only three months. How could I be certain that Saigon was representative of the whole country? Ultimately, I second-guessed myself out of taking any action and resolved to adopt a "wait and see" posture. If I were to formulate any meaningful assessment of South Vietnamese strengths and weaknesses, I would have to break loose from the confinement of my travel restriction and visit the countryside. To this end, I began to explore ways to visit Hau Nghia province.

Somewhere in the annals of military history, a frustrated officer who must have been confronted with a dilemma similar to my travel restriction problem uttered a maxim that has withstood the test of time: "Regulations are written to guide wise men and to restrict fools." Probably for this reason, a persistent search through the bureaucratic jargon of most regulations will uncover a discreetly worded waiver provision. The travel restriction, I learned after a little homework, was no exception. I could travel outside the Saigon area if a valid operational reason existed for the trip.

As luck would have it, our source-hungry analysts responsible for Military Region III (Saigon and the surrounding provinces) decided that they needed to develop new channels of information. They agreed with me that strategically located Hau Nghia was a good place to begin their quest. And, since the cultivation of the Vietnamese intelligence apparatus in a remote place like Hau Nghia was no mean task, an escort officer was needed who knew Hau Nghia and the key personalities who were the object of the mission. Convinced by this irrefutable logic, I allowed myself to be put in for a waiver of travel restriction that would permit a one-time visit to my former home.

A trip to Hau Nghia appealed to me for personal reasons. After all, I had spent nearly two years among the province's rice farmers, sharing hardships with the militia soldiers who had fought guerrillas and North Vietnamese regulars to a standstill. Now I wanted to see what our efforts had wrought. But there was also a professional concern that mandated such a visit, apart from the desire to cultivate new sources. It was difficult to avoid a siege mentality in Saigon, and the propensity for intelligence officers to "worst-case" all analysis had earned for us the appellation of "purveyors of doom and gloom." By the time the North Vietnamese blackened the skies over Saigon with the smoke from thirty-five million liters of fuel, there was enough doom and gloom in the capital for everyone. A brief escape to Hau Nghia would be a timely opportunity to see how the no-war war looked from the countryside. Depending on what we found, it could also be therapeutic. Infected by the malaise of the Saigon garrison, I was probably a good candidate for therapy by early December 1973 as we embarked at dawn for Bao Trai, the province capital.

The road to Hau Nghia took us along Highway 1 to Cu Chi, site of the base camp of the American 25th (Tropic Lightning) Division during the war. At the Cu Chi intersection, a left turn put us on the road to Bao Trai. At the corner, in the shadow of a

bombed-out theater, the bronze statue of an American infantryman of the 25th Division that had been erected in honor of the
25th's sacrifices had disappeared—a casualty of the cease-fire.
I wondered if the Vietcong had destroyed it, or the villagers had
melted it down. During the war, the 25th Division, like so many
American line units, had distinguished itself in combat with the
enemy but had made few friends among the villagers because of
its sometimes heavy-handed approach. It was difficult to develop a sensitivity to the Vietnamese peasants' problems if one was
a nineteen-year-old infantryman from Chicago whose friends
were being killed and maimed by mines within sight of the
villagers.

Before leaving Saigon, I had met with a South Vietnamese
intelligence officer who had confided in me that the military
situation was so precarious that Saigon was vulnerable to
attack. In an agitated voice, the officer, a lieutenant colonel,
had told me that, if the North Vietnamese were to attack out of
their base areas near An Loc, north of Saigon, their units could
be in Saigon within hours. As our sedan crossed the expanses of
a vast swamp that separated Bao Trai from Cu Chi, I resolved
to put this pessimistic theory to the test. Hau Nghia lay astride a
traditional invasion route to Saigon. If my former counterparts
in Bao Trai shared such an outlook, we were in trouble.

Bao Trai's single paved street hadn't changed. Throngs of
black-clad peasants milled around the central market, and the
town's chicken population still scurried about on the dusty
street, foraging for spilled grains of rice. The headquarters of
MACV Advisory Team 43 had been taken over by the government, and only Vietnamese faces could be seen around the
provincial military headquarters. No Americans had lived in
Bao Trai for almost a year.

At the sector G-2 shop, Major Nga greeted us warmly, chiding
me for not making rank as quickly as he and Sang. I introduced
my civilian colleagues as Nga invited us into his office for a
briefing on the military situation. With an exaggerated drama
that had always characterized his briefings, Nga revealed that
he had just interrogated a North Vietnamese defector. According to this source, who had just come from an NVA unit in near-

by Cambodia, Hanoi's forces in northern Hau Nghia were being
regularly supplied by fifty-truck convoys that originated in Svay
Rieng province. The days of long columns of bicycle porters
were over. Hanoi's forces were going modern. Nga related incident after incident of heavy contact with enemy units as the
Communist high command strove to make inroads in Hau
Nghia.

At a local coffee shop, I spotted a group of soldiers from the
305th Regional Forces Battalion. With their black M-16 rifles
balanced on their shoulders, grenades suspended from their
web gear, and purple unit scarves around their necks, they were
on their way to patrol the area west of the city along the Vam
Co Dong River. The platoon sergeant recognized me and called
a halt.

"Troi oi, Dai Uy, di dau vay? Lau qua, Dai Uy oi!" ("Dear
God, where have you been, Captain? Long time, Captain!")

The sergeant was all smiles as he boasted of his unit's exploits.
*"O dau cung co Vietcong, Dai Uy oi, ma cang nhieu thi cang
chet."* ("VC everywhere, Captain, but the more there are, the
more we kill.") His men laughed as they related tales of their
cease-fire heroics. The 305th was killing more enemy and cap-
turing more weapons than they had during the war. But weren't
they disappointed and discouraged because the cease-fire hadn't
ended the fighting? I put the question to their leader.

"Dai Uy," the sergeant replied with a grin that showed his
gold-capped lower teeth, "when you live here and fight as long
as we have, you don't think that the signing of a piece of paper
in Paris can make the Vietcong go away. With us, it's just business as usual." With that, he signaled his men to move out.

I took a couple of snapshots of the high-spirited troops as they
formed up to move out. The patrol headed toward the Vam Co
Dong River as several of the men called out, *"Dai Uy, di chung
duoc khong?"* ("Can you come with us, Captain?") *"Di vui lam,
Dai Uy oi"* ("Lots of fun, Captain"), they chided as I smiled and
begged off. My travel restriction waiver did not cover turning
the clock back to the advisory era. I snapped a final picture as
the olive drab column snaked its way across a rice paddy, looking like anything but a demoralized army on the verge of defeat.

We had lunch at Major Nga's government apartment —
actually little more than a long, cement-floored bay next to the
province G-2 office. In a small patch of dirt outside the door,
Nga's wife had planted marigolds in a garden cordoned off by
spent shell casings. The surprise of the day was the appearance
of our old friend, Private Do van Lanh. Wearing a steel helmet
and the fatigues of the South Vietnamese Army, Lanh greeted
me with a firm handshake and a hug. He had finished basic
training and was assigned as a rifleman in one of Hau Nghia's
militia companies. For a brief moment, my mind flashed back
to 1972, when I had first glimpsed Lanh the day after his capture. Lanh had been led into a room full of South Vietnamese
officers at the request of the South Vietnamese 25th Division
commander. His face still caked with blood from a wound sustained prior to capture, Lanh had endured a browbeating by
the arrogant colonel, whom he had angered by his refusal to be
intimidated. Later that day, I had received special permission
to make Lanh my roommate in an attempt to convert him to
our side. With help from Major Sang, my ploy had worked. Do
van Lanh was flying around in a helicopter with me within a
week, pointing out his former unit's bivouac areas along the
Cambodian border. For his assistance, Lanh had been granted
his freedom, only to be drafted into the army that, only months
earlier, had shot him and pulled him bleeding out of a bunker.
Lanh had told me during one of our many talks in 1972 that he
was through with soldiering. He had no more of the youthful
idealism left in him that had induced him to volunteer to "go
south and strike the Americans." As far as he was concerned,
neither AK-47 nor M-16 would play a role in his life anymore.
Now, as we renewed our friendship, his smile and enthusiastic
description of his life as a government soldier told me that he
had accepted his new lot graciously. Lanh even proudly boasted
about his performance as a reconnaissance scout on a recent
night patrol. I chided Major Nga, who had expressed misgivings
at my plan to pull Lanh out of the POW cage. I had recruited
a trained candidate for service in the most unlikely of places!
What an ironic twist the results of that impulse had taken.

Nga was interested in my impressions of the new province

Hau Nghia Province Chief, Colonel Soan.

chief, Colonel Soan. During the morning, we had accompanied
the colonel on an inspection trip to the Tra Cu ranger base on
the west bank of the Vam Co Dong. A handsome, self-confident
marine, Soan had been decorated by President Thieu for heroism during the battle to retake Quang Tri city in the summer of
1972. Soan's bodyguard was a fierce-looking marine corporal
who sported a captured AK-47 assault rifle that had a red scarf
hanging from its barrel. As a South Vietnamese Navy patrol
boat ferried us across the river, the bodyguard had scanned the
tropical foliage along the riverbank intently. Soan himself
struck me as the kind of officer who would have won the hearts
and minds of American advisors, if not the villagers, during the
American phase of the war. I had spent only two hours with him
that morning but sensed that he was the kind of aggressive officer that our often-frustrated American advisors had preferred.
All too often, our Vietnamese counterparts had exhibited the
calculated, unhurried approach to their duties that characterized the oriental outlook. Mystified by what we saw as a lack
of urgency on their part to attack pressing problems, many of us

reacted by attempting to "take charge" as our military training dictated. It was not the happiest of marriages, that attempted spot-weld of East and West that ended with the signing of the Paris Agreement.

But now, long after Advisory Team 43's departure, I was gratified to see that the Hau Nghia Vietnamese were carrying on effectively. At the Duc Hue district capital, in the shadow of the Hiep Hoa sugar mill, the district chief explained to me that his troops were heavily engaged with a foe that was exerting steady pressure on the populated areas. The illicit trading with the Communists that Major Sang had told me about was a fact of life in Duc Hue, where one needed only to paddle a sampam across the river to barter with the forces of *phia ben kia* (the other side). In the "liberated zones," Communist supply cadre were paying twice the market price for rice and medicines. As we talked, the staccato clatter of automatic weapons fire rang out from across the river. One of Duc Hue's militia platoons had been ambushed by the Communists. The duty officer from the district operations center reported to his superior that the small unit (approximately 30 men) had suffered 5 men killed and 8 more wounded. During the war, we would have called for a medical evacuation helicopter for the wounded men. Now, the district chief admitted sadly with a shake of his head, such support was so scarce that it would not do to wait for it. The platoon was ordered to fashion litters out of the ponchos and rifles of the casualties and make their way back to the river. The district chief told me that Hau Nghia forces had suffered losses of 120 men killed during this rice harvest, a level of casualties that exceeded even that of the 1972 Easter Offensive.

Before heading back to Saigon, we accepted an invitation to join the Tan My village chief and his staff for a beer at the small restaurant that served the village crossroads. While a crowd of teenagers watched the village mechanic struggle with a balky transmission linkage on my sedan, my nervous civilian companions and I picked up on the local gossip. The news was saddening. Lieutenant Ngu, who had worked with me in Duc Hue, had been ambushed and killed recently. The cocky officer had drunk too much beer (at the place where we were sitting) and

Hau Nghia, Major Sang and Major Nga.

insisted on riding his motorcycle back to Duc Hue after dark. As the lieutenant and two sergeants—all three of them on one small bike—headed back, two Communist guerrillas jumped out on the road and sprayed them with their AK-47s. All three men died. Another Duc Hue staff officer now lay in Saigon's Cong Hoa military hospital after being seriously wounded when the Communists ambushed the river patrol boat that was ferrying him and an infantry unit. Captain Ky, one of Hau Nghia's most fearless company commanders, had been shot in the head while leading his unit on a night operation. It was exactly as Major Sang had explained to me in Saigon—Hau Nghia was still at war. The formula for a cease-fire that Henry Kissinger had so laboriously forged in Paris had no meaning in a province that had known almost continuous warfare since 1946. As our sedan crossed the marshlands on the way to Highway 1, I experienced mixed emotions. It had been a gratifying and reassuring experience to learn firsthand that our advisory efforts in Hau Nghia had borne fruit. It was heartening to confirm that not all South Vietnamese military men had succumbed to the pessimism I had observed in the Saigon garrison. Nonetheless, I wondered how long the fabric of South Vietnamese society could endure the debilitating bloodletting of the bogus peace. If Hau Nghia's losses were representative, Hanoi was inflicting severe punishment on the South Vietnamese for their persistent anti-Communism.

THE MANDATE OF HEAVEN

Even though I was impatiently anticipating new duties as an MIA negotiator, I had benefited from the insight into cease-fire politics that my security duties had permitted. As guardian of the "tank" in which our analysts tracked the moves and countermoves of the two sides, I had occupied a ringside seat for the great debate that shaped up as it became evident that the cease-fire was stillborn. Passions had sometimes run high as the intelligence community and our political decision makers struggled to ferret out the meaning of the blatant North Vietnamese buildup.

Observers were divided in their interpretation of events. Some believed that Hanoi's impatient leaders were determined to use their rapidly developing military fist in a general offensive to topple South Vietnam as soon as possible. Few responsible Americans subscribed to this belief during late 1973 and early 1974. The sounders of the trumpets of Armageddon were the worried South Vietnamese, whose government never tired of telling anyone who would listen that the Communists were on the verge of mounting another general offensive. To the South Vietnamese, the question of the hour was whether or not Washington would commit its air power to the battle when the inevitable North Vietnamese onslaught materialized.

Our analysts at the DAO were more cautious. Their estimates reflected a belief that, while the Communists were undoubtedly building up their military forces to support an eventual conquest of South Vietnam, this did not necessarily portend an all-out, country-wide offensive.* Most of our analysts argued that

*A detailed exposition of the intelligence reporting during the cease-fire period is outside the scope of this work. For a comprehensive treatment of this subject, see Col. William LeGro's *Vietnam: From Cease-Fire to Capitulation*, published by the Government Printing Office.

Hanoi would probably continue to launch a series of phased, limited offensives designed to improve its strategic position and demoralize the South Vietnamese Army. As I had seen during the Hau Nghia visit, this tactic was extracting a heavy price in both blood and money from the Thieu government for its refusal to negotiate the political settlement envisioned in the Paris Agreement. When captured Communist documents asserted that "the path of revolutionary violence" must be followed in the south, our analysts interpreted this to mean that Hanoi had elected to use military pressure to force the Thieu government to accept a Communist political role in governing the south. To be safe, though, the DAO estimates left open the possibility that Hanoi might play its military card if American and South Vietnamese reactions indicated weakness and disunity. Hanoi had developed the capability and, hence, had the option to convert its limited offensive into something more serious. For this kind of comprehensive reporting, the DAO analysts acquired the unwarranted reputation in some quarters of being overly alarmist and hawkish.

One regular attendee at the DAO briefings was Frank Snepp, the dapper CIA analyst who subsequently recounted his Vietnam experiences in a controversial book entitled *Decent Interval*. In his book, Frank took a swipe at the "hawkish intelligence analysts at DAO" and erroneously recalled that they "had been predicting a general offensive every month since the first day of the cease-fire."[3] In a unique and imaginative interpretation of American politics in cease-fire Saigon, Frank argued that Colonel LeGro's intelligence organization played into Ambassador Graham Martin's hands by providing the kind of alarmist reporting that enabled the Ambassador to paint a sufficiently grim picture of the military situation to justify high levels of American military assistance.

Documenting an enemy's capabilities is one thing; unlocking his intentions is something quite different. The former task is done with what often is empirical evidence; the latter is a deductive, intellectual process that is hit-and-miss at best. For this reason, none of us really knew Hanoi's specific military blueprint for action in the south. The DAO's civilian intelligence analysts did a creditable job of monitoring and reporting the alarming increase in North Vietnamese capabilities and reminding our national decision makers that these developments broadened Hanoi's range of options. They did not, as Snepp suggested, predict a general offensive early in the cease-fire, and when they finally did make this call, such an offensive came to pass.*

But regardless of where one stood on the analytical debate, life in Saigon had taken on a new flavor as 1973 drew to a close. There was a growing sense that one was sitting on a time bomb and that the North Vietnamese were adding new sticks of dynamite to that bomb every day. Each new move by the Communists upped the psychological ante. When the oil tanks of Nha Be exploded or when a district capital fell to Hanoi's troops, people nervously speculated that we were seeing the beginning of a major push. The history of the Vietnam War was fresh in our minds, a war that was characterized by the unexpected. Ambassador Martin's Special Assistant for Field Operations, retired Army Col. George Jacobson, was living proof that anyone could be overtaken by the unexpected in Vietnam. During the 1968 Tet Offensive, Jacobson had suddenly found himself sharing a house on the grounds of the U.S. Embassy with the last survivor of a Vietcong suicide squad that had seized the compound. Jacobson had waited until the guerrilla emptied his AK-47 up the stairwell, and then killed him with a pistol that had been tossed to him only moments earlier by an MP in the courtyard below. The colonel's colleagues later presented him with his victim's weapon, on which was engraved, "A VC fired this, and missed. The colonel fired back, and didn't."

One incident illustrated the prevailing mood in Saigon at that time—the sense that the next move was up to Hanoi and that no option was too bizarre to rule out. I arrived at work early one

---

*Col. Harry Summers, who became my boss when I joined the MIA negotiations team, says this about Snepp's book: "Since much of Snepp's book . . . is based on his own sources, reading it is much like gambling with a man who rolls the dice in his hat and tells you what his point is." I agree. *Decent Interval* is an emotional, deeply flawed work that must be read with caution.

morning to find all the gates closed and guarded. An alert had been called during the night after the marine security guard at Ambassador Martin's quarters reported that he was under fire. The marine had returned the fire as reinforcements were dispatched to the scene. A contingency plan existed under which a marine reaction force would speed to the Ambassador's quarters in an armored car in the event that it came under attack.

General Murray found an unusually large crowd of curious observers in the command center when he arrived for his morning briefing. The duty officer struggled to retain his composure as he related the evening's events. After the initial alert and the dispatch of reinforcements to the scene, a "FLASH" message containing sketchy details of the attack had been sent to the White House Situation Room and the National Military Command Center in the Pentagon. Ambassador Martin had been awakened and spirited off for safekeeping before it became clear that the whole thing was a false alarm. There had been no attack. Instead, the marine guard had mistaken an exploding safety valve on a hot water heater for enemy fire. The duty officer had sent out a second message directing all addressees to disregard the initial report, but the damage had been done. For those not involved in the ludicrous incident, it was the source of a good laugh. The marines had tested their alert procedures under realistic conditions, although one wondered whether the Ambassador would fully appreciate the humor of the hostile hot water heater. General Murray managed a laugh in spite of the embarrassing messages that had gone out to the world from his office. Humorous though the event was, it served as a reminder that we were living in a country where the unexpected had all too often reigned supreme.

As Hanoi's military strength grew, Saigon's strength ebbed. The oil embargo spawned by the Yom Kippur War had quadrupled the price of oil and triggered international double-digit inflation. The repercussions of this economic ill wind were felt in Saigon. As the costs of ammunition, fuel, and transportation swelled in response to the new oil market, the real purchasing power of the military assistance dollars pledged to the Saigon government eroded. This alone was serious enough to hurt the

Saigon army's ability to fight, but the news was still worse. In Washington, the tone of the debate in Congress pointed to the real possibility that the legislators might sharply cut the President's request for $1.4 billion in military aid for Saigon. Ultimately, Congress appropriated only half this sum, and the effect on the South Vietnamese was devastating.

To both Vietnamese parties, the debate over military aid to South Vietnam meant considerably more than the question of military hardware. Both Hanoi and Saigon viewed the success or failure of the administration in getting its aid bill through Congress as a barometer of the American commitment to South Vietnam. The visible impact of cuts in American aid were the aircraft that the South Vietnamese had to mothball or the damaged tanks that could not be rebuilt because of a lack of funds. Equally important, but less apparent, was the psychological impact of these cuts. Time and again, I heard South Vietnamese military men and civilians bemoan their fate at having been cursed with a faltering ally while the Communists basked in the luxury of two faithful sponsors (the Soviets and the Chinese), each vying to outdo the other in generosity. As I was soon to learn from the Communists themselves during my travels to Hanoi, the North Vietnamese interpreted every congressional vote against aid to South Vietnam as "the voice of the progressive American people protesting their government's neocolonialist policies." The aid issue was a simple equation in which Saigon's psychological and material losses were Hanoi's gains.

In looking back on this period, I believe we witnessed the political and military collapse of South Vietnam in 1974, even though this was not readily apparent to the casual observer. Westerners tend to associate political collapse with a coup d'etat or with the resignation of a chief of state; military collapse brings to mind visions of disintegrating armies and humiliating capitulation. Even though these events didn't occur until 1975, the die was cast during 1974. By autumn of that year, President Thieu was politically bankrupt, convicted in the eyes of his countrymen for failing in the ultimate task—keeping the American aid flowing. Most Vietnamese viewed President Thieu as the best man for the job because of his effectiveness in dealing with the Americans. Thieu meant stability, and stability was Washington's precondition for continued aid. The onerous terms of the Paris Agreement and the cutbacks in American aid thus symbolized to the Vietnamese man in the street that President Thieu had fallen from favor in Washington. The "mandate of heaven" that traditionally lent legitimacy to Vietnamese rulers had come to mean the "mandate of Washington" in Thieu's case. Most of the propaganda themes that the Communists employed found little sympathy among the South Vietnamese population. Exceptions to this statement were twofold: the depiction of President Thieu as a corrupt leader, and the Communist insistence that Nguyen van Thieu was a puppet of the Americans.

Life in Hau Nghia province had exposed me to the corruption that existed in the Vietnamese government and armed forces. I had departed Hau Nghia in 1972, convinced that the survival of South Vietnam depended in part on the success of President Thieu's government in eliminating this problem. It was wishful thinking to dismiss corruption in the Saigon government by rationalizing that most Asian countries were corrupt. It was this tendency that General Murray was referring to when he wrote me about the reaction of the Martin Embassy to corruption:

> Martin's Embassy took no action. Martin, experienced in Thailand and Italy . . . dismissed the issue with a knowing smile and "a little corruption over here oils the economic machinery." Many agreed. I also agreed, but not for that reason. If my family was starving, I'd steal too.

But the problem merited more concern than it was given by our mission, for South Vietnam and its Asian neighbors differed in one significant respect: the Thieu government was engaged in a death struggle with an insurgency backed by some two hundred thousand North Vietnamese soldiers. President Thieu could no more afford to expose a weak flank to the enemy than he could afford to have a hostile American press bent on exposing his regime as corrupt and unpopular. But, while the South Vietnamese economy stagnated, corruption actually increased as government bureaucrats and military men struggled to make economic ends meet. This in turn generated an unprecedented public outcry against the government. Caught between a growing Communist threat and a declining economy, the people of South Vietnam became increasingly indignant over the corruption issue. Time and time again, Vietnamese sought me out to decry the wholesale corruption at all levels. Inevitably, the anger and frustration were directed more and more at President Thieu himself, who seemed unwilling—or unable—to do anything about the problem. "The house leaks from the roof on down" was the expression the Saigonese used to describe their conviction that Nguyen van Thieu was responsible for the pervasive *tham nhung* (corruption) of his regime.

As the problem worsened, responsible military men began to fear that, unless corruption could be checked, the armed forces would be unable to counter the anticipated general offensive. A Military Security Service team investigated the army's strengths and weaknesses and sent out a damning report of its findings to the commanding general of Military Region III. A copy of this report ultimately reached American hands, unquestionably without the approval of the government. The report was a political hot potato, impugning as it did the integrity of many military commanders. One section of the report, entitled "Shortcomings," assessed the morale of the armed forces in these terms:

> Since the cease-fire, military operations of our forces have become less active because of the declining morale of the soldiers, who either did not want to endure hardship or were too confident in the cease-fire agreement. A remarkable factor taking place beside the enthusiastic fighting of the majority of the soldiers is the corruption of a number of command echelons who escape responsibility, avoid hardship, and engage in activities for personal gain. They provide regular leave authorization to soldiers who desire to be away from the unit.

The reference to allowing "regular leave authorization" was an admission of the existence of *linh bong* (flower soldiers). Flower soldiers were permitted extended absences from their units without being declared AWOL. In exchange for this privilege, they usually compensated their commanders with a mutually acceptable sum of money. A flower soldier might appear for unit musters, inspections, and payday, but never for combat operations.

The report also described the worsening economic dilemma of the South Vietnamese Army, in blunt terms:

> Enlisted men can hardly support their families on their small salaries, especially when they are away from home. In September and October 1973, the Commander of Military Region III personally . . . gave instructions to servicemen and cadre of all levels to closely coordinate with one another to effectively prevent Communist collection and purchasing activities. However, satisfactory results have not been obtained because a number of servicemen, being unable to support their families on their low salaries, personally, or through their relatives, do business with the Communists in order to earn a profit. They take the risk of being jailed for such transactions. Particularly, a number of our officers (including field grade officers), who can support their families, enthusiastically engage in activities or support merchants who sell essential supplies to the Communists. They even use manpower and facilities of their units in their personal activities in order to make more money.

Turning to the impact of the American military withdrawal, the report's authors chastised South Vietnamese commanders for their failure to adjust to new conditions:

> Presently, a number of our outposts receive no maintenance. Unit commanders use the reason that they do not receive maintenance materials. The U.S. discontinued the supply of these materials after the cease-fire. Instead of using limited available materials, these units take no actions and their installations deteriorate. The clearing in a defense perimeter can be done with machetes by personnel of the unit. But these units request and wait for a dozer tractor and defoliation chemicals. In a situation where supplies are short, if these units still rely on such supplies, disaster to the units can be expected.

Finally, the report concluded that "the soldiers are only determined to fight the enemy if they have good leaders," and raised this warning:

> If our command echelons, especially battalion and company commanders, continue to do business with the Communists, embezzle public funds, take advantage of subordinates, and devote their attention to private business for personal gain, the army cannot be appropriately improved and strong enough to cope with the Communists.

Almost as noteworthy as the damning revelations of this report was the fact that it found its way into American hands. Someone in the MSS was obviously concerned that the allegations of war profiteering and misconduct would be ignored if they remained solely in Vietnamese channels. Not surprisingly, the contents of the report attracted considerable attention in the DAO, particularly after some of its more incriminating passages were quoted by Colonel LeGro's analysts in the next MISTA briefing.

Could the Americans have done anything about the conditions described in this report? By 1974, the sad answer to this question was "little or nothing." It was simply too late in the ball game for us to exert any meaningful influence on the Vietnamese government to clean up its act. The time to tackle this touchy issue had long since passed—if, indeed, the elusive issue was one that could have been solved.

The problem of corruption in South Vietnam was a complex one, probably meriting a separate book, better written by a Vietnamese. As Americans, we tend to apply our Westerners' yardstick to the situation, neatly concluding that Nguyen van Thieu and all other South Vietnamese who were "on the take" were collectively guilty for their country's fate. Corruption was a major vulnerability that plagued Thieu's image both in Washington and among his people. However, it is also true that many practices we would label "corrupt" in the American military were acceptable conduct in an Asian army whose officers and senior noncommissioned officers earned lower wages than an

American-employed local Vietnamese driver. The salaries of our Vietnamese counterparts were low by any standard, but when subjected to the economic stresses of 1973 and beyond, the result could only be greater abuses. There were, presumably, limits to what, for example, a district chief could skim off before his conduct entered the realm of the unacceptable, but the nuances of this subtle set of practices escaped us. It is doubtful whether any American Ambassador or MACV commander could have ever understood, let alone solved, the complex problem that we labeled "corruption." In any event, by 1974, the system had persisted for too long and too many people were involved for any corrective measures to have enjoyed even a remote chance of success. As one former Vietnamese district chief confided in me long after the fall of Saigon, any attempt to discipline those South Vietnamese officers who were involved in corruption would have required a purge that would have decimated the officer corps. Such a move was simply impractical when the army was locked in a full-scale war in the countryside. The South Vietnamese Army was thus caught in a self-made dilemma. Corruption unquestionably damaged troop morale, as the MSS report so graphically documented, but the advanced state of the disease precluded a cure. To have attempted to cut out the cancer would have killed the patient. Thus the government solution to the problem had been to do nothing. As pressures for reform mounted during 1974, Thieu did remove three of his four corps commanders and cashiered hundreds of field grade officers. But, by that time, his political strength had eroded greatly, and many Vietnamese viewed the shake-up as politically inspired tokenism rather than as a genuine attempt to reform. They were probably correct. Like it or not, we were committed to support a government that was all too often its own worst enemy.

Part III

MISSING IN ACTION

ONLY HANOI KNOWS

"I'm not a political person, Colonel. I'm just a mother who has lost her son. Believe me, I do understand the grief of the Vietnamese mothers who have lost their sons. I can't pass judgment on the rightness or wrongness of the war, but I can understand how you must feel about what has happened to your country. But my Crosley is a good boy who was only performing his duties as a military man when he was shot down. Here is his picture. Could you please check with your government and tell me what has become of him?"

With this emotional appeal to a stoical North Vietnamese negotiator, Dottie Fitton continued her six-year quest for information about her son's fate. It was late September 1974 as we sat around a small coffee table in an old barracks building located at Camp Davis, the Communist headquarters in the heart of Saigon's Tan Son Nhut Air Base. Named for Sp4. James Davis, the first American soldier to die in Vietnam, Camp Davis had housed an American military intelligence unit during the war. Now the compound served as the home and headquarters of several hundred Communist negotiators whose presence in Saigon was one of the most distasteful aspects of the Paris Agreement for the proud South Vietnamese.

On this particular day, I was serving as escort officer and interpreter for Dottie, a graying and bespectacled mother from

Connecticut who had come to Saigon with a delegation of American citizens concerned about their relatives who were listed as missing in action (MIA). In spite of the oppressive heat, the North Vietnamese colonel sipped from a cup of warm tea. A fan spun lazily overhead, barely stirring the tepid air. Outside the window, the large green leaves of a banana tree were motionless under the glaring Saigon summer sun. On the wall behind the Communist officer hung a picture of Ho Chi Minh. Earlier in our meeting, the colonel had lectured Dottie on the many "crimes" committed by the American military in Vietnam, with the clear implication that her son shared in the collective guilt for the suffering of the Vietnamese people. His message had been clear and discouraging: American mothers should call on their government to cease its "illegal involvement in the internal affairs of Vietnam." Washington's continued support of President Nguyen van Thieu's "puppet regime" was the major obstacle to a settlement of all questions, including the missing-in-action problem and the fate of Air Force LTC Crosley Fitton.

Dottie Fitton's persistent quest for information had already taken her to Washington, Paris, Vientiane, and Saigon. As a veteran of several such meetings, the shrewd New Englander was too smart to be drawn into a political debate with an experienced professional like the stone-faced North Vietnamese who now faced us across the table. By emphasizing that she was an apolitical victim of the war—a poor mother who had lost her son—Dottie had avoided a finger-shaking argument that she knew was unwinnable. Before we departed, the colonel expressed his sympathy for her plight, accepted her son's photo, and promised that he would relay her request for information to his government in Hanoi. By deftly playing her hand, Dottie had not given her adversary the opportunity to label her as "impudent" and "unrepentant" for America's alleged crimes. In a strategy session before her audience with the North Vietnamese, Dottie had agreed with our suggestion that it would be fruitless to demand information from the Communists. As we departed Camp Davis, I congratulated her on her performance but cautioned against undue optimism. This was not the first time that one of Hanoi's negotiators had made such a commitment, but we had never seen such a promise yield results.*

I had now been involved in the MIA business for eight months, during which time I was adding daily to my understanding of why the Vietnam War so stubbornly defied our best efforts to defuse it. The missing-in-action negotiations may have been frustrating and tedious business, but they provided the officers of the American delegation a new appreciation for the strength and determination of our Communist adversaries, not to mention a fresh perspective from which to assess our own position. During the war, I had interrogated hundreds of enemy prisoners and defectors in Hau Nghia province, an experience that had provided a good understanding of what motivated "the other side." But, in those days, I had been operationally oriented, concerned more with identifying the enemy's exploitable weaknesses than I was with assessing his strengths.

But the MIA negotiations were an entirely different milieu. Nothing could better symbolize the new ground rules than our advice to Dottie Fitton that her best approach would be a courteous and apolitical appeal to the Communists. No longer were my adversaries frightened prisoners or disenchanted defectors. My sources in 1971 and 1972 had been products of the almost total military defeat of the Hau Nghia Vietcong and the decimation of the North Vietnamese legions that Hanoi had committed to shore up the crippled insurgency. But the Paris Agreement had relegated these events to the scrap heap of history. They had become, in a word, irrelevant. The Communist officers and men who were airlifted to Saigon in January 1973 *were* relevant, and these men viewed their residence under diplomatic immunity in the enemy's capital as proof that they had emerged as winners in the long war. After all, was it not true that the South Vietnamese constitution outlawed Communism? And had I not hunted Vietcong political and military cadre like

*Shortly after the fall of Saigon, Dottie's appeal paid off. One of the first steps taken by Hanoi in its attempts to normalize relations with Washington was to repatriate the remains of several pilots as a gesture of goodwill. Among them was the body of Dottie's son.

animals during my service in Hau Nghia, backed up by virtually every weapon in our arsenal short of "the bomb"? Our avowed objective had always been to prevent the Communists from entering Saigon, but now my colleagues and I were dealing routinely with an enemy contingent that was defiantly ensconced in the heart of the capital—a testament to Communist perseverance and American frustration. The green-clad enemy officers had traversed a long and arduous path from their tunnel hideouts in War Zone D and Cambodia to the security of Camp Davis. One could armchair quarterback the nuances of the Paris Agreement all day, but the fact remained that the signing ceremony in Paris had quickly been followed by the disestablishment of an American headquarters in Saigon (MACV) and the establishment of a Communist headquarters at Camp Davis, almost directly across the street. This reality was not lost on the South Vietnamese, and it was deeply symbolic that no American or South Vietnamese officers ever lived in Hanoi, except as prisoners of war.

My career in the MIA business had begun on schedule in February 1974. Anxious to get off to a good start with Colonel Tombaugh, the hard-nosed Chief of the U.S. delegation, I had vowed to heed the advice of a friend and lay low while I learned the new job. "The Old Man believes that captains should be seen and not heard," was what I was told, and I tried to observe that guidance. Unfortunately, when my security office civilian employees honored their departing military bosses at a rooftop party, no one thought to apply to the local police precinct for a party permit. The gravity of this oversight became clear shortly after midnight, when a squad of Saigon police raided our innocent gathering and hauled more than thirty of us to the local prefecture. As the sole American who spoke Vietnamese, I confessed that I was the organizer of the illegal event, in the mistaken belief that I could talk my way out of such a petty matter. Unfortunately, the local police chief proved to be virulently anti-American (a disease that was becoming common in Saigon), and not even my Vietnamese language could save me from his wrath. My companions were all released, but I was held on the heinous charge of "holding girls closely and dancing without a

MIA Mothers, Mary Raye (left) and Dottie Fitton, with author.

permit." After spending the night under a mosquito net borrowed from one of my jailers, I arrived three hours late for duty on my first day on the new job. I had not done too well at "laying low." Slinking sheepishly into the office, I reported to my immediate boss, Army LTC Hank Lunde. Colonel Lunde was a Norwegian-American whose wartime heroism as an infantry captain in Vietnam had been documented by Brig. Gen. S. L. A. Marshall in *Battles of the Monsoons*. A soft-spoken man with an incisive mind, he was the Chief of the U.S. delegation's Negotiations Division. Lunde listened with patient amusement to my account of the aborted party, then promised me that he would "straighten things out with the Chief." It seemed that Colonel Tombaugh had not been pleased to learn that the new captain had spent the night in jail. I had gotten off to an inauspicious beginning with a demanding boss.

It took several weeks just to review the complex history of the ten-month-old negotiations. The detailed negotiations chronology revealed that the delegation's efforts on behalf of some twenty-five hundred families with MIA relatives had met with delay and frustration. We had entered the negotiations under the naive assumption that the implementation of Article 8(b) of the Paris Agreement (which spelled out the task of resolving the problem of the missing and the dead) would be relatively easy. The files told me that the first officers assigned to the team had commenced negotiations in the belief that MIA information would be promptly exchanged. At the time, it had even been believed that the tour of duty on the U.S. delegation (which was twelve months) was longer than it would take to wrap up the job and head for home.

But by the time I joined the delegation in early 1974, its staff of ten officers and five NCOs had made virtually no progress in resolving the fates of our missing servicemen. The optimistic expectations of the early weeks of negotiations had long since evaporated, and in their place was the sober realization that the Communists could be as implacable in peace as they had been on the battlefield during the war. Initially, the Communists insisted that they were conducting a country-wide collation of data on the missing and the dead in preparation for a prompt exchange of information as called for in Article 8(b). But, as the cease-fire evolved into another phase of the protracted war, Hanoi realized that the South Vietnamese government was not prepared to share political power in the south. As hope for a political settlement faded, so did our hopes for progress in the MIA talks. Humanitarian concerns had fallen victim to the politics of the stillborn cease-fire.

When our side provided the Communists with dozens of folders that established conclusively that Hanoi had captured certain American aviators who had since disappeared—that is, they had not been released in 1973 nor had they been listed as having died in captivity—the North Vietnamese adamantly refused to discuss these cases. When we doggedly insisted that the exchange of such information was an unconditional moral and legal obligation, the Communists dug in their heels and replied with a bewildering array of procedural dodges and excuses, all of which pointed to their desire to exploit the politically sensitive MIA issue in the United States. During the war, Hanoi had parlayed its possession of some six hundred Ameri-

can prisoners into a trump card that had been played during the
Paris negotiations. Now, our wily adversaries were attempting
to play the MIA issue for the same kind of political mileage. As
I read and reread the summaries of the weekly negotiating
sessions and the press releases of the Communists, the Communist price for information on our MIA personnel came into
focus. In Hanoi's words, Washington must "cease its support of
the Saigon government, withdraw its twenty thousand illegal
advisors from South Vietnam, cease its illegal provision of
weapons to the Thieu clique, force the Saigon government to
respect the cease-fire, and, above all, fulfill its commitment to
contribute money to 'heal the wounds of war.' " This latter
Communist demand was a reference to Article 21 of the Paris
Agreement, which committed us to "contribute to healing the
wounds of war and to postwar construction of the Democratic
Republic of Vietnam and throughout Indochina."[1] Hanoi was
determined that Washington should honor President Nixon's
commitment for economic aid of some $3.25 billion—a com-
mitment the President had conveyed to the North Vietnamese in
a letter during January 1973, presumably to provide the Communists with additional incentives for respecting the Paris
Agreement. Stripped of all rhetoric, the Communist position
reflected a firm determination to exact a price for any concessions on the MIA issue. Hanoi's position was unshakable.
Progress on the MIA issue depended on progress in other parts
of the Paris Agreement. The North Vietnamese were clearly prepared to weather any criticism that their policy was tantamount
to an unsavory "bartering for bones."

   The impasse appeared irresolvable. Our side firmly insisted
that the MIA question should not be linked to the other provisions of the Paris Agreement, and President Nixon strongly
advocated continued support for the Thieu government. Our
guidance from the Embassy was clear. The United States would
not sacrifice its ally in exchange for information on our missing
personnel, no matter how badly we desired a breakthrough in
the negotiations. For its part, Hanoi seemed equally committed
to its belief that stalling on the MIA issue would generate still
another source of domestic pressure on the Nixon adminis-

MG John E. Murray, Defense Attaché.

tration to abandon the Saigon government. The polarization of views could not have been more complete. The cease-fire had not ended the war of words any better than it had stopped the shooting.

While I immersed myself in the tangle of documents that traced the negotiations, the war raged on unabated. By now, regular features of General Murray's morning briefing were status reports on the siege of Phnom Penh, the Cambodian capital, and the status of the South Vietnamese rangers who were defending an encircled base at a place called Tong Le Chan in northern Tay Ninh province. Like so many of the former American bases now occupied by President Thieu's overextended forces, Tong Le Chan was a remote border camp of questionable strategic significance. But because the North Vietnamese had long since surrounded and cut off its defenders, the base had assumed a symbolic importance out of proportion to its military value. Since the stubborn President Thieu had vowed to yield no territory to the Communists, Tong Le Chan and several similar remote outposts now hung like logistical albatrosses around the neck of the South Vietnamese Air Force, which was forced to run a continuous aerial resupply program to keep several hundred miserable soldiers in food and ammunition.

The siege of Tong Le Chan was symptomatic of fundamental flaws in the peacekeeping mechanism of the Paris Agreement.

One of the protocols to the agreement established a four-nation International Commission for Control and Supervision (ICCS) to supervise the cease-fire. The intention of the agreement's drafters was for the ICCS teams to be deployed throughout South Vietnam, to include presence at certain predetermined entry points for military hardware. Theoretically, this would enable the commission to control the introduction of military manpower and supplies into the country and to investigate violations of the truce. In reality, the ICCS, like our MIA team, was an early victim of the political deadlock between the two sides. To make matters worse, the ICCS included two Communist and two non-Communist countries (Poland and Hungary; Canada and Indonesia).* The problem was that the organization operated on the principle of unanimity. No investigations of alleged cease-fire violations could be conducted unless all four members agreed. Predictably, when the Communists were the apparent violators, the Poles or the Hungarians vetoed the investigation. If the Saigon government's forces appeared to be guilty, then the Iranians or the Indonesians would nix the probe. With their organization thus paralyzed, ICCS personnel whiled away their time sunning at the DAO pool, thereby earning a pair of nicknames for their moribund organization. The quick-witted Saigonese insisted that ICCS stood for *"I'm Cho Coi Sao"* ("Wait quietly and watch how things turn out"). Not to be outdone, Saigon's English-speaking community argued that the letters stood for "I can't control shit."

The four officers who worked in my office became known as the "think tank" in deference to our job of preparing initiatives and responses for use in the weekly negotiations sessions with the Communists. To accomplish this task, we received limited guidance from the Embassy's Political-Military Affairs Section. Most of our time was spent drafting statements for delivery by the Chief during the negotiations, or in writing position papers on the many facets of the MIA question.

*Shortly after the ICCS deployed to Vietnam, the Canadians decided that their presence was futile and withdrew, to be replaced by Iran.

Every Tuesday and Thursday morning at ten o'clock, representatives of the four parties to the negotiations met at a conference site located on Tan Son Nhut Air Base.* Seated around a large, circular conference table covered with green felt, the American and South Vietnamese delegations would spar for three hours with the two Communist delegations, in vain and tedious attempts to convince our Communist adversaries that we should get down to business on the exchange of MIA information. But the Communists would have none of it. On many occasions, the entire three hours would elapse without even an agreement on the agenda for the day. If the American or the South Vietnamese delegate spoke first, it was predictable that he would offer a proposal for discussion of a specific MIA case. Typically, the United States would press for an answer to an earlier query on the fate of a pilot who had been captured but not repatriated. The Communist replies seldom varied. Week after week, the Hanoi delegate and his Vietcong colleague would ignore our appeals for commencement of substantive discussions and subject us to long-winded, strident statements condemning the United States for initiating, waging, and prolonging the war. Over and over, they reminded us of our "crimes against the Vietnamese people" and our "sabotage of the Paris Agreement." To support their position, they would often cite the views of "the progressive American people," among whom they numbered Jane Fonda, Senators Kennedy and Fulbright, and other doves in the U.S. Congress. As backup officer at these sessions, I took notes for use in our reporting requirements and supplied the Chief with an occasional hastily scrawled note if I picked up something unusual in the monotonous Communist diatribes. After several weeks of such exposure, I came to dread these charades.

But as repugnant as I found the repressive features of the Hanoi government, one could see how the North Vietnamese

---

*The four parties to the Four-Party Joint Military Team were the United States, the Republic of Vietnam (South Vietnam), the Democratic Republic of Vietnam (North Vietnam), and the Provisional Revolutionary Government of the Republic of South Vietnam (the Vietcong).

position would be compelling to the people of the north. Captain To, a member of the Hanoi delegation, departed from his government's normal rhetoric one day as we conversed during a coffee break:

> Of course we have information on many of your MIA personnel, and in some cases even the remains of your pilots we shot down. And you must know that we do not like to keep them. Their graves defile our ancestral soil and are ugly reminders of the horrors of the bombing of our country. So we want to give them back. But why should we give them to you for nothing? Your government has done so much damage to our people and our land that it must pay. That is your obligation, and even your president committed himself to this. So we will not give you what you want just because you ask for it or demand it.

Had I been a North Vietnamese, I would undoubtedly have agreed with Captain To. But, as I had seen during the war in Hau Nghia province, General Giap's artillery had inflicted extensive damage in the name of "liberating the oppressed southerners," most of whom wanted no part of Hanoi-style Communism. There were simply no blacks and whites to the situation by 1974, and all parties to that unfortunate conflict could assume a share of the blame. President Nixon had pledged to the American people that we would spare no effort to provide the fullest possible accounting of our missing servicemen. All of us who grappled daily with this responsibility did our utmost to fulfill this commitment. Unfortunately, it was beyond our power to compel the Communists to accept our view that the MIA question was a purely humanitarian matter that should not be linked to other political portions of the cease-fire agreement. The days when we could force the Communists to do anything had long since passed.

THE BIG LIE

"Someone in Hanoi must have read *Mein Kampf* and *The Goebbels Diaries*," I called out to my office mate as I struggled through the tedious morning ritual of reading the daily transcripts of Radio Hanoi. Even though the themes seldom varied, we scanned the copy regularly for any signs of change in Hanoi's hard line on the MIA question. Today's lead item was a smug attack on "Governor General Martin," the Communists' mocking nickname for Ambassador Graham Martin. Martin, the Hanoi propagandist preached, should "recognize the futility of his attempts to prop up the puppet army of Nguyen van Thieu." As usual, General Murray and the Defense Attaché Office were accused of being the "control headquarters" for an alleged "secret army of twenty thousand illegal American military advisors."

The allegations were false, but there were compelling reasons why they had become indispensable parts of Hanoi's daily litany. Even though only a handful of American military men remained in Vietnam after the cease-fire, the North Vietnamese knew that the Saigon government's ties to Washington represented one of its major political weaknesses. The xenophobic South Vietnamese were responsive to the charge that their president was a creature of the White House. Furthermore, the withdrawal of the American military had left the Saigon government and the South Vietnamese people standing alone in opposition to North Vietnamese Communism—an image that Hanoi could not allow to take hold. A fundamental article of faith preached by Hanoi was that the Vietnam War was one of outside aggression (American), *not* a civil war caused by southern antipathy for Communism. By repeated insistence that the American military and political role in the south continued, Hanoi legitimized the need for continued heavy sacrifices "to eject the foreign aggressors from Vietnamese soil."

But like all good propaganda, the Hanoi line contained a grain of truth that made it more readily believable. Several thousand American contractor employees (many of them ex-military men) were assisting the South Vietnamese to maintain their air force, although their presence was not a violation of the Paris Agreement, which required a complete American military withdrawal only. It was also quite true that the Thieu government depended upon American aid for its existence, although Saigon was no more dependent upon Washington than Hanoi

was on Moscow and Peking. But the charge that these contractor employees constituted General Murray's "secret army"
was a particularly ludicrous notion to anyone familiar with life
in cease-fire Saigon. The contractors were a mixture of retired
military men and assorted expatriates whose motives for Vietnam duty were often questionable. Collectively, they were an
uncouth lot that thrived on the cheap liquor and women that
life in Saigon afforded. Discipline was not their middle name.
General Murray once described the life-style of Saigon's American expatriates as "sybaritic." We had to consult a dictionary to
decipher what the colorful general meant, after which everyone
agreed that he had aptly described the beast.* If the nefarious
Washington war hawks were covertly maintaining troops in
Vietnam, they had hardly recruited the elite of American society for the mission, and they could not have tapped a more
unlikely candidate to be their leader. Major General Murray
had seen duty during World War II as a member of a gun crew
on a merchant tanker, then later as a rail transport officer in
Italy. An American General Giap he was not. President Nixon
had promised continued military assistance to the Saigon government, and General Murray was the well-schooled technician
tasked to implement this commitment.

Article 7(a) of the Paris Agreement permitted the one-for-one
replacement of expended military equipment. General Murray's
mission was to ascertain South Vietnamese needs, work out the
priorities, and administer funds that were appropriated by Congress to keep the Saigon army in business. To accomplish this
task, Murray and his staff of fifty officers were augmented by
eight hundred to one thousand American civilians and a sizable
staff of Vietnamese employees. It was a massive undertaking
that was made even more demanding by the fact that the cease-
fire never succeeded in stilling the guns. As General Murray

---

*On the other hand, as one friend (a former contractor in Vietnam) reminded
me, these men played an important role in Vietnam throughout American
involvement, to include sharing the risks of death or injury with the military.
Like the early settlers who built the railroads and canals of America, or the
men who built the Alaska pipeline, "work hard, play hard" was their ethic.
They did both.

would recall, his mission was "the first time in our history—
perhaps any history—that we had the task, with a mere fifty
military, to totally support a million alien folks in battle."

I didn't envy General Murray his job. When the Military
Assistance Command, Vietnam, furled its colors, it bequeathed
to the unfortunate general a continuing bloody war rather than
the "era of national reconciliation and concord" envisioned by
the authors of the Paris Agreement. MG John Murray, logistician, found himself thrust by history into the eye of a highly
sensitive political and military hurricane. There was nothing
decent about Saigon's "decent interval."

Not that the slightly built, Brooklyn-bred Murray was overcome by the unexpected magnitude of his role. As an attorney
with a command of English equaled only by his candor and
blunt wit, he approached his job with an impressive intensity
and dedication. Always outspoken, General Murray made no
attempt to conceal his positive feelings toward the Vietnamese,
nor did he hide his conviction that the vindication of a decade
of American and Vietnamese sacrifice depended on successful
Vietnamese adjustment to our sudden pullout. The general
knew better than anyone that logistics was the Achilles' heel of
the Vietnamese military machine in 1973. His job was to compensate for this deficiency within the constraints of the Paris
Agreement, which clearly forbade any further American advisory role in Vietnam.

As the level of hostilities escalated, General Murray sometimes found himself uncomfortably situated directly in the line
of fire between the strong-willed Ambassador Martin and his
political opponents. Prime candidates for this role were congressional liberals, certain members of the press, and even Murray's own superiors in the chain of command. The general
recalls his position at the time as a no-win proposition. He once
related to me that "Ambassador Martin used to tell me that it
was either him or me when we disagreed. Then he'd add that
there were not too many people standing in line for his job."
General Murray preferred to avoid the Embassy's intrigues
altogether—a desire that became less and less achievable as his
tour progressed.

The feisty Murray was not one to run away from a fight. When he learned that the Department of Defense was about to eliminate hostile fire pay for his fifty officers, he dispatched an indignant protest to the Pentagon. Suspecting that the move to eliminate our combat pay was a political ploy to signify the termination of hostilities in Vietnam, Murray's challenge to Washington was a classic. "Maybe it's an attempt to whitewash the inside of a coal bin," he led off. "If so, then I want to know about it." The general explained that his staff officers were sometimes unavoidably exposed to enemy fire in the performance of their duties, and that to cut their combat pay of sixty dollars per month was thus unfair, and hardly deserving of attention as a cost-cutting measure since it involved a miniscule amount of money. We heard no more of the move to cut our combat pay. Our outspoken boss had made his point.

General Murray rejected the notion that we were assisting the South Vietnamese for the politically cynical purpose of delaying an inevitable Communist victory to save face for the Nixon administration. If he had believed that this assumption underlay our efforts in 1973 and 1974, I am convinced that he would have resigned rather than associate himself with such a policy. By 1973, many Americans in Saigon had become disenchanted with our Vietnamese ally, but General Murray was not one of them. A close personal friend of many of his Vietnamese counterparts, he identified with their cause and agonized over the limits imposed by the U.S. Congress on the use of American military power in Southeast Asia. Frustrated by congressional reluctance to continue funding the beleaguered South Vietnamese, he regarded any refusal to live up to our commitment as an unconscionable breach of trust. Saddled with the thankless task of explaining the acts of the tight-fisted Congress to the South Vietnamese, General Murray became increasingly disillusioned as the outlook for peace dimmed.

One day in early 1974, the general announced that he desired to address all military personnel in the DAO theater. The summons was unprecedented and triggered a wave of speculation. Many of us knew that the general was becoming embittered. Was he now going to announce his retirement? Ten minutes before the appointed hour, some seventy military men representing all four services had assembled in the theater. When the general strode briskly down the aisle, his expression signaled that he had called the meeting to get something off his chest. After confirming that all military personnel were indeed present, he began to speak. His voice was calm, but firm:

> This won't take me long, but I don't want anyone to get the idea that, because my delivery is brief, I don't mean exactly what I say. We are assigned here in Saigon to implement the policies of our government. In all matters pertaining to this mission, the chief spokesman for our government is Ambassador Martin. It's his show. Any and all statements of policy released to the press must come from the Ambassador or his press officer. *No one* in this office, myself included, has the authority to discuss the current situation with members of the Saigon press corps without specific authorization. If the Ambassador should choose to delegate this authority to me or anyone else, then and only then will we share our opinions about the military situation. Until we receive such authorization, we will respect the fact that the sole authorized channel of communication to the press is the United States Embassy.

Then the general came to the point:

> Recently, there have been stories appearing in the press quoting "informed American military sources in Saigon." Now, if there are any "informed American military sources in Saigon," they are in this theater right now. I want you all to understand that we are forbidden to communicate with the press unless specifically directed and authorized by the Embassy. If members of the press approach you for your opinion of the situation, you should refer them to the South Vietnamese military, which is carrying on without American combat forces. It is *their* war; let *them* explain it. Finally, I want you all to know that, if a member of my command violates this policy and it comes to my attention, I promise you that I will lock, bolt, and barricade the gates of mercy!

With that, the general snatched up his hat and stalked out of the theater, leaving all of us with the thought that one colonel expressed aloud: "Boy, what an ass-chewing he must have gotten from the Ambassador!"

One thing was abundantly clear to all of us. From now on, we would be wise to avoid the company of anyone remotely connected with the press. In the event of a leak, anyone who consorted with journalists would be automatically suspect. The general's uncharacteristic ultimatum unquestionably bore the Embassy's trademark. It was a stern warning that portended draconian measures. At a minimum, the transgressor would earn a one-way ticket home under less-than-honorable circumstances.

The public relations nerve had long been official Saigon's most sensitive spot, as reflected in the instructions General Murray had received when he assumed his post. General Murray recalls that the Terms of Reference that established the DAO created a "number of bosses" for him in the chain of command. The DAO's activities had to be coordinated with several layers of military headquarters in Thailand, Hawaii, and Washington. "I had many bosses," Murray remembers, "but not the Ambassador, with whom I was 'to cooperate and fully inform.' The one clear exception was public relations. That was placed entirely under the Ambassador by a separate message. I was to take my marching orders on public relations from him."*

Relations with the media in Vietnam had been a sticky problem for as long as I could remember. Early in my tour as an advisor in Hau Nghia, I had been warned about the dangers of talking to reporters. At that time, the guidance was clear; we would not talk to a reporter unless he had a letter of introduction from the MACV Public Information Office. Even then, talking to the press was risky business. Everyone knew that a MACV-sanctioned journalist had badly misquoted a district senior advisor in our province, and that the candid remarks of

*However explicit MG Murray's marching orders were, they contained the seeds of conflict and misunderstanding. For Ambassador Martin was most certainly the head of the U.S. "Country Team" in South Vietnam. He, and only he, could make the claim that he was the President's personal representative, a grant of power that he exercised until his departure in an evacuation helicopter.

another officer had caused such a reaction from the Embassy
that the hapless officer had been counseled for his indiscretion.
Most of us would have preferred to shake hands with a leper
than to entrust our careers to a journalist in 1972. By the time I
returned to Vietnam in 1973, I had developed a strong sense of
caution about the media.

For this reason, I was initially uneasy upon learning that my
duties on the MIA team included the role of press officer. But I
needn't have worried, for it soon became clear that virtually all
dealings with the media were centralized downtown at the
Embassy. I prepared many press releases on the MIA talks for
Embassy approval, but few ever made it past our State Department colleagues. I even wrote a thirty-four-page "White Book,"
a report to the American people on the first year of the MIA
talks, but it, too, failed to clear the Embassy. Nor was I overworked in arranging press conferences for our delegation chief.
I can recall only two such occasions during my fifteen months
on the job, and the Embassy played the leading role in arranging both. The Embassy's Political-Military Affairs Section kept
our delegation on a short public relations leash.

This situation quickly became one of the most frustrating
features of our job. Without strong ties to the media, we for-
feited a useful weapon in our battle of wits with the Communists. In our view, the Communists were clearly responsible for
the deadlocked talks, and we wanted to mount a press campaign
to exploit their vulnerability. When our initiatives repeatedly
failed to receive the Embassy's blessing, we felt that we were
missing an opportunity to saddle the North Vietnamese with
responsibility for the MIA impasse. Stonewalled by Hanoi's stall
tactics at the conference table, we sought to bludgeon our
adversary publicly for his callous behavior. The Communists
had used the POW issue to their advantage during the war, and
we saw an opportunity to beat them at their own game. But the
Embassy held firm, and the MIA issue was kept at a low sim-
mer. Our superiors evidently believed that the blame for the
deadlocked talks already rested at the feet of the Communists
and that any press campaign that we might launch would
invite accusations that we were playing politics with the MIA
question.

One of the most enlightening, yet sobering, features of duty in cease-fire Saigon was the opportunity to observe the never-ending war of words from a box seat. At times, I felt that our crude attempts to match the North Vietnamese in the art of influencing world opinion resembled a kid from the neighborhood gym trying to stand up to the heavyweight champion of the world. No one has described Hanoi's mastery of the manipulative art better than Tom Wolfe:

If the United States was seriously trying to win the battle of world opinion—well, then, here you had a real bush-league operation. The North Vietnamese were the uncontested aces . . . One of the most galling things a pilot had to endure in Vietnam was seeing the North Vietnamese pull propaganda coup after propaganda coup, often with the help, unwitting or otherwise, of Americans. . . .

For example, the missions over . . . an important transportation center in the Iron Triangle area. For two days they softened the place up, working on the flak sites and SAM sites in the most methodical way. On the third day, they massed the bomb strike itself. They tore the place apart. They ripped open its gullet! They put it out of the transport business. It had been a model operation. But the North Vietnamese are now blessed with a weapon that no military device known to America could ever get a lock on. As if by magic . . . in Hanoi . . . appears . . . Harrison Salisbury! Harrison Salisbury—writing in the *New York Times* about the atrocious American bombing of the hardscrabble folk of North Vietnam in the Iron Triangle! If you had real sporting blood in you, you had to hand it to the North Vietnamese. They were champions of this sort of thing. It was beautiful to watch. To Americans who knew the air war in the north firsthand, it seemed as if the North Vietnamese were playing Mr. Harrison Salisbury of the *New York Times* like an ocarina, as if they were blowing smoke up his pipe and the finger work was just right and the song was coming forth better than they could have played it themselves.[2]

Our organization experienced Hanoi's penchant for the propaganda coup on a number of occasions, but several episodes are particularly memorable.

Shortly after the cease-fire, the U.S. Air Force commenced weekly liaison flights to Hanoi to carry representatives of all four MIA delegations to the North Vietnamese capital. These missions were flown to enable the North Vietnamese delegation to communicate directly with its government in the hopes that this would facilitate the exchange of MIA information. During the first several trips, which included a day's layover in Hanoi, our Air Force C-130 crew wore their flight suits on guided tours of the city hosted by the North Vietnamese. A regular feature of these tours was the opportunity to purchase souvenirs, the most popular of which were metal combs engraved with Chairman Ho Chi Minh's credo, "Nothing is more precious than independence and freedom." Engraved in Vietnamese on the opposite side of the combs appeared the words, "Wreck of the 4,000th American aircraft," Hanoi's smug boast that the combs were made from melted parts of our fallen jets. Needless to say, our hosts delighted in selling them to American airmen.

Then the North Vietnamese announced that the Air Force crews should only wear civilian clothes into downtown Hanoi. The official explanation was that the sight of American pilots in flight suits "enraged and infuriated" the citizens of Hanoi, who recalled the "brutal carpet bombing of their city by the U.S. Air Force." Since the North Vietnamese were the hosts and could call the shots for the Hanoi trip, the Air Force complied with this request. Some months later, on one of my trips to Hanoi, one of the employees of the Hoa Binh ("Peace") Hotel told me that our crews had "refused to wear their uniforms into the capital because they were ashamed of their air piracy and afraid of Hanoi's outraged citizens." After demanding that the crews wear civilian clothes, the Communists had apparently told their people that the Americans themselves had made the decision.

After a year of negotiations, Hanoi finally agreed to repatriate the remains of twenty-three American prisoners who had died in Communist POW camps (some of whom had died from torture inflicted by their captors). In negotiating the release ceremony, the Communists stipulated that no members of the Saigon press corps would be allowed at Hanoi's Gia Lam airport, where the remains would be turned over to our delegation.

B–52 piece on display in Hanoi.

We accepted this condition because we had no desire to turn the solemn occasion into a public relations circus. When the long-awaited day arrived, our team of negotiators arrived in Hanoi only to discover that the Communists had invited more than one hundred members of the Hanoi press corps to cover their "humane gesture." As the army of Communist-bloc and leftist reporters recorded the events, a North Vietnamese spokesman read a lengthy, prepared statement that lauded Hanoi's act as proof that his government was "scrupulously implementing" the Paris Agreement. No mention was made of the fact that Hanoi had stalled for more than a year before finally repatriating the remains. Nor did the statement mention Hanoi's rejection of our request to return the remains of an unidentified twenty-fourth American discovered by our team during an earlier visit to a Hanoi cemetery. The North Vietnamese argued that this American had been discovered dead in the wreckage of his aircraft. Hence, technically, he had not died in captivity, and the repatriation of his remains would thus have to be separately negotiated. Subsequently, we tried repeatedly to reopen this case, but Hanoi would not discuss it. The remains of the man we dubbed "the twenty-fourth American" remained in Communist hands.

The Communist military delegation at Camp Davis held a press conference every Saturday morning at ten o'clock. It was the only regular show in town, and the press could always be counted on to show up in force to hear the senior Communist spokesman, Colonel Vo Dong Giang. I routinely sent my Vietnamese press assistant to cover these conferences, and Monday mornings in the office were usually traumatic as she angrily reported on the latest Communist accusations. It was not uncommon for the Vietcong spokesman to bombard the press with hostile propaganda, to include calling for President Thieu's overthrow. Usually, the obliging Communists would end the conference by posing for pictures and distributing transcripts of their statements to assist the press in accurately quoting their positions.

Under such circumstances, we needed all the help we could get in our efforts to counter Hanoi's finely tuned propaganda machine. Such help certainly included good relations with the press. Unfortunately, this was simply not the case in Saigon. The legacy of mutual distrust and misunderstanding that developed during the war continued to haunt us during the cease-fire period. Six months on the Joint Military Team had convinced me that my wartime hostility toward the press was unhealthy. Much of our difficulty stemmed from a tendency toward oversensitive reactions to criticisms often implied in questions from inquisitive reporters. In defense of the press, I believe that the vast majority of journalists endeavored to maintain professional and objective attitudes toward our problems as we struggled to find the "light at the end of the tunnel." It is easy to understand how the glaring discrepancy between the military's official optimism at the end of 1967 and the sudden explosion of South Vietnam's cities during Tet of 1968 had triggered skepticism and undermined official Saigon's credibility. The tragedy of the resulting mutual distrust was that the press and the military tended to perceive each other in extreme terms. Just as I had left Vietnam in 1972 convinced that the press corps was dedicated to discrediting our efforts in Vietnam, a regrettably large number of reporters likewise concluded from our defensive posture toward them that we had something to hide. If we were unfair in questioning the loyalty and professionalism of the press because reporters asked tough questions that often exposed our weaknesses, the press was equally unfair when it accused the military of pursuing a policy of deliberate deceit. To be sure, the Saigon command's perpetual optimism invited suspicion; and, to make matters worse, some incidents of deliberate misstatements quite clearly occurred. Still, the press and the American people never quite understood that most of the optimistic reporting during the war resulted from inadequate comprehension of the forces at work, not from some coordinated and sinister plot to hide the truth. The Americans who made inaccurate assessments and predictions because of their naivete and misinterpretations of reality vastly outnumbered those who made misstatements grounded in malice and deceit.

Unfortunately, we never succeeded in penetrating the barriers between ourselves and the press in Saigon. Thus, as Press Officer for the U.S. delegation, I found myself in the absurd position of physically avoiding the members of the Saigon press corps as the military situation deteriorated and they began to dig for sources. Jim Markham of the *New York Times* may recall his attempts in March 1975 to pump me for information during our noontime swims in the DAO pool. I would swim my laps around the pool and then seek out a cabana on which to recover. Jim would flop down beside me and commence his interrogation. I knew from his informed questions on the snowballing disaster then under way in Hue and Danang that he had pieced together an accurate picture of events. On a couple of occasions, I swore that his sources were better than mine. But I dared not confirm or deny the accuracy of his efforts, lest I be identified as "an informed American military source in Saigon." My only recourse was to squirm and play dumb, thereby contributing to the legacy of distrust that had already done so much harm.

Looking back now, I can see that the whole problem was stupid and avoidable. Locked as we were in a war of words with the grand masters of opinion manipulation, we desperately needed a relationship of mutual trust with the press. In Saigon, our reluctance to deal regularly and openly with the media ignored the fundamental tenet that journalists must produce copy for their editors. If adequate copy cannot be obtained from authoritative sources, reporters will invariably obtain it elsewhere.

HANOI

"Hanoi is truly beautiful, Dai Uy. In the center of the city lies the Hoang Kiem Lake, with a temple in the middle on a small island. You would really like it!" The speaker was one of the many khaki-clad North Vietnamese prisoners I had interrogated during the war. Like most of General Giap's troops, he was short and lean, with a deeply suntanned face from the many months he had spent trudging down the infiltration trails of Laos and Cambodia. His nostalgic recollections of Hanoi were not unfamiliar to me, for I had heard them from his comrades who had been fortunate enough to fall into our hands alive in Hau Nghia. These were the men who would literally live to fight another day, and their fond memories of Hanoi had long since filled me with curiosity about the enemy's capital city. After all, Hanoi was the nerve center of a small, peasant country that had fielded an army of light infantry that had outlasted our country on the battlefield. True, Hanoi's regulars had never decisively defeated the U.S. Army in a major battle, but, when the guns stilled and the decisions of the politicians were implemented, it was General Giap's troops that clung to their positions in South Vietnam while the U.S. Army completed its withdrawal.

During my frequent verbal sparring sessions with those North Vietnamese prisoners, I had been intrigued by the success enjoyed by the Hanoi government in mobilizing its population to accept the horrendous sacrifices of the long struggle for national reunification. It was impossible to ignore the bravery of the North Vietnamese regulars we had fought in Hau Nghia province. Hanoi's troops had seldom surrendered unless they were wounded or out of ammunition. During interrogation, most of them exhibited a firm belief in the justice of the war against what they had been told was foreign aggression. The initial interrogation was always difficult. Convinced that they were about to be tortured and executed, my sullen sources would invariably clam up and stoically await their fate. Conditioned to expect the worst, Hanoi's men would only open up after I had undermined their defenses with humane treatment. When they did begin to talk, they told of their deep admiration for Ho Chi Minh and of their pride in their country. Many of them had volunteered for the army because they believed it was their "solemn obligation" to liberate their southern cousins from American oppression. Raised from infancy to revere *Bac Ho* (Uncle Ho), pliable young North Vietnamese soldiers were easily convinced by their political officers that the South Vietnamese people were brutally enslaved by the barbaric and cruel Americans, the same Americans whose aircraft were bombing their villages in the north. As one North Vietnamese prisoner told me, "When the commandant of the training center asked us who would volunteer to go south and strike the Americans, we were all caught up by the emotion of the moment. We felt very patriotic and raised our hands to the man. Some men even went to the local tattoo parlors and had the words, *Xuong Nam, Giet My* ('Go South and Kill the Americans') inscribed on their chests."

Not that such intense feelings of regional pride were confined only to Hanoi's soldiers. One could sense it among Vietnamese of all three regions—north, central, and south. And in the south, it was even evident among the native North Vietnamese who comprised a large proportion of the South Vietnamese officer corps. Deep pride in the customs, culture, and beauty of their northern homeland was a part of being North Vietnamese, even among those who had fled the north after the division of the country under the 1954 Geneva Accords rather than live under Ho's Communism. My northern friends proudly explained to me that the north had always been the home of the educated elite of Vietnamese society. If I desired to speak correct Vietnamese, they admonished, I must learn the Hanoi dialect. Large numbers of the North Vietnamese who came south in 1954 were Catholic, and these families were tightly knit, thrifty, and hard-working. As one northern acquaintance patiently explained to me, "We never had any choice but to work hard in the north. The climate was cold, the soil less fertile, and the rivers less controllable than in the south. The aggressive, almost Western approach to life and its problems seen among us northerners derives from these realities. We had to be strong."

Not surprisingly, the South Vietnamese saw their northern neighbors somewhat differently. My southern friends insisted that the North Vietnamese were arrogant, tightfisted, and untrustworthy. Northerners were infected with a superiority complex that made them pushy and uncompromising. If I were foolish enough to marry a northern girl, the southerners counseled, she would save all my money, but I would live on spinach and water lilies as she nagged and bullied me into an early grave. One joke popular among the South Vietnamese insisted that the North and Central Vietnamese ate *Ca ro cay* (a carved wooden fish), which, when dipped in fish sauce and licked, would last forever and precluded the need to buy fresh fish at the marketplace.

But the North Vietnamese scoffed at such insults. Southerners, they pointed out, were lazy, shiftless country folk who were given to drinking, gambling, and free spending. Marry a southern girl, I was warned, and you will labor all your life merely to keep ahead of her spending habits. As proof of northern superiority, they pointed proudly to the fact that most of them had fled the north in 1954 with little more than the shirts on their backs. Now, a scant twenty years later, ethnic North Vietnamese comprised a disproportionately large segment of South Vietnam's economic, political, and military leadership. In South Vietnam, a poor North Vietnamese family was indeed a rarity. Undisciplined and uneducated northern children were rarer still.

As an American, I found the north-south rivalry amusing, but also valid. During the war, many an American advisor observed that the northern officers in the South Vietnamese military were usually more direct and aggressive in their approach to problems. In contrast, southerners seemed less inclined to mount a frontal attack on a given problem. Southerners seemed to approach life in the deliberate and patient fashion that our instructors at Fort Bragg had ascribed to all Vietnamese during our advisory training. The typical southerner's approach to any endeavor usually incorporated the key principle that "tomorrow's another day," a propensity that caused no end of frustration for countless Americans during the war.

I had seen the manifestations of this dichotomy, and thus turned a deaf ear on the insistence of one well-educated, Hanoi-born officer who tried to convince me that the north-south distinction was a fiction fostered by the French as part of their colonial philosophy of "divide and rule." Article I of the Paris Agreement reaffirmed the unity of Vietnam, but many fundamental differences existed between north and south over and above the ideological split that had been the cause of so much bloodshed. I had already seen the results of twenty years of American-backed "nation-building" in the south. A trip to Hanoi would give me the opportunity to see what the North Vietnamese had done with their half of the country since the signing of the Geneva Accords.

We were airborne in a lumbering C-130 cargo plane over the South China Sea—Hanoi bound. Our estimated flight time from Saigon to the Communist capital was less than four hours. Four hours to travel a distance that had taken some of the North Vietnamese officers seated across from me more than one hundred days when they had trudged on foot into South Vietnam to do battle with the tall, long-nosed soldiers of the 1st Cavalry Division and the 101st Airborne.

Our aircraft had departed Saigon at eight that morning with the Americans and South Vietnamese on one side, the Communists firmly entrenched on the opposite side. The DMZ, I joked to my South Vietnamese opposite number, ran down the middle of the aircraft. This was my first trip, and from the lack of traffic between the two sides, I deduced that fraternization was frowned upon. The South Vietnamese were particularly stiff whenever we were in the presence of the Communists, for it was no secret that our ally resented the legitimacy that the presence of Communist negotiators in Saigon implied. Prior to boarding the aircraft, curt South Vietnamese police officials made no attempt to disguise their feelings as they scrutinized ID documents and forced each Communist delegate to pose for mug shots on the tarmac. Later that night, they would again subject each Communist passenger to this drill as they disembarked from the C-130. The South Vietnamese never missed an opportunity to remind their adversaries that they were not welcome in Saigon. We had forced the South Vietnamese to accept the terms of the Paris Agreement, but they were not obligated to like the results.

Shortly after takeoff, I summoned up my courage and crossed the "DMZ," taking a seat between Major Tien and Sergeant Ha, two members of the Hanoi delegation. The weekly negotiating sessions were structured and provided little opportunity to meet our counterparts. If I were to ever have a meaningful dialogue with them, it would have to take place during the weekly liaison flights. I had given the matter considerable thought as the day of the flight approached and decided that it would be foolish to allow shyness or a closed mind to mar this opportunity.

Major Tien wore an ill-fitting khaki tunic adorned with scarlet and gold collar tabs. An olive drab pith helmet hung on the bulkhead behind him. Except for the collar tabs, the only insignia on his uniform was what we jokingly referred to as his "Ho Chi Minh Good Conduct Badge," a small red and gold pin affixed over his right breast pocket in the shape of a profile of Chairman Ho. I guessed that the major was around fifty-five years old. His hair was graying, and crow's-feet had appeared at the corners of his almond-shaped eyes. Tien extended his hand and greeted me with a thin, humorless smile.

"Chao, Dai Uy. Dai Uy co khoe khong?" ("Hello, Captain. Are you feeling well?")

"Da, cam on Thieu ta. Toi khoe lam. Con Thieu ta, thi sao." ("I'm fine, thank you, major. How about you?") I deliberately used the polite, deferential form, as I would to a senior officer in the Saigon armed forces. This preliminary exchange of greetings lasted several more minutes as the major asked me a battery of personal questions common to Vietnam, but which most Westerners would regard as a bit nosey. How old was I? Did I have a

wife? Any children? How long had I studied Vietnamese, and how long had I been in Vietnam? I had been pumped in a similar manner by hundreds of curious Vietnamese during the past three years, but, coming from Major Tien, the questions made me uneasy. "Don't make it too easy for them to do your dossier," the intelligence officer in me cautioned—"make them work for it." Then Tien steered the conversation to the war, making no attempt to be diplomatic. As I would later learn, his question that was really a statement was typical of Hanoi's negotiators.

"Dai Uy, tell me something. You are an educated man. Why did the Americans come to our country, intervene in our affairs, cause so much destruction, and kill so many people? Surely you know about what happened at My Lai and elsewhere in our land."

"Major," I replied, "let me ask you a question. Is it not the policy of your government that soldiers must stay close to the people and treat them well?"

The major nodded his agreement. On my right, the baby-faced Sergeant Ha leaned closer so that he could understand my accented Vietnamese.

"There, you see, Thieu ta. That's exactly what our soldiers are taught. Our policy is the same as yours. But, sometimes, mistakes can be made at a lower level. Surely you would agree that a lower-level cadre might make a mistake and disobey your government's policy?"

"No, Dai Uy," replied Tien with a determined shake of his head. "Such a thing is possible, but not in our army. No cadre would ever make such a mistake. The policy is clear and understood by all. These are our people. Nothing like My Lai could ever be committed by liberation forces."

"I've got you now," I thought to myself. "In that case, Major, you must explain to me why your troops massacred thousands of civilians in Hue during the 1968 Tet Offensive." I glanced triumphantly at Sergeant Ha, who by now was almost sitting in my lap as he strained to monitor the debate over the drone of the engines.

"Dai Uy," Tien responded with a glare, "the thousands of innocent civilians killed during the general uprising in the cities of South Vietnam in 1968 were killed in the cross fire of the battles, mostly by the massive firepower of the American military. Our liberation forces scrupulously heeded their orders to protect civilian lives and property."

"But surely, Thieu ta, you cannot deny that the bodies of several thousand citizens of Hue found by our forces in mass graves outside the city had been executed and buried by your forces. People whose hands had been tied behind their backs certainly weren't killed in any cross fire. I think that some of your local commanders got carried away there the same as Lieutenant Calley at My Lai."

The old major's jaw was set now. "Dai Uy, the only citizens executed at Hue were convicted by liberation courts of treason. Such courts administered revolutionary justice according to law, and your claim of thousands of victims of our forces is incorrect. All our commanders know the correct policy and adhere to it. Such excesses may be possible in your army, but never in ours. You have listened too much to your government's propaganda."

Our conversation was leading nowhere, but I was intrigued by the way the major handled himself. The stubborn old revolutionary was not about to let his guard down and openly discuss the conduct of "liberation armed forces." It occurred to me that he actually believed what he was saying. After all, unless he had been an eyewitness to the Hue slaughter, or had spoken to one, it was hardly likely that he would have read about such excesses in *Quan Doi Nhan Dan* (People's Army), the North Vietnamese Army newspaper. Still, it was difficult to accept the idea that he could believe so firmly in the total discipline of his forces in combat, particularly if he were a combat veteran himself. I interpreted his intransigence as a disciplined determination to yield nothing to an American adversary, particularly in front of Sergeant Ha, who had clung to every word of our exchange.

Major Tien signaled a truce by slumping back in his chair and closing his eyes, his fascination with the new American officer clearly at an end for the moment. No doubt he had decided that I was no better than other Americans—impudent and arrogant.

How could I dare to criticize liberation forces when the American army had come thousands of miles to intervene in a nation where it had no business in the first place?

Tired of political rhetoric, I turned to the bright-faced sergeant. He was a security guard. Armed with a Chinese K-54 pistol discreetly hidden by his tunic, his job was to guard the North Vietnamese cargo during loading and unloading. (Like the baggage of the passengers themselves, Communist cargo was diplomatically immune from search.) Unlike the dogmatic Major Tien, Sergeant Ha turned out to be a pleasant traveling companion. A twenty-three-year-old native of Hanoi, Ha had been a law student before his induction into the army. His spirits were high on this trip, for he would soon see his wife, who was pregnant with their first child. Sergeant Ha was more interested in talking about his hopes for a son than he was in proving his ideological purity in a political debate.

The sergeant expressed curiosity about a book I was carrying. I explained that the book was Col. Robinson Risner's *The Passing of the Night*, an American prisoner of war's account of life in a Hanoi prison. This brought the feisty old Major Tien to life.

"I've heard about this book, Dai Uy. Surely you must know that it is a slander against the Democratic Republic of Vietnam. Our policy was one of leniency toward captured personnel."

I had read enough accounts of Hanoi's "leniency" to know better, but decided to go one more round with the major anyway. Could I break down his ideological rigidity? "Thieu ta, I don't believe it was your government's policy to torture prisoners (a white lie), but, in war people sometimes become emotionally involved and do regrettable things. After all, the American pilots captured by your people had just attacked your country. Under such circumstances, I can understand why Colonel Risner and other prisoners were not welcomed to Hanoi as honored guests, and why some of them were mistreated by your interrogators."

Tien shook his head. "No, Dai Uy, you still don't understand. No officer would dare to strike a prisoner. We are trained to explain the facts about the war so that they can understand that they were the tools of their government in its dark scheme to

NVA Sgt. Tran Ha.

perpetuate the colonial rule of our country. Even progressive Americans like Jane Fonda and Ramsey Clark have visited our POW camps and verified our humane treatment of prisoners. You cannot believe the lies of a man like Colonel Risner."

I had played my experiment to the end of its usefulness, deliberately challenging the major several times to speak openly, to abandon his plug-in answers, and to discuss the problems of wartime ethics and conduct. But he had refused the bait. The dogmatic old veteran either could not, or would not, let his guard down and accept my challenge to a free exchange of views. Or did he perhaps consider that we had indeed engaged in such an exchange? Was he, to use General Murray's description, "not lying, but transmitting lies"? Or was he afraid of the consequences if he yielded a single point to me and I reported his words to my superiors? I couldn't know, but I had gained some insight into the mentality of our adversaries from the encounter. Dealing with the likes of Major Tien was considerably more challenging than extracting information from frightened and malleable prisoners and defectors in Hau Nghia province.

My first glimpse of North Vietnam was Hanoi's Gia Lam airport, nestled among the paddy lands across the river from the city. As we taxied past the rows of Soviet-built aircraft stored there, I caught sight of the terminal building, a pale green stucco structure that was almost deserted. Red flags hung around the area in profusion, while a scarlet and gold banner proclaimed in Vietnamese, "Hearty welcome to the delegations of international women arriving to participate in the Fourth Vietnam Women's Convention." A small welcoming party greeted us on the tarmac, only a few feet from the spot where our prisoners of war had been repatriated twelve months earlier. Led by a major named Huyen, the reception committee was all smiles as we descended from the C-130's cargo deck. At Huyen's side was a bushy-browed second lieutenant who served as his interpreter. In the terminal, we sat down for tea in a small alcove. Here we would hear from our hosts what the itinerary of the day was to be. As we talked, a photographer hovered around us, snapping away like he owned stock in Eastman Kodak. As the new man on the scene, I was photographed from all angles. A civilian with Mayor Huyen introduced himself as Mr. Quang, a member of the "Committee on Receiving Foreign Visitors" from the Ministry of Foreign Affairs. "No doubt a member of the *Cuc Nghien Cuu* [Research Bureau—Hanoi's secret service]," I thought.

Major Huyen was all smiles as he announced a trip to the National Art Museum, followed by lunch at the Hoa Binh Hotel. There, he announced, we would be given an opportunity to purchase North Vietnamese handicrafts. We would then enjoy a "typical Vietnamese meal," which turned out to be an eight-course extravaganza that no North Vietnamese peasant could afford, after which we would return to the airport for yet another opportunity to purchase souvenirs before departing.

We boarded an old red and white bus for the trip to downtown Hanoi. Across from the terminal, the long barrels of an antiaircraft battery protruded from their emplacements. After crossing the railroad tracks, our bus rattled down the main street of Gia Lam, a small village that lies directly across the Red River from Hanoi itself. On our right lay the twisted and gutted remains of the Gia Lam railroad yards, still unrepaired

thirteen months after the end of the bombing. An old steam
locomotive lay on its side, its body pockmarked with hundreds
of gaping holes from the exploding bombs. Directly across the
street, a row of small shops and shanties stood untouched, convincing evidence of the "surgical bombing" skills of the U.S. Air
Force. A large blue sign with an arrow indicated "Hanoi" to
the right, and I experienced a moment of apprehension. I was
about to venture into the heart of a city that our B-52s had
heavily bombed just before the signing of the Paris Agreement,
and I suddenly became very aware of my khaki uniform. "The
rail yards are just the beginning," I thought, as our bus wound
its way up the approach ramp to the famous Paul Doumer
Bridge. Beside the ramp, a huge crater had been blown in the
earth by what Major Huyen smugly described as "a stupid
smart bomb." The crater was full of brown water, and a gaggle
of half-naked children were seine-fishing in its murky depths.
Our air force had dropped spans of this bridge several times
during the war, but Major Huyen boasted that "the people"
had rebuilt it the last time in forty-four days.

The United States had dropped more bombs on North Vietnam than the total tonnage dropped in both theaters during
World War II, and the furor over the 1972 Christmas bombings
was fresh in my mind. I was thus mentally prepared for the
worst as we snaked down the circular ramp and entered Hanoi.
While serving in West Berlin, I had seen photographs of the
damage wrought there by strategic bombing. Some of the ruins
in Berlin's Tiergarten still stood, more than two decades after
the end of the war. Surely Hanoi would still be a shattered city.

But as we headed down Dien Bien Phu Boulevard, I experienced a sobering revelation. Instead of a sea of chimneys amid
mountains of rubble, block after block of intact buildings
greeted my eyes. Hanoi was largely undamaged, with only
occasional evidence of destruction or rebuilding. The city had
clearly been spared by our B-52s. Hanoi was not a Berlin, a
Tokyo, or a Dresden. Nor by any stretch of the imagination had
it been "carpet-bombed." The stucco buildings in the center of
the city were much as I imagined Graham Greene would have
remembered them, and most of the bombs that had fallen on the

downtown area had clearly been aimed at the giant iron bridge. I almost laughed aloud when I realized that Hanoi's propaganda had flimflammed me into swallowing the image of an indiscriminately devastated city. (I wasn't the only one taken in by the propaganda of North Vietnam's Ministry of Information. World opinion convicted our air force of carpet-bombing Hanoi on extremely meager evidence, a myth that has been impossible to kill. Even in the memoirs of a man as experienced and educated as George Ball, one can read about the Nixon administration's "brutal carpet-bombing" of Hanoi.) It was not a reassuring feeling to realize how badly we had been finessed by Hanoi's propagandists.

Not that signs of the recently ended war were absent. The U.S. Air Force had indeed struck virtually every military target in and around the capital, and, in the process, "collateral damage" had occurred. Hanoi's tour guides were adept at displaying the results of what were largely accidents of war, the most widely publicized of which was the sad fate of the Bach Mai dispensary. Bach Mai had the misfortune to lie across the street from a military airfield and petroleum storage depot, and it had paid for this by absorbing a string of bombs. The tragedy of Bach Mai had been costly to the North Vietnamese, but it had been doubly costly to the United States. Every foreign traveler or journalist who visited North Vietnam received a complimentary trip to Bach Mai to witness irrefutable proof of American brutality. Once again, the North Vietnamese managed to turn the tables on us and literally snatch victory from the jaws of defeat. Using Bach Mai as a showcase, Hanoi's propagandists had convinced the world that the Christmas bombings unleashed by President Nixon represented an indiscriminate campaign of terror against innocent civilians. In fact, the 1972 bombings were restrained and limited compared to the punishment inflicted on the Germans and Japanese during World War II. The loss of life among Hanoi's civilian population at the hands of our air force was tragic, but it was nothing compared to the slaughter that could have resulted if we had bombed indiscriminately, as charged by the North Vietnamese. As callous as it may sound, the 1972 Christmas bombings were

Major Huyen and author in Hanoi.

probably a testament to progress in the technology of aerial bombardment since World War II. As our bus wound its way through the streets of downtown Hanoi, it seemed almost inconceivable that we could have dropped so much ordnance in and around that city and still left it virtually intact.

When I expressed my astonishment at the absence of bomb damage, Major Huyen insisted stubbornly that "the people have completely rebuilt the city." If he was right, then "the people" must have mastered the techniques of aging new buildings sixty or seventy years. Actually, it was quite easy to identify those structures near the bridge and elsewhere that had recently been rebuilt. I saw nothing during that first visit or subsequent visits to support Major Huyen's contention that we had unleashed our machines of war against innocent civilians and nonmilitary targets.

On the contrary, the evidence pointed to the opposite conclusion: namely, that the North Vietnamese were well aware of our bombing accuracy as well as of our pilots' targeting restrictions. Good examples were the controversial Red River dikes, which world opinion tried and convicted us of bombing. It had not taken the North Vietnamese long to determine that we were deliberately sparing the dikes, and they reacted by emplacing mobile antiaircraft batteries in their shadow to secure them from attack. In still another show of respect for the accuracy of the alleged "indiscriminate" bombing, cowering citizens of Hanoi and military convoys filled the streets outside Hoa Lo prison (the "Hanoi Hilton") during the Christmas bombing raids. The Hanoi population knew that the raiding B-52s could and would avoid bombing our own captured aviators.

Perhaps the most memorable feature of the face of Hanoi was its cold austerity. Gazing out the window of the bus at what North Vietnamese prisoners had called the "great socialist rear base," I felt a sense of total disbelief that this could be the nerve center of our courageous and determined enemy. The Saigon I had left that morning was a montage of colors, fast-moving vehicles, crowds of shoppers, and the mixed sounds of Western and Vietnamese music blaring from the stalls of sidewalk vendors. Hanoi could not have been more different. Saigon was a festive place for thousands of prosperous Westerners who kept it humming with daily injections of hard currency. In Hanoi, I saw only Vietnamese faces.

The atmosphere in Saigon was much like Hong Kong — crowded streets lined with overflowing shops, fine restaurants, and art dealers. Indian and Chinese merchants dominated the gold shops and custom tailor businesses, and the black-tressed beauties of the South Vietnamese capital exhibited a charm unequaled in the Orient. After living in Saigon for the past six months, I could not have been more jolted by the stark contrast of Hanoi.

"Austere" is perhaps not the best term to describe Hanoi in 1974. Actually, the city was drab, run-down, and depressing. Hanoi's tree-shaded boulevards conveyed the sense of a formerly attractive neighborhood that had been allowed to run down by its residents. French-inspired beige stucco buildings with dark green shutters and red tile roofs predominated, but the paint had long since begun to peel from them all, and the ornamental shrubberies once so elegant and pruned now had overgrown the screenless open windows. The municipal streetcar network that crisscrossed the center of town still functioned, but peasants and city dwellers alike moved about mostly on foot. Most of the people were uniformly attired in ill-fitting, pajamalike suits of black, blue, or brown cotton, while here and there, the olive drab tunics of the People's Army or the mustard-colored uniforms of the public security police could be seen. Strange-looking carts equipped with balloon tires and pulled by plodding oxen moved undisturbed through the heart of the city. Few motor vehicles were visible except for the gray lorries of the government and occasional buses crammed to overflowing with passengers. Army jeeps in use to haul the dependents of the soldiers were further testimony of a transportation shortage in the capital.

Saigon literally teemed with humanity—not so Hanoi. I saw only a few shops, though I did spot a free market in an alley off the main street in which a large crowd of dark-clad peasant women hunched over a long row of produce baskets and haggled over goods as Vietnamese are wont to do. Across the street, another group of people queued up outside a building labeled *"Hoc Tap Xa,"* a government food cooperative. But the feature of the face of Hanoi that struck me as most unusual was the lack of young people among the population. An inveterate girl-watcher, I noticed that the city's residents consisted almost exclusively of the very old or the very young. Elderly people were everywhere, usually tending small children. With the exception of the baggy-trousered soldiers on leave, I spotted few people of either sex in their twenties, thirties, or forties.

By the time I boarded the C-130 for the return flight to Saigon, I had spent less than six hours on the ground in Hanoi. Only six short hours, but what I had seen and what I had not seen left an indelible imprint on my mind. Hanoi had indeed reminded me of Berlin, but not the Berlin of 1945. Instead, the stark, colorless austerity recalled the streets of East Berlin and the East German city of Magdeburg, both of which I had glimpsed during my tour in Germany. There was something distinctly similar about the contrast between East and West Berlin and the different faces of Saigon and Hanoi. In West Berlin and Saigon, one was surrounded by relative prosperity and a sense of vibrancy. East Berlin and Hanoi mirrored austerity and conveyed the feeling that the people were struggling for a fulfilling life in spite of the system. Glancing out the window of the bus at the peasants of

Gia Lam hunched against the fifty-degree March chill, I thought
of the lush, tropical warmth of South Vietnam and remembered
what my North Vietnamese friends had told me of the hard life
in the north. Now I could better understand their description of
the toils of life in the Red River Delta, and why the Communists
so strongly desired to reunify the country. Ho Chi Minh had unquestionably settled for the poorer half of Vietnam in 1954.

The face of Hanoi told me better than anything else how
much the Communists had paid for their relentless prosecution
of the war in the south. The run-down buildings and the almost
total absence of any signs of a consumer economy were grim
reminders of the sacrifices endured by the unfortunate twenty-
four million North Vietnamese in the name of Ho Chi Minh's
dream of one socialist Vietnamese state. Even Major Huyen had
candidly admitted, "We spend our national wealth on the over-
riding problem of national defense and have nothing left over to
paint buildings or invest in luxuries." As our bus recrossed the
railroad tracks and approached the airport, I reflected on the
irony of it all. The North Vietnamese population had been kept
in a state of almost continuous mobilization for twenty-five
years on behalf of liberating their southern cousins, yet they
clearly needed liberation more than the prosperous peasants
and merchants in the south. In spite of this, driven by Chairman
Ho's assurances of ultimate victory and unhindered by organized domestic opposition, the Hanoi government had been able
to persist in its remarkably successful campaign to sell the justice of the war to its citizens and to the world. "We will succeed
in unifying our country," Major Huyen insisted, "because the
current division of Vietnam is unnatural. We threw off the
Chinese yolk after one thousand years and defeated the French
after one hundred years. So you see, your country's ten-year
attempt to dominate our people is nothing to us. Once your government faces this reality and ceases its attempts to control our
people, there is no reason why we cannot be friends. After all,
Chairman Ho was so inspired by American democracy that he
quoted your Declaration of Independence in our Proclamation
of Independence from the French. So you see, Dai Uy, we really
have much in common."

Back in Saigon that evening, I reflected on Major Huyen's

words and on the sobering realization that the citizens of the
backward city I had just visited had successfully supported
almost continuous warfare since 1946. Hanoi was drab and
unimpressive when held against the American yardstick of
affluence and materialism, yet I had been impressed by what I
had seen in a different way. I had seen for myself the source of
strength for the hundreds of thousands of young North Vietnamese who had trudged for more than a hundred days down
the infiltration trails to face the overwhelming firepower of the
American military. I was not completely certain that the struggle would never go away as long as North Vietnam was ruled by
men who carried the torch passed by Ho Chi Minh. Ho was
their strength, even though he had been dead since 1969. His
image and his words were omnipresent in Hanoi. Chairman Ho
Chi Minh dominated North Vietnam just as his alabaster statue
dominated the foyer of Hanoi's National Art Museum. The
paintings in this museum depicted Ho, the gentle leader, inspir-
ing the peasantry; Ho, the teacher, patiently guiding the children; Ho, the strategist, planning brilliant victories in the caves
of Tay Bac; and Ho, the leader, urging young soldiers on to
battle. His exhortation, *"Khong co gi quy hon doc lap va tu do"*
("Nothing is more precious than independence and freedom"),
was emblazoned over doorways and on billboards throughout
Hanoi. *Bac Ho* (Uncle Ho) was the source of inspiration for
North Vietnamese society, and the government played up his
memory as the source of its legitimacy. Ho's successful struggle
against the Japanese and the French had made him a populist
deity who was the subject of the songs and folklore heard by
North Vietnamese young people for twenty-five years. Ho had
told his people that their struggle against the United States was
like the struggle between the elephant and the mouse: The
smaller combatant with the will to win would inevitably triumph when its lumbering adversary tired.

Shortly after the signing of the Paris Agreement, the government erected a large billboard in the center of Hanoi. On it
appeared a mural, dominated by a heroic caricature of a Vietnamese soldier standing triumphantly astride the wreckage of a
fallen American jet aircraft. "Hearty congratulations to the

resistance of the entire Vietnamese people," the caption read. "We have defeated the Americans and saved the country!" Now, with the American military almost completely out of the picture, one could understand why the single-minded Hanoi government viewed Uncle Ho's cherished "final victory" as only a matter of time.

"NINE STREAMS"

We called it "Nine Streams." If the Embassy gave its approval, the project would finally enable us to score one on the Communists. Ever since the cease-fire, we had been frustrated and disappointed in our dealings with Hanoi's representatives. Time after time, the crafty Communist negotiators had skillfully used procedural obstacles to avoid meaningful business in the MIA talks. A favorite Communist ploy was the demand that agreement on the "modalities" for implementing the MIA provisions of the Paris Agreement must precede any actual exchange of information. At other times, Hanoi's representatives insisted piously that "continuing combat in the liberated zones" precluded any efforts to collect information on the missing and the dead. Even though the reasons varied from day to day, the message was always the same. Concrete measures to resolve the fate of the missing and the dead were "not yet possible."

We hoped that the Nine Streams initiative would expose the Communist tactics for what they were—transparent and cynical attempts to manipulate American public opinion by deliberately stalling the talks. We had already detected disturbing signs that this Communist gambit was achieving some success. Impatient with our failure to unravel the mystery of at least some of the twenty-five hundred MIA cases in the year since the cease-fire, the MIA lobby had become increasingly critical of Washington. In Saigon, we were frustrated by the Communist stonewalling and disturbed by the implication that we were not doing everything possible to accomplish our mission. Our worst fear was that Hanoi would somehow succeed in laying the blame for the deadlock on our doorstep. The Nine Streams project was an attempt to fix the blame where it belonged—at the feet of the Hanoi government. The project was born in March 1974.

"The 29th of March 1973 is a date that will be forever emblazoned in the history of our people; the day the last American left South Vietnam."[3] So wrote the North Vietnamese author of an article in *Thong Nhut (Reunification)*, a Communist weekly that I had picked up a few hours earlier in the lobby of Hanoi's Hoa Binh Hotel. The paper had attracted my attention because it was a commemorative edition celebrating the first anniversary of the American military withdrawal from South Vietnam. As our aircraft droned southward high over the South China Sea, I amused myself by reading the Hanoi version of our withdrawal. In the article, a Hanoi journalist provided an eyewitness account of the departure of the last American "aggressor," a GI who had boarded a DC-9 aircraft on 29 March under the watchful eyes of two Communist control officers. This is Hanoi's account of that historic moment.

> The last American soldier to board the airplane was named Bienco. The victors shook his hand, wished him well, and presented him with a postcard depicting Hanoi's single-pedestal pagoda. The shocked Bienco gaped at them for a moment, stammered his thanks, and boarded the plane. Its doors closed, and MAC DC-9 #40619 taxied away, lifting off and disappearing into the heavens. It was 4:25 P.M., Hanoi time.[4]

I wondered if the parting gesture described in the article had actually happened. "Would the Communist officers have done this?" I asked my South Vietnamese counterpart in the next seat. He took the article and gave it a glance before replying with contempt, "It's pure propaganda, Dai Uy. The North Vietnamese don't give anyone anything—ever. They're so stingy that when they defecate, they hide the results for fear someone will get it." I laughed. So much for the "Era of National Reconciliation and Concord" that the Paris Agreement was supposed to create.

My eyes fell on another column in the paper. Under the headline, *"Danh cho Quan Doi My—Nhung cai Chet Ky Quai"* ("Reserved for the American Military—Bizarre Deaths"), appeared a collection of anecdotes about the war. To my surprise, two of the stories described incidents involving missing and dead Americans. The first article was entitled "Starved to Death at Nine Streams." ("Nine Streams" in Vietnamese folklore refers to the Gates of Hell.)

> It is the end of 1967. Three American advisors and a unit of puppet special action raiders parachuted onto Mom Xoi hill of the Western Highlands. No sooner had their feet hit the ground when they were fiercely attacked by the Rang Dong (Sunrise) Engineering Group. The puppets found an escape route and fled. The three American advisors moved into the uninhabited valley known as Nine Streams. It is certain that they didn't understand the awful meaning of this name. This area does have nine streams, but there is nothing to eat there, despite what was shown on the sketch of the area they carried with them. After several days here, two of the Americans died, their bodies contorted with hunger. When our Liberation Forces entered the Nine Streams area, they found the surviving American breathing weakly. They had to pry open his mouth and force in some rice soup.[5]

The Nine Streams episode was followed by another anecdote entitled "Died of Thirst":

> The American corporal R. Ri-Vo, service number 466-723 was a member of the marines stationed on top of Hill 845 in Khe Sanh. Surrounded by Liberation Forces, the marines could hardly speak due to thirst-parched throats. The sunny month of May in Khe Sanh is terribly hot. Many Americans died or were near death from thirst, and they fought with one another over drinking water. At the foot of Hill 845 flowed a stream, whose blue waters beckoned.
>
> On 24 May 1965, R. Ri-Vo went down the hill in search of water. He was neatly captured by Liberation Forces. R. Ri-Vo said, "Many of my friends have died of thirst. I selected this course of action in order to survive!" But after that he was killed by a bomb dropped from a B-52![6]

The two articles posed an opportunity for exploitation in our negotiations with the Communists. Even though both stories

were probably fictionalized accounts dreamed up by some
Hanoi propagandist, there was a remote possibility that we
could cross-check the facts in them and match them up with
specific MIA cases. We could then surface the stories as evidence that the Communists were deliberately withholding information about our MIA personnel. In the more likely event that
the two stories were fiction, Hanoi would be hard-pressed to
admit it. Such an admission would have meant that the North
Vietnamese government was propagandizing its own people.
Properly exploited, the Nine Streams articles would enable us to
embarrass the Hanoi government and call attention to its bad
faith on the MIA question.

I shared my discovery with LTC Lunde, who urged me to
work out a negotiating initiative based on the two articles. If
nothing else, they might serve as a new tactic in our never-
ending efforts to get the stalled talks moving. It would be satisfying to score a public relations coup of our own for a change.

I attacked the new project with a will. Step one was to check
the list of American servicemen who had died in captivity—a
list the Communists had given to us in Paris at the time of the
signing of the cease-fire agreement. Forty-one names appeared
on this list, but none of them resembled the Vietnamized "R.
Ri-Vo." Nor could we correlate the partial service number that
appeared in the article. Another check confirmed that there had
been no marines deployed on Hill 845 near Khe Sanh on 24 May
1965. A review of the Department of Defense master MIA list
drew a blank on Corporal Ri-Vo. Finally, we checked with our
colleagues at the Joint Casualty Resolution Center in an attempt
to match the events in the anecdote with any actual MIA cases,
again with negative results. Similar efforts to pin down the
events in the Nine Streams anecdote were equally fruitless.
Either the stories were fiction or the facts had been greatly dis-
torted. Armed with this information, I drafted two requests for
information to the Vietcong's Provisional Revolutionary Government (PRG) delegation, since both the Nine Streams area
and Khe Sanh were now located in "liberated zones" of South
Vietnam. These requests treated both cases as legitimate MIA
business. Concerning the Nine Streams story, the request read
as follows:

Request your delegation obtain additional information on these three Americans. In particular, the U.S. delegation requests information on the names of these three Americans, the locations of the graves of the two deceased Americans, the exact date of their death, and the fate of the one captured American. Our delegation has no record of any U.S. POW being repatriated who was captured under the circumstances described in this article.

The Ri-Vo case provided an even better opportunity to exploit a Communist weakness, and we forwarded this pointed query in a separate memo:

Since Corporal "R. Ri-Vo" was a captive of the PRG military when his death occurred, the PRG is responsible for resolving his status under the terms of Article 8(b) of the Paris Agreement. Therefore, the U.S. delegation requests the PRG delegation to provide the following information:

a. Why was Ri-Vo's name not on the PRG list of those who died in captivity?
b. Where are his remains interred at this time?

To supplement these two requests, we prepared a strongly worded statement for Colonel Tombaugh to read at the upcoming negotiations session.

The entire proposal amounted to an ambush of the Communists with a piece of their own propaganda. The plan called for the colonel to read the two anecdotes, pass the Communists the requests for information, and deliver his statement. Among other things, the statement chastised the Communists for their choice of war stories to entertain the North Vietnamese population. The following excerpts are taken from the colonel's statement:

First, the U.S. delegation deplores the fact that the tragic deaths of our servicemen on the battlefields of Vietnam should be so callously exploited in the propaganda organs of North Vietnam. The death of Corporal Ri-Vo, or the suffering of the three Americans in the Nine Streams valley are matters unsuitable for such heartless exploitation. The U.S. delegation would like to remind the North Vietnamese delegation that information of the type contained in these articles should rightly be exchanged in the forum of this organization. This is in keeping with Article 8(b). The U.S. delegation is shocked that such vital information on American casualties is withheld by North Vietnam only to appear in a North Vietnamese newspaper for the entertainment of the North Vietnamese population.

The U.S. delegation would like to point out that no one resembling Corporal R. Ri-Vo's name or description appears on the list of those who died in captivity turned over by the Provisional Revolutionary Government. Must we thus assume that the PRG list is not, in fact, a complete list?

Finally, the U.S. delegation would like to repeat its disappointment that this vital information should surface on the back page of a Hanoi newspaper, rather than here at the conference table, as clearly dictated by the Paris Agreement. The U.S. delegation hopes that the Hanoi delegation will take steps to insure that this unfortunate tactic will not be employed again.

Finally, our strategy proposal called for a follow-up attack in the form of a press release designed to keep the Communists on the defensive. The proposed release challenged Hanoi to "confirm the two stories as either fact or propaganda." Having done my homework, I forwarded the entire proposal through LTC Lunde to Colonel Tombaugh.

Later that afternoon, Lunde called me into his office and smiled broadly as he suggested that my sharp eyes might yet enable me to live down the night I had spent in a Saigon jail. Colonel Tombaugh had enthusiastically endorsed our Nine Streams gambit. His reaction appeared on an office routing slip that Colonel Lunde suggested I save for posterity. The Chief seldom displayed such enthusiasm.

This is excellent! A really top-notch tactical maneuver and the type of action which should be used to "pressure" the PRG as a part of a larger policy. Please prepare all in final—I will push this through the Embassy as a "type-action" required. Dependent upon PRG response—we should be prepared with a hard-hitting news article on this. I believe this is the type of thing which possesses enough "news value" that it might be exploited by our "news hungry" press corps.

Predictably, the Embassy gave our proposal its blessing, but nixed the proposed press release. Armed with the official go-ahead, we planned to confront the Communists at the 11 April 1974 negotiations session. All of us looked forward with unconcealed satisfaction to the prospect of at last taking the initiative in the stalled talks.

The big day arrived, and Colonel Tombaugh fired the first salvo in the Nine Streams campaign. Waving a copy of *Thong Nhut* in front of the surprised Communists, he launched into his statement with the melodramatic flair that we had all become accustomed to. The Chief delivered his statement as if he were lecturing a roomful of naughty grade-school children. Colonel Tu, the North Vietnamese delegate, began to write rapidly on his pad, while LTC Son, the Vietcong delegate, leaned over and whispered something to his deputy. Both officers adopted expressions that conveyed total unconcern, and neither man replied to Tombaugh's pointed demands for an explanation of the articles. We had expected this, knowing that it would probably take the Communists a few days or even weeks to devise a response to our unexpected move. Our plan was to press the point and relentlessly taunt the Communists to respond to our inquiries.

At first, all went well. At the next meeting, Colonel Tombaugh pressed the Communists for an explanation of the articles. Once again, our demands fell on deaf ears, and we reveled in the belief that our opponents were squirming under the pressure of our attack. Rather than respond to our queries, the Communists subjected us to their oft-stated position that resolution of the MIA question must await American and South Vietnamese acceptance of a true cease-fire throughout Vietnam. The lack of progress on the MIA issue stemmed from the "stubborn insistence" of the United States and South Vietnam on continuing the war. As usual, the Communist accusations dealt solely with alleged American and South Vietnamese violations of the Paris Agreement, while conveniently ignoring Hanoi's ongoing infiltration of troops into the south, which had commenced on the first day of the cease-fire.

On 18 April, the Communists finally unveiled their tactic to counter the Nine Streams campaign. In response to Colonel

Tombaugh's demand that he reply to our Nine Streams queries, LTC Son countered with a lengthy statement in which he warned that the U.S. delegation should abandon its Nine Streams campaign. According to Son, the United States had used information on the missing and the dead for radio propaganda broadcasts during the war, and was therefore in no position to criticize either the Hanoi government or the PRG for the Nine Streams articles.

Colonel Tombaugh sat impassively during LTC Son's statement, but I knew what he was thinking. As soon as we returned to the office, I phoned the United States Information Service (USIS). If we had made any radio broadcasts during the war that used the names of fallen Communist soldiers, USIS would know about it. I reached Wayne Hyde, who confirmed that we had beamed several programs of casualty information to North Vietnam. I listened in silence as Wayne described how the South Vietnamese station Voice of Freedom had broadcast the names of North Vietnamese soldiers killed in the south in 1966. Apparently the program had been an attempt to counter Hanoi's persistent fiction that the North Vietnamese Army (NVA) was not fighting in the south. Wayne also confirmed that, in 1972 and 1973, the Voice of America had broadcast the names of more than eight thousand North Vietnamese POWs in programs beamed at North Vietnam. In an effort to weaken the Hanoi government's domestic support for the war in the south, we had aired the names of NVA prisoners, their dates and places of birth, their parents' names, and even their date of infiltration into the south. The programs had also identified wounded North Vietnamese prisoners, named fifty men who had defected, and even given the names of ten North Vietnamese who had been killed in action in Cambodia.

In view of these broadcasts, we were in no position to continue our attacks on the Communists for the Nine Streams articles. We had railed at Colonel Son for exploiting the fate of Corporal Ri-Vo and three other Americans, but our side had played loose with the names of thousands of Communist soldiers. Colonel Son's salvo had hit us in a vital spot. Quietly, with no fanfare, we dropped the matter.

The Nine Streams affair had taught me an important lesson. Insofar as the war was concerned, everyone's hands were a little dirty. In the future, I would be more cautious in proposing bold attacks on our adversaries, lest the accusers once again become the accused.

Part IV

SOUTH VIETNAM FACES
THE INEVITABLE

THE YEAR OF THE TIGER

Somewhere in Vietnam's Central Highlands, an elderly village midwife awoke late one night to the sounds of something moving outside her door. When she opened the door to investigate, she discovered a magnificent tiger, whose jaws were easily large enough to swallow her in one bite. The frightened woman fainted, but the nimble tiger caught her as she fell. Gently placing her on his back, the beast disappeared into the night before anyone could stop him. At his lair deep in the jungle, the tiger revived his captive by licking her hands. When she awoke, the startled midwife discovered a beautiful tigress writhing in pain on the forest floor as she tried in vain to deliver her cubs. With a reassuring word and a skillful twist of her hands, the midwife performed her magic. The grateful tiger looked on as she assisted the tigress in delivering three tawny male cubs. Shortly thereafter, surprised villagers in the paddies looked up and saw their midwife enter the village—riding proudly erect on the back of the majestic tiger!

The year 1974 was the Year of the Tiger. During Tet, the three-day Lunar New Year holiday, Vietnamese mothers entertained their children with the traditional Tet fables that had been passed on from generation to generation. These fables were but one part of the myriad of customs and rituals associated with Tet, all of which had to be respected to enhance the prospects for a prosperous and happy new year. I had long since ceased to smile at Vietnamese customs and beliefs; thus, on this particular occasion, I listened attentively as a friend related the saga of the tiger and the midwife. As he finished the story, I thought wryly to myself that it had become dated. The tigers of Vietnam's rain forests were all but extinct, thanks to twenty-five years of warfare. Now, if the legendary midwife could somehow revisit the scene of her deed, she would no doubt find the tiger's lair occupied by the soldiers of the North Vietnamese Army. One year after the signing of the cease-fire, the opposing Vietnamese factions continued to slaughter one another in the jungles and rice paddies. "National reconciliation and concord" had proven to be easier said than done. If the Vietnamese people were to find happiness and prosperity in 1974, they would have to rely on more than tiger tales.

It was a year when it was difficult to be an American in Saigon, for it was simply not easy to observe the undoing of an ally for whom so many sacrifices had already been made. The ordeal of watching the balance tip inexorably against the South Vietnamese—and this is what happened during that pivotal year—was compounded by the knowledge that 1975 promised to be worse in every respect.

Still, the deep personal reservations about the prospects for South Vietnamese survival that I had experienced in 1973 had not been borne out by the performance of President Thieu's troops during that first year of the cease-fire. My fears and pessimism had been more of a visceral reaction than an empirically supportable position. It was one thing to write home about the dangers of collapse and possible American evacuation, and something quite different to support such a claim. In fact, the South Vietnamese military had acquitted itself well during 1973. In the province of Chau Doc in the Mekong Delta, South Vietnamese rangers had scored an impressive victory in ejecting Hanoi's 1st Division from its redoubt in the Seven Mountains region. In the Central Highlands, the ARVN 23rd Division had worn down the North Vietnamese 10th Division after weeks of bloody position warfare and forced the northerners to yield the decimated village of Truong Nghia. During 1973, South Vietnamese territorial forces militia had played a significant role in reestablishing control over 10 to 20 percent of the country's "contested areas," a euphemism that often was used to describe areas that were under de facto Vietcong control. But these operations had been costly. The first year of "peace" had cost the lives of 57,000 Vietnamese combatants (12,000 South Vietnamese, 45,000 Communists). This slaughter was inflicted on a combined north and south population of 42,000,000, and would equate to the loss of 283,000 American soldiers in one year if our nation were to suffer equivalent losses. (We only lost 250,000 men and women during the three years and nine months of World War II.)

And yet, in spite of the losses, the strategic position of the South Vietnamese military when fireworks ushered in the Year of the Tiger could have been much worse. If 1973 was the first round of the cease-fire bout, South Vietnam had won it handily.[1]

But 1974 was to be the turning point in the fortunes of the Saigon government. At the beginning of the year, one could argue that South Vietnam had a chance of survival, despite the continuous Communist buildup and the growing American disenchantment with the war. This was not the case twelve months later. By the end of the Year of the Tiger, the only unanswered question concerned the timing of the impending Communist victory. How much longer could the South Vietnamese stave off the inevitable?

The year began on a bizarre note when South Vietnam waged a futile war with Communist China over a tiny group of offshore islands known as the Paracels. We watched apprehensively as the two sides squared off for a showdown. Stimulated by the prospect of offshore oil deposits, both countries had dispatched forces to the Paracels. While a South Vietnamese naval task force approached the islands to reinforce the tiny garrison there, Chinese naval units approached from the north. Our intelligence reported ominously large numbers of Chinese MIG fighters were overflying the area, unchallenged by the South

Vietnamese Air Force (which lacked radar coverage of the Paracels; the Chinese Air Force was operating under the radar umbrella provided from nearby Hainan Island).

Concern intensified in Saigon when we learned that an American civilian was on board one of the threatened Vietnamese naval vessels. His name was Gerald Kosh, a former Green Beret captain who worked at the U.S. consulate in the city of Danang. Believing that the Paracel resupply mission would afford a good opportunity to observe the Vietnamese navy, Kosh had made a hasty decision to accompany the force. Now, unaware that the task force was steaming to a confrontation with a superior Chinese force, Kosh was aboard the HQ-10, a destroyer-class vessel.

When the Embassy heard that an American was on board the HQ-10, the reaction was predictable: Get him off that ship—the sooner, the better. Tension in the operations center soared as Chinese MIG activity escalated and the two naval forces closed. Our liaison officer at Vietnamese Naval Headquarters finally persuaded the Vietnamese to transmit a message directing the adventurous Kosh to leave the HQ-10. Kosh dutifully obeyed and disembarked on the main island with the South Vietnamese reinforcements. In Saigon, we relaxed somewhat when word reached us that he was safely on terra firma.

Shortly thereafter, the battle erupted, and a Chinese ship-to-ship missile sank the HQ-10 with great loss of life. Kosh had almost been the first American casualty of 1974. Then disaster really struck. Chinese MIG fighters began to strafe the main island in preparation for an amphibious landing. Kosh had jumped out of the frying pan into the fire. One final transmission from the Vietnamese garrison on the island confirmed that Chinese troops were landing. Within minutes, the battle was over, and Gerald Kosh was taken prisoner by the Chinese, along with the survivors of the Vietnamese garrison.

The Embassy explained to the press that Kosh had been an observer on what he had thought would be a routine mission. The explanation was substantially true. Kosh worked for the DAO Coordination and Liaison Section, and one of his main responsibilities was to report on the state of readiness of the South Vietnamese armed forces. He was neither a CIA agent nor an advisor to the Vietnamese; he had merely "gone along for the ride," and the ride had led to internment on the Chinese mainland. Kosh was detained and questioned for eleven days before his release in Hong Kong with a group of South Vietnamese prisoners, thus ending one of the strangest episodes of the cease-fire.

The Paracels defeat did nothing to help the morale of the South Vietnamese, despite the government's attempts to use the episode as a rallying point. The "Heroes of Hoang Sa" (the name of the islands in Vietnamese) received a warm, government-sponsored welcome when the Chinese released them. Government propaganda banners and television programs temporarily redirected their wrath at the Chinese, while, within the military, a debate raged over who was responsible for the setback.

While the South Vietnamese fought the wrong war against the wrong enemy, Hanoi's leaders made fundamental decisions about the direction of the war in the south. According to the account of Hanoi's Senior General Van Tien Dung, the North Vietnamese decided by late 1973 that the cease-fire was a failure. President Thieu's refusal to negotiate a political settlement giving the Communists a share of power in the south convinced Hanoi that military measures were required to pressure their opponent into political concessions. As long as Thieu's forces could push the NVA around in the south, the South Vietnamese president would remain in an uncompromising mood. Thanks to the steady buildup of its forces in the south during 1973, Hanoi now had the clout to put an end to this situation. In a series of classified pronouncements, North Vietnamese leaders gave new guidance to their commanders. The era of attempted compromise was over: "The path of the revolution in the south is the path of revolutionary violence . . . since the enemy fails to implement the agreement and continues to pursue Vietnamization. . . . We have no alternative but to destroy the enemy and liberate the south."[2] To accomplish this, the North Vietnamese high command directed military preparations that would enable its forces to stand up against the firepower of the South Vietnamese by the end of 1974. Hanoi's commanders were ordered to "seize the initiative in order to change the battlefield situation and to facilitate large-scale offensives to be launched everywhere in 1975."[3]

Acting on these orders, North Vietnamese forces in the south began to step up their attacks, and 1974 became a year of increased bloodletting. The newly equipped North Vietnamese Army revealed its increasing mastery of the combined arms attack as NVA infantry, armor, and artillery attacked in well-coordinated formations. The clumsy attempts of the 1972 Easter Offensive, when Communist tankers had attacked without infantry support, were a thing of the past. Hanoi's second attempt to undo South Vietnam by unleashing a modern, conventional force would belie any notion that the war in the south was a people's war.

In October 1974, North Vietnamese leaders met to evaluate the results of their directives. After a series of meetings, they unanimously adopted a four-point assessment of the military and political situation. This assessment appears in General Dung's account of the cease-fire period and contains strikingly accurate perceptions of the overall situation. Taken together, Hanoi's conclusions indicate that North Vietnamese leaders believed that they had turned a decisive corner in the war, and that conditions were now favorable for a military showdown with the Thieu regime.

The first point in the North Vietnamese estimate dealt with the shifting balance between the opposing armies. Hanoi concluded that "the puppet troops were militarily, politically, and economically weakening every day and our forces were quite stronger than the enemy in the south."[4] Our mission in Saigon was slow to grasp the truth of this assertion, but Hanoi's agents had reported accurately. The events of 1974 had sapped the strength of the South Vietnamese military, both materially and psychologically. Throughout the summer, South Vietnamese attention was focused on developments in Washington. When Congress voted to fund only $700 million in military aid, and President Nixon, overwhelmed by Watergate, resigned, the South Vietnamese were stunned. (The administration had requested $1.45 billion.) The Saigon government needed President

Nixon's hard-line commitment to its cause almost as much as it needed the aid bill. These two setbacks alone would have eroded the fighting spirit of the Vietnamese, but they were accompanied by stepped-up combat, escalating corruption, and worsening economic stagnation. The result was an unprecedented crisis in morale. The average South Vietnamese GI had been forced to fight more and make ends meet on less ever since the American withdrawal. Now the Vietnamese had to face the stark realization that their major ally was losing faith in their cause. Bitterness and disillusionment became widespread.

During the summer of 1974, the DAO conducted a survey to determine the economic status of South Vietnamese military men. Interview teams of Vietnamese nationals queried more than 6,600 South Vietnamese servicemen concerning their economic conditions. The final report was prepared by Tony Lawson, then the Director of Special Studies. Its conclusions painted a grim picture of conditions in the Vietnamese armed forces. More than 90 percent of the men polled indicated that their pay and allowances were insufficient to meet their families' needs for food, clothing, and shelter. More than 88 percent affirmed that their standard of living had eroded since 1973, and most bachelor soldiers stated that they could not afford to marry. An annex of quotations attached to Lawson's report showed all too clearly the economics of the cease-fire. These are only a few samples of comments by South Vietnamese officers:

> An ARVN artillery commander: The use of artillery ammunition is now very limited. The present allocation cannot satisfy the present battlefield requirements. . . . We should move as often as possible in order to avoid the enemy's counterfire, but because of lack of fuel, the commander did not allow us to do so.

> An ARVN regimental commander: Due to the shortage of fuel, there are many difficulties in the evacuation of wounded troops from the battlefield. We have to use hammocks and hondas for this operation. This aggravates the state of the wounds and exhausts the wounded soldiers during evacuation.

> An ARVN battalion commander: The soldier's life is miserable. Not only their food is poor, but uniforms are also very hard to get. Our unit is receiving only 50 percent of the authorized quantity of uniforms. . . . If the government feels pity for the

soldiers, it should immediately provide the soldiers with the needed supplies. We don't ask for anything else. We are afraid that if we ask for too much, we may receive nothing.

Another ARVN battalion commander: Government leaders are so unskillful that they did not formulate an economic plan for the country when the American troops were stationed in South Vietnam; therefore, after the withdrawal of the American troops, the entire Vietnamese people became stricken by poverty, the officers and the troops are in famine.

Helicopter pilots are robbers, since each time they transport supplies to this unit they request some rice, or a portion of dry rations, or some money as a bribe. If their request is not satisfied, they refuse to unload the supplies with the excuse that the landing zone is not secure.

An ARVN regimental commander: The use of ammunition has been limited, while the regiment has frequently made contact with the enemy. Thus, I once personally paid five thousand piasters to RF troops to get one case of M-79 grenade launcher rounds.[5]

Upon hearing that the interview team worked for the Americans, one respondent caustically remarked that "the Americans inquire into the ARVN troops' living conditions merely to be aware of the fact, not for rendering further assistance." Still another respondent defiantly told the interviewers: "If the [needed] support cannot be obtained from the Americans, then the Vietnamese people can continue fighting in the way their ancestors did. I blame the Americans for such a deteriorated situation in South Vietnam."[6]

The Lawson Report concluded with this prophetic warning:

It is quite clear that South Vietnamese military personnel are forced to live at less than reasonable subsistence levels, and that performance and mission accomplishment are seriously affected. Day-to-day survival in the face of worsening economic conditions has caused a deterioration of performance which cannot be permitted to continue, if the South Vietnamese military is to be considered a viable force.[7]

The North Vietnamese were also aware of these difficulties. Communist infiltrators in virtually every government military unit kept Hanoi posted on what the Communists labeled "the increasing contradictions among the puppet soldiers." Hanoi could keep its fingers on Washington's political pulse by reading the *New York Times* and the *Washington Post*, which contained encouraging evidence of the growing congressional disenchantment with the Thieu government.

But the most significant contribution to Hanoi's understanding of conditions in the ARVN had been the actual battlefield tests that it had been subjected to by the North Vietnamese Army. In August 1974, for example, North Vietnamese forces seized the district capital of Thuong Duc, then repulsed repeated South Vietnamese attempts to retake the town. Thuong Duc thus became the first district capital that was permanently lost during the cease-fire. General Dung described this operation as "a test of strength with the best of the enemy's forces," and made it clear that, in this battle, Hanoi's forces had finally demonstrated superior firepower over the weakened South Vietnamese.[8] Commenting on the impact of cuts in American aid to South Vietnam, General Dung observed cryptically: "Nguyen van Thieu was then forced to fight a poor man's war."[9]

The second pillar of Hanoi's estimate concerned the vital question of continued American involvement in the war. According to Hanoi, "The United States was facing mounting difficulties both at home and in the world, and its potential for aiding the puppets was rapidly declining."[10] With the "reactionary" Richard Nixon out of the White House, Hanoi unquestionably felt less constrained militarily. One of my Communist counterparts insisted shortly after the Nixon resignation that Nixon had been "stubborn" and refused to "recognize the reality of the American defeat in Vietnam." Translated, this meant that Hanoi feared Nixon's penchant for such heavy-handed shows of force as he had displayed in 1972 and 1973 when he had ordered renewed bombing and the mining of North Vietnam's waterways. Another North Vietnamese officer told me that the Watergate revelations of official corruption in Washington were "no surprise" to him. "I have been an Americanologist for years," he boasted, "and I was therefore not surprised to hear that Nixon was corrupt. After all, President Thieu is corrupt, and the father cannot be better than the son."

General Dung relates that, in the wake of Nixon's resignation, Hanoi's major concern was the single question: "Would the United States be able to send its troops back to the south if we launched large-scale battles that would lead to the collapse of the puppet troops?"[11] The Hanoi leadership discussed this issue "heatedly," according to Dung, and ultimately deferred to the judgment of Party First Secretary Le Duan, who argued that, "having already withdrawn from the south, the United States could hardly jump back in, and no matter how it might intervene, it would be unable to save the Saigon administration."[12] In arriving at this conclusion, Le Duan assessed Washington's position as follows:

> The internal contradictions within the U.S. administration and among U.S. political parties had intensified. The Watergate scandal had seriously affected the entire United States and precipitated the resignation of an extremely reactionary president— Nixon. The United States faced economic recession, mounting inflation, serious unemployment, and an oil crisis. Also, U.S. allies were not on good terms with the United States, and countries who had to depend on the United States also sought to escape U.S. control. U.S. aid to the Saigon puppet administration was decreasing.[13]

How valid was Le Duan's conclusion? By the end of 1974, it was tested by a bold North Vietnamese initiative on the battlefield—the seizure of Phuoc Long province. President Nixon had promised President Thieu that the United States would reintervene militarily in the event that Hanoi failed to respect the cease-fire. In his letter of 5 January 1973, the President urged Thieu to sign the Paris Agreement and made this persuasive commitment:

> Should you decide, as I trust you will, to go with us [to sign the ceasefire], you have my assurances of continued assistance in the postsettlement period and that we will respond with full force should the settlement be violated by North Vietnam.[14]

I was on a Christmas leave in the States when Hanoi's forces assaulted Phuoc Long province. By the time I returned to Saigon, the Communist flag flew over the provincial capital of

Phuoc Binh, just seventy-five miles north of Saigon. There had been no American application of "full force" in response to Hanoi's seizure of the town. A disgraced Richard Nixon could only observe helplessly from the sidelines at San Clemente, while President Ford's hands had been tied by congressional restrictions. Nor were there any South Vietnamese plans to retake the town from the superior Communist force. A successful counterattack was deemed impossible by the South Vietnamese General Staff, primarily for logistical reasons.

In Hanoi, North Vietnam's leaders correctly interpreted their Phuoc Long victory as firm proof that Le Duan's assumption had been valid: America would never reintervene militarily in Vietnam. The Communists now had a green light for using their military forces to conquer South Vietnam, and they knew it.

Within a week of the fall of Phuoc Long, I began to receive phone calls and visits from long-lost Vietnamese friends. Two of the intelligence officers whom I had met at Fort Huachuca suddenly contacted me for the first time in more than a year, and I even heard from an interpreter who had worked with me during my tour in Hau Nghia province. Of course, all of them had some pretext for getting in touch, but I knew the real reason for my sudden popularity. If the military situation continued to deteriorate, an American friend in Saigon would represent a possible avenue of escape. Not to be outdone in prudent prior planning, I discreetly began to ship my possessions to the States through the military post office. August 1975 would mark the second anniversary of my arrival in Saigon and the end of my tour. I wrote to my parents and told them not to be alarmed by the sudden flow of packages—I would be home before August.

The third element of Hanoi's appraisal of the military and political situation was an assessment of its own capability to support "revolutionary violence" in the south. Could "the great socialist rear base" sustain the kind of military operations required to topple the "stubborn puppet clique"? Like the other conditions, this one had vastly improved. In General Dung's words, "We had created a chain of mutual support, had strengthened our reserve forces and materiel and were steadily improving our strategic and political system."[15] Six North Viet-

namese reserve divisions were now available to support the sixteen front-line divisions already deployed on southern battlefields or in neighboring Laos and Cambodia.

In Saigon, our intelligence analysts continued to track the
infiltration of North Vietnamese personnel, weapons, and equipment. The monthly threat briefing now concluded with a sobering estimate: Hanoi had enough supplies and ammunition stock-
piled in the south to sustain a major offensive on the scale of the
1972 onslaught for at least twelve months. Equally ominous
was the organizing of Hanoi's line divisions into army corps to
facilitate the command and control of multidivisional operations. Aerial photography now revealed seemingly endless convoys of Molotova trucks laden with war materiel moving openly
down the modernized infiltration routes. The arduous one hundred–day trek from North Vietnam to the rubber plantations
north of Saigon had become a two-week drive. General Dung
described the newly completed roads, trails, and pipelines as
"endless lengths of sturdy hemp ropes being daily and hourly
slipped around the neck and limbs of the monster who would be
strangled with one sharp yank when the order was given."[16]

Finally, Hanoi's leaders analyzed South Vietnamese society,
the subtleties of which had always eluded them. In spite of the
many "contradictions" in the southern political system, the
"oppressed" South Vietnamese people had refused to recognize
their plight and had twice (in 1968 and 1972) ignored Hanoi's
call for a "general uprising." Ironically, Hanoi seemed to
fathom the moods of the American people better than it understood the South Vietnamese peasantry. In a final assessment of
the southerners' mood, Hanoi's leaders concluded that "the
movement to demand peace, national independence, and
Thieu's overthrow in various cities was gaining momentum."[17]
If the peasantry was not in a revolutionary mood, then at least
the city dwellers were.

There was an element of truth in this assessment. By late 1974,
many South Vietnamese *were* fed up with President Thieu, and
they had unquestionably grown weary of the continued bloodletting. Thieu had become the visible object of their wrath and
frustration at what was happening to their country, and they

blamed him for everything. When three hundred Catholic priests formed the "People's Anti-Corruption Movement for National Salvation and Peace Restoration," open demonstrations against President Thieu became increasingly common. In September 1974, the anti-corruption movement published "Indictment #1" in a Saigon newspaper, a vitriolic attack that accused President Thieu and his wife of every conceivable form of corruption. The government ordered all copies of the paper confiscated, but to no avail. Contraband mimeographed copies of the charges freely circulated in the city, one of which even found its way into my in-box, courtesy of an anonymous anti-Thieu employee. Many Vietnamese blamed the provisions of the hated Paris Agreement on Thieu, despite the fact that Hanoi and Washington had negotiated the treaty bilaterally. One officer even told the DAO survey team that President Thieu's anti-Communist credentials were suspect!

> Servicemen now have less confidence in the government, since the President's statements and actions seem quite contradictory. An obvious example of this is the fact that the Communist delegation has been allowed to stay in Tan Son Nhut and has been provided with air-conditioned sedans to move in Saigon.[18]

By August 1974, it was clear that President Thieu was losing most of his popular support, although he retained the loyalties of the South Vietnamese Army officer corps from which he had emerged. When I briefed our new commander, Col. Jack Madison, I described Thieu's increasingly isolated position and ventured that, for the first time since the cease-fire, a coup d'etat was a distinct possibility. "The likelihood of such a coup," I commented, "increases as the economic situation deteriorates and the 'no war, no peace' policy continues to result in casualties and refugees."

By year's end, nothing had transpired to change my mind. Public disenchantment with Thieu had penetrated the enlisted ranks of the military, but it had not yet affected the vast majority of the officer corps, who saw stability under Thieu as the only way to withstand North Vietnamese pressure. When the

Congress authorized only $700 million for military aid in fiscal year 1975, many South Vietnamese concluded that Thieu himself was the major reason for American disenchantment with their cause. Thieu then cashiered a number of corrupt government employees and military men, but his enemies were not appeased—they would settle for no less than his departure.

As conditions worsened, anti-American sentiments became more common. In our office, one of the Vietnamese secretaries showed up one morning with a book entitled *How the Americans Killed a Vietnamese President*. The work interpreted the assassination of President Ngo Dinh Diem as an American-directed outrage against the Vietnamese people. As President Thieu's fortunes declined, increasingly large numbers of Vietnamese had begun to revise their recollections of the Diem era; they now tended to forget the excesses of Diem's secret police or the fact that many Saigonese had celebrated in the streets on learning of the demise of the Ngo regime.* The Diem era had been a time of relative peace. Thus, the Americans, who, according to the author of the book, were responsible for the assassination, were guilty by implication for the suffering that followed. On the day before the anniversary of the anti-Diem coup, the Embassy ordered all American offices closed at 2:00 P.M. Americans were strongly urged to go to their quarters and remain there until the following Monday to avoid confrontations with the "Third Force," as the anti-Thieu opposition had come to be called.

Outside the gates of Tan Son Nhut, I skirted around a violent demonstration as I headed for my quarters. Angry demonstrators had set fire to a national police jeep after several thoughtless riot policemen had roughed up Father Tran Huu Thanh, the Anti-Corruption Movement leader. The "Third Force" insisted that their goal was to create a "government of national unity" that would be capable of resisting the Communists unhindered by corruption. But, to Hanoi's leaders, the demonstrations portended a "general uprising" in the cities and proved that con-

*President Diem's brother, Ngo Dinh Nhu, was widely feared and hated. Diem himself was relatively popular and respected, but the government's image suffered from the excesses perpetuated by Nhu in Diem's name.

ditions were ripe for yet another attempt to reunify the country.

As I cooled my heels in the billet that weekend, I wrote home that Thieu was a fool for waiting until the eleventh hour to tackle corruption. The tragedy of South Vietnamese politics was the fact that no one except the Communists waited in the wings to replace Thieu. For better or for worse, Nguyen van Thieu was still the only alternative to another series of debilitating coups such as had followed the assassination of President Diem. This time, however, the North Vietnamese Army was poised for the kill, and South Vietnam's generals knew better than anyone that they could risk no such shenanigans. Besides, Thieu continued to enjoy American backing, even if the mood in Washington was less than ideal.

Nguyen van Thieu was fast approaching political bankruptcy in South Vietnam by the end of 1974, but this did not mean that the South Vietnamese people were yearning for "liberation." Nonetheless, Hanoi could never officially forswear its insistence that the South Vietnamese people had a grass-roots longing for socialism. But, by late 1974, even the North Vietnamese leadership had all but abandoned the notion that the South Vietnamese workers and peasants would spontaneously rise up against their government and welcome their North Vietnamese liberators. As my counterpart in Hanoi once told me, "The southerners have been seduced by American wealth into accepting the Thieu regime. We will have to educate them." South Vietnamese peasants had repeatedly expressed their distaste for Communism by "voting with their feet" wherever Hanoi's troops appeared. North Vietnam's leaders were well aware by 1975 that the only solution to this problem was the military seizure and subjugation of the south. No matter that the southern peasantry did not yet appreciate the blessings of socialism—they could learn.

"WHEN THE TIME IS RIPE, THEY WILL STRIKE"

Tinh was eighteen years old. Hundreds of Americans knew him as the friendly bellhop at Saigon's Embassy Hotel. Several of my neighbors in the billet at 192 Cong Ly Street had virtually adopted Tinh and his younger brother, Minh. If one dropped in on Joan Pray or Jerry Jablonski, Tinh and his friends were an ever-present part of the social equation. Joan and Jerry had met Tinh during their stay at the Embassy before they moved to permanent quarters. Tinh's perpetual smile and willingness to assist them in their adjustment to life in Saigon had quickly led to a close friendship. Tinh was like a son to Jerry Jablonski, even though Jerry had his own family in Washington, and Tinh's parents were alive and well in Saigon.

When Tinh received his draft notice, we held a going-away party for him in Jerry's apartment. I scrounged up a set of army fatigues, a flak jacket, and a steel helmet, and, with great ceremony, we suited up our teenaged friend for a picture-taking session. The pictures show a beaming face under the oversized steel helmet as Tinh struggled to strike heroic poses for the camera.

Tinh, receiving his gift at his going-away party.

But Tinh had no desire to be a war hero and dreaded the prospect of reporting to Quang Trung Training Center for basic. The escalated fighting had produced heavy casualties by then, and he had no desire to *hy sinh* (sacrifice himself) on the battlefield. The illegal deferment market was rampant in Saigon, and Tinh was solicited by the recruiting sergeant. For a sum of money, the sergeant could insure that Tinh would be assigned to rear duty upon completion of basic training. Sorely tempted, but distrustful of the sergeant, Tinh and his family rejected the offer, only to fall victim to the spiteful sergeant, who kept Tinh in the recruiting office until his papers expired. When Tinh left, he was promptly arrested and charged with failure to carry valid identity documents. In a confused series of events, Tinh's American friends became involved, a collection was begun to bail him out, and he was eventually freed through the intervention of one of Jerry Jablonski's Vietnamese liaison officers (for the price of two lunches). Once freed, Tinh reported for his military training.

Six months later, Tinh was dead, killed by a mortar round in the Delta during one of his first combat operations. Shocked, Tinh's American friends attended his funeral at the National Cemetery. The cemetery sits on a hill just west of the Long Binh Highway in Bien Hoa. Guarding the entrance was the statue of an exhausted soldier sitting on a rock, his helmet tilted back, a carbine across his lap. It was a poignant work of art, inscribed with the words, *"Thuong Tiec"* ("Mourning"). As the funeral procession passed the statue, one of my Vietnamese passengers told of the sculptor's difficulty in locating a model for the work. None of the superstitious Vietnamese soldiers wanted to invite tragedy by allowing his image to sit outside a cemetery. By day, according to my passenger, the statue kept his silent vigil; but, at night, the local people insisted that they had seen him come to life and smoke a cigarette as he stood his lonely watch over his fallen comrades.

When we buried Tinh, the South Vietnamese were reporting more than four hundred combat deaths each week. At Bien Hoa, the magnitude of this sacrifice took on real meaning. During Tinh's graveside service, I stood near two long rows of open

Statue at entrance to cemetery.

graves, each more than one hundred meters from end to end. Next to them were three more rows of fresh graves, each grave a mound of earth covered by a red and yellow South Vietnamese flag. One week later, I returned for a traditional second graveside service and noticed with horror that all of the graves had been filled, and that workers were busily digging three more rows. I counted almost four hundred new graves. In a nearby tent, twenty fresh wooden coffins were awaiting burial. I left Bien Hoa that day, haunted by the piteous graveside wailings of the bereaved Vietnamese women and shaken by the realization that Saigon's official casualty figures were clearly deflated. I knew that all four military regions had large national cemeteries, and that many militia soldiers were customarily interred in their native villages. If four hundred South Vietnamese had been buried in Bien Hoa during the past week, then God only knew how many had actually died, but the total was certainly much higher than the number reported by the Ministry of National Defense.

Tiny Whitfield was an American civilian contractor. A native of the Florida panhandle, Tiny worked for Northrop, helping the South Vietnamese Air Force maintain its fleet of F5 fighter aircraft. I had met Tiny while serving in Hau Nghia province, during one of my forays into Bien Hoa city. The short, round Florida cracker had married a girl from the Delta in 1969 and swore repeatedly that he would never leave Vietnam as long as there was work. Where else could he make twenty thousand dollars a year, tax-free, and live in a villa with two servants?

But by August 1974, Tiny had changed his plans. Thoroughly fed up and ready to call it quits, Tiny explained to me that working with the Vietnamese Air Force at Bien Hoa had become a daily battle of wits between the American contractors and their Vietnamese counterparts, a battle that Tiny and his friends usually lost.

"Every time we get a bird fueled up and ready for a test flight," Tiny complained, "we can't find the pilot who's supposed to fly it. By the time we run him down, they've done stole all the gas out of the damn aircraft, and we have to start all over again!" According to Tiny, morale at the Bien Hoa base was so poor that many pilots came to work and spent the day figuring out how to avoid flying. The threat from Communist antiaircraft fire had become so formidable that few pilots wanted to risk being shot down. Those aviators who did fly dropped their bombs from so high that accuracy was almost nonexistent.

"I've tried for three days to get one F5 tested," Tiny fumed, "and we have already had to refuel it twice, even though it has yet to leave the ground. The damn VC are so close that they hit us with rockets the other night, but we still can't get no one interested in flying." Carrying an extra steel helmet and flak jacket I had loaned him, Tiny left my apartment, grumbling that Northrop could care less about his safety. To the best of my knowledge, the situation Tiny described had not been reported, so I related his plight to a colonel in the DAO Air Force Division. The colonel listened attentively and thanked me for the information. When the next weekly wrap-up went out, I looked in vain for any mention of declining morale in the air force.

Bill Laurie was a former military intelligence officer, one of the few who learned to speak Vietnamese well. As a civilian intelligence analyst in the DAO Current Intelligence Section, his area specialty was Military Region IV, the Mekong Delta.

By early December 1974, Bill was deeply concerned about a series of ominous indicators in South Vietnam's populous "rice bowl," and he expressed his concern in a pessimistic analysis that was included in the DAO "Weekly Wrap-Up." Embassy reaction came quickly from Deputy Chief of Mission Wolfgang Lehmann. Bill recalls the dispute in these words:

The report noted several developments and changes in VC/NVA operations during the previous several months, changes that indicated the Communists were saving up for something big. On the surface, not much had changed in terms of *numbers* of incidents. There was still a war going on, and, to the casual observer, that was about all there was to it. But our analysts noted that there was a sudden decrease in VC/NVA use of their heavy weapons: 122- and 107-millimeter rockets; 120- and 82-millimeter mortars. Now we were observing shellings and harassment fires by 60- and 61-millimeter mortars, and a drift away from combat engagements initiated by the Communists. All of this was taking place at a time when wet season rains allowed supplies to come in across the Plain of Reeds and when fuel cutbacks to the ARVN 7th Division had restricted it to a reactive posture— ruling out preemptive spoiling attacks that it had conducted the previous year with great success. At the same time, captured documents had alerted us that the Communists knew about and intended to exploit South Vietnamese fuel and munitions shortages.

In sum, something was in the wind, and those of us who knew the Delta smelled a rat. Hence, the report concluded that we would probably witness the heaviest fighting in the Delta since the Tet Offensive and that the attacks might well be on the scale of the 1968 onslaught. This time, however, the targets would not be the headline-grabbing seizure of cities and towns, but rather the ARVN itself. The Communists would direct attacks on Saigon's military forces in the Delta to force the expenditure of skimpy manpower reserves and even skimpier supplies, to accelerate the hemorrhage of casualties, and to compound the difficulties South Vietnamese forces were experiencing because of the aid cutbacks and a crippled economy.

The report was sent to the Embassy, and returned shortly thereafter with the handwritten comments of the Deputy Chief of Mission, Wolfgang Lehmann. He was incensed and equated pessimistic reports, however valid they may have been, with naive defeatism or some such thing. There was nothing in the way of rational critique. No one was going to tell him about the Delta, since he had served there as consulate general for some months—from which he had collected a number of preconceived notions. Among the comments most clear in my mind were "Crap!" "Can this be substantiated?" and "Where did you get your info?"—all in glaring red ink.

Shortly thereafter, the roof fell in on the Delta when the enemy launched what was far and away the biggest and most widespread campaign since 1968, during which he expended more munitions against more targets than during the Tet attacks. The attacks were well coordinated between VC military regions for the first time, and Communist troops came out fighting, willing to take casualties, and going like hell to draw blood. Not to seize capitals or anything like that, but to make the South Vietnamese military burn itself out in response, to throw more sand in the gearbox by forcing the South Vietnamese to expend vital manpower, supplies, and armaments. Vinh Binh province all but disappeared in a "black hole" of noninformation, and other pockets of the Delta became obscured by the dust of combat.

That Saturday, in a highly unusual occurrence, Mike Hanson and I were summoned to the Embassy to explain matters to Mr. Lehmann and his staff, despite the fact that the whole scenario had been clearly laid out in the report that had been dismissed as "crap" only a week earlier. If the report erred, it was in *underestimating* what would take place. Regrettably, this incident was all too common. When experienced "Delta hands" attempted to call attention to the post-cease-fire deterioration of security in Military Region IV, our estimates fell on unreceptive ears in the Embassy. Any balance that we were able to impart to the Embassy's upbeat reporting had to be accomplished through military (DAO) channels.

I knew a young Vietnamese soldier named Nguyen van Ba, who served in a militia company in the Delta province of Chuong Thien. Year in and year out, Chuong Thien was one of South Vietnam's bloodiest battlegrounds. Ba occasionally came to Saigon to visit his family. On one of these visits near the end of 1974, he shared this story with me:

Our company commander's name was Suong. He was well liked by the men because our company never took any casualties under his leadership. The VC had passed the word through the people to the captain that he should not conduct operations into the outlying hamlets, and especially not into the Rung Tram forest. Whenever our unit left the outpost on an operation, the captain would have us "test fire" our weapons as we approached the operational area. The Vietcong, warned of our approach, would melt away. On these operations, we walked through the hamlets without searching or checking ID cards. We never contacted the VC, and no one ever tripped a booby trap. Back in the outpost, we slept at night without fear of mortar or sapper attacks. The VC had told the captain through the people that if we left them alone, we could live in peace together. Both sides respected the rules.

Then one day the MSS came and arrested the captain for accommodation with the enemy. Everyone was sorry to see him go—his men, the villagers, and probably the Vietcong. Under his command, the war had gone away. His successor was a hard man—a northerner—and he quickly changed everything. We began to search the hamlets and run aggressive operations into the Rung Tram area. Casualties from booby traps mounted, and our outpost began to receive mortar fire several times a week. After that, our company began to shrink from losses like all the others in Chuong Thien. Now, our guards stay alert at night because of the danger of a sapper attack.

No one in Saigon was more stricken than General Murray by the decision of the U.S. Congress to cut the Vietnam aid bill by 30 percent. He was convinced that the South Vietnamese faced a military showdown with the Communists, and he believed firmly that both American aid and air power were essential to South Vietnamese survival. In his end-of-tour report, the general offered these prophetic views on North Vietnam:

It could collapse internally. Russia and China, or both, could dry up the pipe; for that matter, nature in these parts could typhoon it to virtual submission. All these and more could happen. But they probably won't.

If the past records anything, it's their everlasting obstinancy. They will keep coming.

Their future big offensive is plainly written in the daily events that are casting their shadows of a showdown.

They are not building roads for tourists. Constructing pipelines to support the oil industry. Piling up ammo caches just to make pyrotechnic displays. Pushing in tanks, field guns, and ack-ack just for the logistical exercises.

When the time is ripe—they will strike. And strike with violent power. And perhaps this time with air power.

General Murray had done everything possible to insure that Washington understood the urgency of South Vietnam's dilemma. When his superiors in the Pentagon requested guidance on the impact of reduced aid on the South Vietnamese military, Murray cabled bluntly that the prospects for South Vietnamese survival diminished as aid levels dropped below $1 billion (the administration had requested $1.45 billion). If U.S. aid dropped to the $750 million level, the general warned, "Funds would not support hard-core self-defense requirements. Any chance of having Hanoi see the light and come to the conference table would be sharply diminished." If aid fell to the $600 million level, the general suggested that the United States might as well "write off RVN as a bad investment and a broken promise." [19]

The news of President Nixon's resignation and the slash in military aid to the $700 million level hit Saigon only a few days apart. General Murray, who was about to retire, responded readily to an Embassy request that he speak candidly to the press on the plight of the South Vietnamese. In an interview with a *New York Times* reporter, Murray unloaded on the congressional aid cuts. The South Vietnamese are "sacrificing blood for the lack of ammunition," he argued passionately. He called attention to the fact that, despite the wishful thinking of Congress and the American people, the war in Vietnam continued to produce heavy casualties. [20]

Even though the Embassy authorized the interview, the general's blunt rhetoric triggered a sharp reaction from Washington. General Murray recalls the resulting brouhaha:

Then came the uproar from the Pentagon telling me "not to get out in front." In effect challenging State's authority to give me instructions and attempting to renege on the past agreement when the heat got scorching [DOD and State had agreed that the Defense Attaché would be subordinate to the Embassy in the area of public relations].

I was miffed by the Gerry Freidheim phlegm. Only a few days before at a Pentagon news briefing as the spokesman for the Defense Department, when asked a question about Vietnam, he replied, "We don't have anybody out there anymore." If so, then what the hell were you and I doing there? And when the stuff hit the fan what was he doing? Sending a message to a phantom?

Everything I said was authorized, and I was for it. What I did was restrain Ann Bottorf [DAO Public Relations Officer] from tipping off the higher headquarters that I was going to say it. And say it for publication. A technical violation . . .

Can't you imagine it? If I had tipped off CINCPAC et al that I was going to tell the press the sorry facts about our eye-opening eyedropper support, you know what would have happened? I'd be directed to furnish a prepared statement and instead of saying that the poor little guys "are sacrificing blood for lack of ammunition," I'd be directed to recite some bland prose like: "As the result of prudent fiscal restraints, the Armed Forces of South Vietnam have been obliged to appropriately modify their episodic combat methodology toward the maintenance of a cease-fire equilibrium."[21]

I dropped by General Murray's office the day after the *New York Times* interview hit the street. The general had just hung up the phone in disgust as I entered the room. It had been his third remonstrating phone call from the Pentagon. "I've had enough of their phone calls," he fumed. "I just told them that if I get one more call telling me to shut up, I'll hold a retirement press conference in Hawaii and really sound off—to include revealing the names of those who tried to shut me up." The general was furious over the congressional aid cut because he knew that it portended the end of South Vietnam. With his departure from Vietnam and his retirement imminent, the conscientious Murray felt like a rat abandoning a sinking ship. It was naive and self-deluding, he argued, for Congress to believe that reductions in aid would force compliance with the cease-fire. A weakened South Vietnamese military could result only in increased North Vietnamese militancy. Within a few days of the blowup

over his news release, General Murray departed Saigon and
went into retirement, disillusioned and deeply disturbed by his
unsuccessful efforts to influence what he regarded as cynical
and shortsighted policy.

During a September 1974 interview in Chicago, he prophesied
that South Vietnam would be hard pressed to survive another
year because of the reductions in aid. "What we are doing now
is sadistic," Murray argued, pointing out that South Vietnamese
casualties mounted as American aid declined.[22] But the con-
science-stricken general's voice was ignored like a cry for help in
downtown Manhattan. The risks of involvement were too high.

We met in the air-conditioned conference room of the United
States Information Service (USIS) in Saigon. Our group, known
as the "Hanoi Watch Committee," convened every Thursday
afternoon to exchange information on North Vietnam. Seated
around the polished conference table were representatives from
the CIA, State Department, the DAO, USIS, and the JMT. At
one particularly memorable session in late July 1974, a heated
discussion focused on the subject of Hanoi's intentions in the
south. CIA analyst Frank Snepp had started the debate by sharing the latest hot intelligence. We listened intently as Frank provided a detailed recounting of the contents of the latest top-
secret directive that had been issued by the Communist high
command. The order informed all Communist cadre, "If the
South Vietnamese government continues to be defeated, it will
agree to implement the cease-fire, including the establishment
of the National Council of National Reconciliation and Concord
and agreement on the demarcation of zones of control." Frank
pointed out that the new order marked the first time that the
Communists had mentioned to their cadre the possibility of a
political settlement with President Thieu's government.

Jack Mace was more cautious. The DAO analyst pointed out
that the new Communist directive also asserted: "We must continue to push the South Vietnamese so we can deliver a decisive
blow in the spring of 1975." Arguing that the new information
was insufficient evidence that the Communists had opted for a
political settlement, Jack pointed out that continued increases

in North Vietnamese infiltration and the recent establishment of enemy corps-level commands pointed to an impending offensive.

Snepp countered by reviewing the latest intelligence. One source had allegedly stated that "the Soviets have cut aid to Hanoi and think that the Chinese have also. There is no major offensive in the offing." Another source claimed that the North Vietnamese were asserting that "peace is assured in the south now," and "we are seriously occupied in solving urgent economic problems now. The Thieu regime doesn't need to be pushed over the brink now. It is deteriorating all by itself." Frank cited yet another source who had stated, "The Soviets are telling the North Vietnamese that Thieu is no pushover but will fail as the United States cuts aid." To further buttress his case, Frank quoted several different sources who had all insisted that Hanoi had been put on notice by Moscow and Peking. If a major offensive were to be launched, there would be no replacement military aid for combat losses such as had been sustained during 1972. Still another of Frank's sources had provided this enticing tidbit of information: "The North Vietnamese are bitter at the Soviets for cutting back military aid. They feel constrained in the military sphere."

But Jack remained unconvinced, pointing out that Hanoi already had enough aid on hand to sustain a major military push in the south for many months. He refused to accept the validity of either the alleged Soviet aid cuts or the reputed split between Hanoi and Moscow. He felt that the war was building up to a decisive military showdown, not a resumption of political talks. When the end came, it would come with a bang, not a whimper. (President Thieu continued to urge his people to "kill all the Communists in Vietnam if necessary," and fight "to the last bullet and the last grain of rice.") Jack saw the emergence of the new North Vietnamese corps headquarters as a portent of offensive activity, whereas Frank leaned toward the less dramatic interpretation that the North Vietnamese had created the new command structure to facilitate the logistical support of their troops in the south.

The debate between Jack Mace and Snepp once again underscored the classic dilemma of the intelligence officer. Estimating enemy capabilities was relatively simple, but fathoming the enemy's intentions was an elusive task. In this instance, Frank and Jack simply put a different interpretation on the same set of facts. Two years later and long after Saigon had been renamed Ho Chi Minh City, Hanoi's General Dung resolved the argument in Jack's favor. In his discussion of Hanoi's preparations for its 1975 offensive, Dung wrote:

> To stage large-scale annihilating battles and firmly defend the newly liberated areas, it was no longer advisable to field only independent or combined divisions. In 1974 army corps were gradually formed and deployed in strategic areas most vital to insuring mobility. . . . This represented a great step to maturity for our army and, at the same time, the most active step in preparing forces for the future general offensive.[23]

On 16 August 1974, I briefed Colonel Madison, pointing out that the superpowers had already created in Vietnam a volatile situation that they could perhaps no longer control:

> Are North Vietnam's economic problems so serious that they restrict Hanoi's options in approaching the question of reunification? The North Vietnamese are hard; they are used to sacrifice. Their leaders are dedicated to reunification. The increasingly uttered conclusion that "Hanoi has opted for long-term economic development at the expense of a quick solution in the south" makes the assumption that Hanoi's leaders think and act as Westerners—an assumption that has always led us to grief. There may be no quick solution in the south in the cards at this time, but it is my view that if Hanoi's "aging leaders" saw the opportunity, no amount of typhoons, hog cholera, or additional sacrifice by the DRV peasantry would deter them from striking the final blow of their cherished revolution. The North Vietnamese may not launch a general offensive to topple the South Vietnamese government if they perceive that it is not necessary. Indeed, the current phased offensive, however costly to Hanoi, is showing signs of bringing about unprecedented economic and morale problems in the GVN. However . . . the capability, and the will, for a prolonged offensive exists. I do not believe Soviet

or Chinese pressure, economic problems, or American threats
will deter Hanoi if invoking this option appears necessary.

Shortly after my briefing to Colonel Madison, I made another
trip to Hanoi. The tree-lined boulevards of the North Vietnamese capital were bedecked with colorful displays of flags
representing the Hanoi government and its PRG "ally." Scarlet
and gold banners hanging at the intersections urged the people
to "implement the transportation offensive!" When queried,
Major Huyen replied innocently that the transportation offensive involved the repair of North Vietnam's roads and railroads
that had been destroyed during the American bombing. When I
countered that his government had just recently announced the
completion of reconstruction in the north and the commencement of a "new phase" of "economic development," the major
replied with a benevolent smile.

Part V

THE AXE BEGINS TO FALL

"HOGWASH!"

Eighteen days after the North Vietnamese seized Phuoc Long province, Major Le Tan Dai emerged from the jungle and approached a unit of surprised South Vietnamese troops. The major was a survivor of the battle for Song Be city, the province capital, in which North Vietnamese armor had penetrated into the ARVN lines and shelled the South Vietnamese command bunker from point-blank range.

Dai told a grim story. Song Be had been under artillery fire for several weeks before the enemy assault on 3 January. Two North Vietnamese divisions had attacked after a three thousand–round holocaust of artillery fire, supported by tanks, anti-aircraft units, and elite sapper troops. Opposing this formidable array of forces had been four militia battalions and a handful of lightly armed Popular Forces platoons, reinforced by one battalion of ARVN infantry and two companies of airborne troops. Thus, when the North Vietnamese launched their final assault, they had achieved a four-to-one superiority of forces. The outcome of such a lopsided battle was never in doubt. South Vietnamese defenders fought bravely; Dai himself watched his desperate soldiers climb onto the backs of the buttoned-up NVA tanks in futile attempts to throw hand grenades into the hatches. When the Hanoi regulars finally hoisted their banner over the province headquarters, less than 850 of the 5,400 South Vietnamese soldiers committed to the battle survived.[1] Major Dai, still in shock over the calamity he had witnessed, expressed deep sorrow to his debriefers that "the rest of the free world does not understand, nor care. I feel very bad," he lamented, "and believe that my country may fall, but I will die fighting for it. The problem I will have to understand is why it fell when so many Americans and Vietnamese have died for a good cause."

Even as Major Dai related his tragic odyssey, in Washington President Ford's administration prepared to request additional funds to support Cambodia and South Vietnam. On 28 January, the President requested a supplemental appropriation of $522 million, of which $300 million was to be provided to South Vietnam. The President was swimming against the congressional tide on this issue, but he was determined to use all of his influence to live up to his predecessor's commitments to South Vietnam. On the heels of this request came an exodus of congressional leaders to Saigon to determine for themselves if the unpopular request was really required.

By far the largest of these delegations was led by Congressman John Flynt of Georgia. During late February and early March 1975, the Flynt delegation joined up with Oklahoma Senator Dewey Bartlett and Congressman Paul McCloskey of California, both of whom had also come to Saigon for a firsthand look at the situation. Other members of the delegations included the pipe-smoking Congresswoman Millicent Fenwick of New Jersey, Congressman William Chappell of Florida, Congressman Donald N. Fraser of Minnesota, Congressman John P. Murtha of Pennsylvania, and the brash and often controversial Congresswoman Bella Abzug of New York. During their weeklong visit, the legislators had the opportunity to attend briefings at the U.S. Embassy, at the DAO, and at the headquarters of South Vietnamese Joint General Staff. Some of the visitors conscientiously attended everything on the itinerary, while others showed little interest in briefings. Congresswoman Abzug, for example, was particularly independent. She arrived firmly determined to see "political prisoners" and meet with members of the anti-Thieu "Third Force." General Cao Van Vien, then

Congressional delegation arrives at Tan Son Nhut and is met by Colonel Bao.

Chairman of the Joint General Staff, described his impressions of the congressional visitors with typical Vietnamese politeness:

> The backgrounds of the visiting U.S. congressmen were as diverse as their opinions on the issue of U.S. aid and the Vietnam War. Some were for, others were against it. There were those who came with open minds, and there were also those who appeared heavily prejudiced. Some were courteous and modest; others were rude and contemptuous; still others were completely detached and indifferent. But no matter who they were or how they behaved themselves, they were all received with equal warmth and sincerity.[2]

When we learned of the impending congressional visits, Colonel Madison directed us to gear up for another briefing. The MIA issue remained a volatile one in the States, and it was a rare legislator who could pass through Saigon without some display of interest in our operations. In this case, the congressmen had requested that we arrange audiences with both Communist delegations at Camp Davis so they could discuss the MIA issue face-to-face with our adversaries. To prepare them for this confrontation, we scheduled a working breakfast briefing. Colonel Madison assigned me as the escort officer/interpreter for the Camp Davis meeting; LTC Harry Summers, who had replaced LTC Lunde as my boss, would provide a background briefing to our visitors at breakfast.

The day of the visit arrived, and Colonel Summers presented our guests with a detailed account of the stalled talks. The colonel explained that the Geneva Convention, the International Red Cross, and the United Nations General Assembly had all affirmed the obligation of belligerents to exchange information on the missing and the dead. To the Communist claim that progress on the MIA issue must await the day when the entire Paris Agreement was "strictly implemented," Summers responded that the weight of international legal opinion dictated the exchange of information *during conflicts*, even in the face of other unresolved issues. While several of the legislators took hasty notes, the colonel concluded his presentation by pointing out that Communist foot-dragging on the MIA issue for the purpose of extracting political concessions from the United States "ignores the imperatives which have been adopted by civilized nations."[3] The colonel had argued clearly and persuasively, laying the blame for the impasse where it belonged, at the feet of the Communist delegations. Now we could only hope that our visitors would handle themselves well in the sessions to come.

I rode to the meetings in a sedan with Congressman Flynt, who pumped me for additional details about the vulnerabilities of our negotiating opponents. I told the congressman that the Vietcong delegation had provided us with a list of forty-one Americans who had died in their jungle prison camps, but had steadfastly refused to discuss the repatriation of their remains for more than twelve months. The congressman asked me to repeat the figures, which he jotted down on a small piece of paper.

A mob of reporters surrounded our vehicles at Camp Davis, our first clue that the Communists had decided to make the

Seated, left to right: Representatives Fenwick, Abzug, Flynt, Bart-lett, Fraser, Chappell, McCloskey.

sessions a public affair. As we climbed out of the sedans, report-ers and photographers surged around our party, thrusting microphones under the noses of the congressmen and asking questions that were unintelligible because of the confusion. The crush was so great that I momentarily became separated from Congressman Flynt. By the time I fought my way back to his side, the white-haired Georgian was protesting vigorously to Colonel Bao, our North Vietnamese host. Using the Commu-nists' interpreter, Flynt was telling Bao that the presence of so many reporters would render a meaningful exchange of views impossible. But Colonel Bao would hear none of it. He smiled, ignored the congressman's protest, and invited us into the con-ference site, which, by this time, was swarming with reporters. Off to my left, I spotted Congresswoman Abzug. She had skipped our morning briefing to pursue her contacts with the anti-Thieu opposition, but she now flounced into the conference room, dressed in a garishly flowered dress and her trademark, a white hat that looked like an upside-down wastebasket. Maj. Jim Sabater, my Marine Corps office mate, gave me a look of resignation as Abzug greeted a North Vietnamese officer as if he were her long-lost brother. Jim had been assigned as a body-guard for Abzug, who, alone among the visitors, apparently did not feel comfortable around South Vietnamese. As we entered the conference room, Congressman Flynt grabbed me by the arm and ordered, "You just stay right by my side from now on, son."[4]

Congressman Flynt and Senator Bartlett took seats at one end of a long table, directly opposite Colonel Bao, who sat in front of a large marble bust of Ho Chi Minh. The rest of the party sat along both sides of the table. The room was small, and all of us were hemmed in by the crush of reporters, who pushed and shoved us and one another rudely as they attempted to secure good vantage points for observing and recording the show. Our North Vietnamese hosts made no attempt to restrain the press, whose grinding cameras, shouted instructions, and maneu-vering made communications difficult.

I elbowed my way to a place between Congressman Flynt and Senator Bartlett, only to discover that the North Vietnamese had ordered an English-speaking officer to eavesdrop on my conver-sations with the two legislators. The pesky North Vietnamese Lieutenant Thanh insisted on hovering over my shoulder, strain-

Author talks to Flynt; NVA lieutenant takes notes.

ing to catch what I was saying to the Washington visitors and recording whatever he could pick up in a small notebook. I leaned over and hissed into his ear, *"Di cho khac di!"* ("Beat it!"), but he refused to budge.

The heavy-jowled Colonel Bao opened the meeting with the suggestion that the American visitors should ask all of their questions first, after which he would reply to them all at one time. The cagey Washingtonians recognized Bao's ploy as a device that would give him the floor last and enable him to avoid specific answers. Congressman Flynt responded with a counterproposal that Colonel Bao should answer each question as it was posed. But the inflexible Bao had his marching orders, and he stubbornly insisted that the visitors should speak first. Flynt and Bartlett stood their ground. Each question should be answered in turn. Faced with such determined resistance, Colonel Bao compromised, inviting Congressman Flynt to ask a question and promising that he would then answer it "with an answer that will take twenty minutes." After a year of dealing with Colonel Bao and his cohorts, I knew what that meant, and so, apparently, did Senator Bartlett. The senator shot me a resigned glance as he realized that we were about to be subjected to a prepared statement. By now, Congressman Flynt had wearied of this procedural bickering, and he posed a question: "When did Hanoi plan to release information on American MIA personnel?"

Bao replied by launching into a twenty-minute prepared statement condemning the United States for its "illegal intervention" in the internal affairs of the Vietnamese people, and assailing the Ford administration for "perpetuating the war and making the exchange of MIA information impossible." It was precisely the line that Colonel Summers had predicted we would hear.

The impatient Flynt replied caustically that Bao's statement bore no relation to his specific question. "In fact," Flynt noted, "your remarks were clearly read from a prepared statement, which your interpreter then reread from his script. I am certain that if I had asked about the weather in Hanoi, your answer would have been the same." Several reporters laughed openly, but Colonel Bao sat stoically through Flynt's sarcasm.

Senator Bartlett and I had a whispered exchange, during which he suggested an approach to unhinge the Communists. I nodded my enthusiastic agreement with his idea, and he took the floor. Removing an MIA bracelet from his wrist, the square-jawed senator explained to Colonel Bao that the officer whose name appeared on the bracelet had been shot down over North Vietnam and was listed as missing in action. "I would ask that you record Captain Fieszel's name, rank, and service number," Bartlett continued, "and I would like to remind you that a resolution of the United Nations General Assembly of November 1974 makes it obligatory for your government to take immediate steps to resolve Captain Fieszel's fate. He was shot down in 1968, about seven years ago, and his wife wants to know where he is or where his remains are. I go back to Oklahoma in about two weeks. Now what am I going to tell Mrs. Fieszel when we're paying a lot of money to send a flight from here to Hanoi once a week with the express purpose of providing information on MIAs, and we haven't received one bit of information?"

Colonel Bao attempted to deliver a second, hastily prepared statement, but the angry Oklahoman interrupted: "Excuse me, but your remarks have nothing to do with our specific questions. In fact, in Oklahoma, where I come from, they have a

Seated, left to right: Captain To, interpreter, LTC Bao; listening to Senator Bartlett's demand for information on Captain Fieszel.

word for your remarks, and that word is 'hogwash.' What about Captain Fieszel? What do I tell his wife? Do I tell her that you have refused to answer?"

By now, the MIA bracelet had been passed down the long table to Bao, who fingered it uncomfortably as Senator Bartlett badgered him. Visibly uncomfortable under fire, the barrel-chested North Vietnamese passed the bracelet back to our end of the table. "You may tell the captain's wife," he snapped, "that I will check with my government on the case of her husband."

Congressman Chappell of Florida then took the floor:

I came to Vietnam in the spirit of objectivity, in an attempt to learn about the true situation over here so that I can vote cor- rectly on the important issue of aid to South Vietnam. I had hoped after this conference here today that the other members of this delegation and I would be in a position to go back to Amer- ica and say that what we had learned would give us an oppor- tunity to foster peace in this area of the world. As I said, I came here with an open mind and have tried to be objective. But, now that I have had the opportunity to meet here with you and hear your side of the story, I have come to some conclusions. I want to say to you in all candor that I don't believe you people ever intended in the first instance to abide by the agreement made in Paris. Nor do I think that you intended to honor your obligations and exchange information on MIA personnel. For over two years now, the United States has flown your delegates to Hanoi every week at a cost of more than $600,000 a year so that you could collect information from your government on our MIA personnel. Up to now, you have not given us information on even one MIA case. You complain about violations of your dip- lomatic privileges and immunities and state that your water and electricity is [sic] always shut off, yet I see you living very com- fortably here in Saigon. Furthermore, all this is at the expense of the U.S. government and the South Vietnamese government. You have not paid a single penny for all of this since the cease-fire. You claim to be humanitarian, yet, in December 1973, your military forces ambushed an unarmed U.S. search team, mur- dering in cold blood two [sic] U.S. military officers.* As for my-

---

*Only one American officer was killed in this ambush.

self, what I have learned here has helped me to make up my mind. When I return to the United States, I intend to share what I have learned here, and, when asked, I will vote for the $300 million in supplemental aid to the Republic of Vietnam.

An uneasy silence descended on the room as Chappell finished his defiant speech. Bella Abzug, who had said little up to this point, ended the silence with a conciliatory statement: "I think that North Vietnam's repatriation of the remains of the twenty-three servicemen who died in captivity and Colonel Bao's consent to query his government about Captain Fieszel's case show that the spirit exists to take steps to alleviate the grief of America's MIA families," she cooed. Abzug then went on to propose that the Hanoi delegation should agree to receive more requests from the U.S. delegation on specific MIA cases, and then check the requests against its records in the north. "Such actions," she concluded, "would be an enormous step toward building goodwill and establishing normal relations between the United States and the Democratic Republic of Vietnam." I winced at her naivete and clear lack of information about our negotiations. If she had attended our morning briefing instead of hobnobbing around Saigon in search of anti-Thieu sentiments, she would have known that we had been passing specific queries on MIA cases to Hanoi for two years with no results.

The confrontation with Colonel Bao had lasted almost ninety minutes, and we still faced a meeting with delegates from the "Provisional Revolutionary Government"—the Vietcong. Outside the conference room, a green-clad Vietcong soldier signaled us to follow him to the second conference site. As we walked along a row of broad-leaved banana trees, Senator Bartlett vowed that he would not let the Vietcong representative get away with manipulating the meeting as the North Vietnamese had done. I braced myself for the confrontation.

At the PRG's conference room, we were met by MG Hoang Anh Tuan, the senior Vietcong officer in Saigon. A large, red, blue, and gold Vietcong flag and a photo of Ho Chi Minh hung on one wall. We took our seats directly opposite General Tuan.

Trouble began right away. Before Tuan could open the meeting, Senator Bartlett took the floor and announced that he had a question. By the time the surprised Tuan had nodded his assent, the aggressive senator had already begun to pose his question.

"The United Nations General Assembly Resolution of 1974 requires belligerents to exchange information on the missing and the dead during a conflict," he announced. "Why has the PRG failed to take a single step to exchange MIA information under Article 8(b) of the Paris Agreement?" Our Washington visitors had obviously absorbed the key points of Colonel Summer's breakfast pep talk. Senator Bartlett was fed up with Communist stalling after less than two hours of combat. Across the table, General Tuan was shuffling a typewritten document. Senator Bartlett and Congressman Flynt exchanged glances as they realized that we were about to be subjected to another prepared statement.

The Communist general ignored Senator Bartlett's question and began to read a statement that sounded like a carbon copy of Colonel Bao's remarks. Congressman Flynt groaned audibly in disgust and turned to Bartlett for a brief whispered exchange. The senator turned to me with a wink and said, "Watch this."

"Thank you for your comments, General Tuan," Bartlett interrupted in a loud voice. Tuan stopped speaking abruptly, clearly perturbed at this blatant breach of protocol. The senator continued, usurping the chairmanship of the meeting. "I believe Congressman Flynt now has a question."

Congressman Flynt joined the fray with a vengeance. "If, as you say, you are interested in seriously implementing the Paris Agreement, then why has your government refused to repatriate the bodies of forty-one American servicemen who died in your prison camps?"

General Tuan glared coldly at the impudent Americans from behind his tinted glasses. "I was explaining this systematically by showing the overall problem of the Paris Agreement and the continued intervention of your government in Vietnam, but, regrettably, I was interrupted. Allow me to continue, since we have only five minutes of time remaining. The real problem is the American continuation of the war . . ."

"No!" Congressman Flynt interrupted. "I want to know why you haven't returned the forty-one bodies. Where are they?"

Vietcong MG Hoang Anh Tuan.

Well schooled in the art of dodging questions, Flynt recognized the tactic when he saw it.

Tuan again attempted to forge ahead with his speech: "After the signing of the Paris Agreement, the United States illegally continued to perpetuate the war, making it impossible for the treaty to be implemented while hundreds and thousands of Vietnamese are miserable and dying each week."

Flynt was livid by now. "I'm sorry," he thundered, "but I don't want to hear this. I want to know where the forty-one bodies are. Where are the forty-one bodies?"

I was enjoying the whole routine. I had sat through many such prepared statements while my boss listened in silence, constrained by the niceties of diplomatic protocol. Congressman Flynt was subject to no such restraints. General Tuan finally gave up in disgust, but not without a parting shot. "I thought you came to exchange views, to try and understand more clearly the situation in Vietnam. I will not be forced to answer such a question, and I believe the American people will understand." Tuan glanced at his watch, snatched up his papers, and announced, "I see that our time is up." Springing to his feet, he stalked out of the room, followed by his aides and interpreter. I looked at my watch. Exactly fifteen minutes of the agreed thirty-minute session had elapsed.

Senator Bartlett had the last word. "Good!" he pronounced with a satisfied grin. The reporters scrambled for the door.

I couldn't conceal my delight as our sedans departed Tan Son Nhut. Our visitors had now experienced firsthand what we had endured since the cease-fire, with one major exception. They did not have to sit still and listen to the Communists' eternal lectures. The Communists had clearly believed that they could orchestrate the meetings to their advantage—a serious miscalculation. The visitors from Washington had quickly divined the Communist plan and reacted accordingly. The independent legislators were not content to come halfway across the globe to be used as drawing cards for a Communist propaganda spectacular. Nor were they inclined to sit passively and be lectured at by the likes of Colonel Bao and General Tuan. The public forum that the Communists had created by inviting the media could be used by both sides. Colonel Bao and General Tuan had just learned the hard way that nothing is more formidable than an American legislator in a roomful of reporters.

It also seemed that our adversaries had seriously underestimated the volatility of the MIA issue in the United States. If they thought that Congresswoman Abzug's sympathies with anti-Thieu forces meant that she would speak out against administration policy during a conference on the MIA issue, they were sadly mistaken. Brash and outspoken she was, but dumb she was not. The Communists apparently did not understand that the "dove" image might be politically healthy on the issue of military aid to the Thieu government, but that a soft stand on the MIA issue was political suicide. Hence, Congresswoman Abzug sat in subdued silence while her hawkish colleagues raked the Communists over the coals for their MIA stonewalling.

On balance, the whole affair had boomeranged on the Communists. General Tuan's premature walkout was an obvious reaction to Congressman Flynt's aggressive pursuit of a simple answer to a simple question, and it was so perceived by the press. *Stars and Stripes* gave the confrontation front-page coverage under the headline, "US Solons in Showdown with 'Lying, Murdering' NVA." The Communist press referred to the congressional visit as an "abortive operation" and explained the embarrassing confrontation this way:

> To top the programme, the CIA even engineered an incident between Dewey Bartlett and William Shappell [sic] and the representative of the DRVN members of the Joint Military Four-Party Commission in charge of the search for MIA's and KIA's graves.[5]

Our superiors at the Embassy were relieved that the congressional visit had ended on a positive note. At least some of our visitors had gone away determined to support the supplemental aid bill, although none of us thought that it stood much of a chance of passage. Congress seemed intent on charting a strange course: It would somehow end the war by weakening one of the antagonists. As South Vietnamese Gen. Cao Van Vien remembers it, "The impression left behind by the departing visitors was one of pessimism and premonition. The atmosphere was charged with rumors and speculation, all detrimental to the national cause."[6] President Thieu himself was deeply affected by his encounter with the congressional visitors, whose behavior convinced him that further hopes for American aid were futile. Within days, this fatalistic conclusion would influence him to make a decision that would change the course of the war.[7]

"TO RESTORE THE MOON TO ITS FULL GLORY"

It didn't take Clausewitzian genius to figure out after the fall of Phuoc Long province that the military situation was becoming perilous. Even before Congressman Flynt and his colleagues descended on Saigon, the handwriting was on the wall. Already in January 1975, shortly after the Phuoc Long debacle, Hanoi's 968th Division had moved from Laos across the border into the Central Highlands, thus further tipping the ratio of forces against the South Vietnamese in this remote area. As Bella Abzug rattled around Saigon in her futile search for two hundred thousand political prisoners, infiltration figures monitored by our analysts in the DAO showed that North Vietnamese reinforcements were arriving in the south in record numbers. Colonel LeGro's analysts prepared a summary of these statistics for our visitors, putting the situation in clear language. The rate of infiltration had increased so dramatically that by the end of March, the number of North Vietnamese troops scheduled to arrive in South Vietnam would exceed the number that had arrived during the first half of 1973. Infiltration of this magnitude was unprecedented in the history of the Indochina War.[8]

The LeGro document also provided the congressional delegates with a sobering summary of the North Vietnamese buildup since the cease-fire. Enemy tanks had increased from one hundred vehicles at cease-fire time to more than seven hundred; artillery pieces numbered more than four hundred, up from one hundred; Hanoi's combat and support units had swelled by eighty-eight thousand men; and this force was backed up by logistical stockpiles of ammunition, food, fuel, and medicine that were adequate to support twelve months of offensive operations.[9] The Monthly Threat Assessment for January concluded (correctly) that all indicators portended major offensive activity. Our DAO analysts speculated that the anticipated offensive was "expected to assume country-wide proportions, and a number of indicators point to the introduction of strategic reserve divisions from North Vietnam."[10] All of these facts were laid before the visiting legislators, who could decide for themselves which were greater—North Vietnamese strengths or South Vietnamese weaknesses.

While Colonel LeGro's analysts composed their delphic predictions in Saigon, Hanoi's General Dung paid a farewell visit to several of the strategic reserve divisions in the north. At one installation, troops of the North Vietnamese 1st Corps responded to his exhortations for victory with shouts of *"Quyet Thang! Quyet Thang!"* ("Determined to Win! Determined to Win!") At Tan Ky city in southern North Vietnam, Dung had bid farewell to the 316th Division a month earlier. The 316th was being dispatched to join three other NVA divisions in an assault on the highland city of Ban Me Thuot, the first blow of the great offensive. The target had been carefully selected to insure surprise and easy victory. Ban Me Thuot was an isolated town in a difficult-to-reinforce area and was defended by less than one South Vietnamese division. Dung recalls that he recited a poem to the departing troops to describe "the common bitter score that must be settled by all Vietnamese":

> In our country after thirty years of bearing arms,
> The moon still remains divided into halves.
> Beckoning are battlefields, opportunities, and duty,
> Now is the time for us to set out together with the people of the
>   entire country,
> To restore the moon to its full glory.

Dung then warned the assembled troops that the South Vietnamese foe was "stubborn, cunning, and experienced." He then hurled a challenge at the men of the 316th:

> However, he is an enemy without a just cause who suffers from historical defeat, who is beset with all kinds of difficulties, growing poorer and poorer, both morally and materially, and declining in terms of both position and strength. It would be unjustifiable if the 316th Division could not defeat the puppets, considering their general decline and the rising position of the southern revolution.[11]

In Saigon, the experts were divided on where the Communist hammer would fall. As late as January, Tay Ninh province appeared to be the most likely target. Located on the Cambodian border some forty-five miles northwest of Saigon, Tay Ninh was threatened by more than three divisions supported by ten battalions of medium and heavy artillery. Communist forward observers perched on nearby Nui Ba Den (Black Virgin Mountain) directed deadly accurate fire against the city, which had been almost totally evacuated by the end of January. Like Ban Me Thuot, Tay Ninh was lightly defended, in this case by part of the 25th Division. My Vietnamese contacts at the Joint General Staff Headquarters were convinced that the North Vietnamese would move first to sever Tay Ninh from Military

Region III. Few of them doubted the Communists' capability to accomplish this feat, and their pessimism was not without foundation.

In mid-January, the South Vietnamese had tried to eject the North Vietnamese from their positions atop Nui Ba Den. For more than a week, helicopter gunships, artillery, and air strikes had pounded the enemy positions in preparation for the assault. But, when South Vietnamese heliborne troops attempted to land on the mountain slopes, they had been driven off by heavy enemy fire.[12] Convinced that Tay Ninh would be the next province to fall, I briefed Colonel Madison that the province could be overrun almost at the discretion of the North Vietnamese. But I was mistaken. While we were all transfixed by the Tay Ninh situation, General Dung's forces were massing around the highland city of Ban Me Thuot under strict radio silence.

The North Vietnamese refrained from any major offensive moves in late February. We speculated. Was the lull due to the presence of the congressional delegations in Saigon? Certainly Hanoi's leaders would have been foolish to initiate any major military moves while the legislators were in Saigon assessing the need for additional military aid to the Thieu government. Once again, we were wrong. As it turned out, the lull was the proverbial calm before the storm. General Dung's forces had not yet finished the complex series of moves required to isolate and attack Ban Me Thuot, and all units were under strict orders not to do anything that would tip the hand of the coming attacks.

Shortly after the congressmen departed, attacking North Vietnamese forces cut Routes 19 and 21, the only two east-west arteries linking the coastal region of Military Region II with Ban Me Thuot. The target city was then further isolated by the severing of Route 14, which linked it with reinforcements in Pleiku city to the north. Suddenly, attention became riveted on the Central Highlands. Tay Ninh was quickly forgotten as the debate focused on a different question. Would the North Vietnamese attack the northern highland cities of Pleiku and Kontum, or was their target Ban Me Thuot to the south? General Phu, the Military Region II commander, received warnings from his own G-2 and from the Joint General Staff G-2 that Ban Me

Thuot was the target, but he chose to ignore these warnings and prepare for an attack against Pleiku and Kontum.[13]

At this time, I happened to meet Larry Budow, a foreign service officer visiting in Saigon. Our meeting had been a chance encounter in the "White House," the DAO VIP guest house, where I had dropped by while escorting Congressman Flynt. Larry explained that he was in Saigon with a visiting State Department delegation. Headed by retired Ambassador Spencer King, this group had come to Vietnam to inspect our Embassy. I had learned about the King delegation's visit from a friend in the Consular Section of the Embassy. He had explained that public law required periodic inspections of all American embassies, similar in some respects to the annual IG inspections in the military. My friend also confided in me that the Saigon Embassy had tried to fend off this particular inspection with the claim that it was too taxed by the demands of the continuing war to devote time to such administrative exercises. But Washington had ultimately forced the inspection on the Embassy and selected Ambassador King to head the delegation, partly because he was senior in rank to the very senior Ambassador Graham Martin.

I spent only a few minutes with Larry that afternoon, just long enough to field a few queries about my background and to sense that the King delegation was fishing around for information that extended beyond the scope of internal Embassy operations. As we parted, Larry alerted me that I might soon hear from him. The Ambassador, he explained, was interested in learning about Vietnam.

The following morning I received an invitation. Ambassador King requested that I make reservations at the Chinese restaurant of my choice and meet him and his party at his quarters for cocktails. On the telephone, Larry Budow explained that the Ambassador wanted to talk to me about my experiences in Hanoi. Before I left the office, I told Colonel Summers of my premonition that Hanoi would not be the sole topic of discussion that night. Before heading home to change, I paid a brief visit to our DAO Library.

I easily located Ambassador King in *Who's Who*, which told

me that he was a Yale graduate whose career included atten-
dance at the U.S. Army War College. His last post had been as
the U.S. Ambassador to Guyana. Larry had also told me that
the Ambassador was accompanied by a Mr. Ed Swift, of the
Swift Packing Company. Swift, too, merited an entry in *Who's
Who*, which revealed him to be another Yale graduate, as well
as a high-ranking officer in the family business.

We indulged in a sumptuous feast of delicacies at Cholon's
My Le Hoa Restaurant that evening, where I passed around
pictures of Hanoi and fielded questions. After dinner, the Ambassador invited Ed Swift, Larry Budow, and me to his suite for
a drink. Over a gin and tonic, the conversation turned immediately to the war. Ambassador King came straight to the point.
How were the South Vietnamese doing?

I was nervous and asked for his assurances of confidentiality.
Ambassador Martin could have forced me out of the country in
a moment for presenting an uncleared, out-of-channels, contradictory report on the plight of the South Vietnamese. The Ambassador nodded understandingly and assured me that I could
speak openly.

Emboldened no doubt by the drinks, I poured out my fears for
the South Vietnamese in the face of an all-out North Vietnamese
offensive. My pessimistic views were out of step with the official
position of the U.S. mission, which was that the South Vietnamese military would give a good account of itself in the impending battles. The January Threat Assessment, for example, had
concluded, "If reported (Communist) plans are executed, in the
near term, the Communists will probably experience continued
success, to include overrunning of some district towns; however, increased Communist losses may prove prohibitive in the
long run."[14] Some of us in the DAO did not agree with this
assessment. I told Ambassador King that the South Vietnamese
military was a completely demoralized force that had lost all
confidence in President Thieu as a leader and in the United
States as an ally. I even melodramatically ventured the opinion
that the North Vietnamese could defeat South Vietnam within
ninety days if Hanoi's commanders acted boldly.

The Ambassador and Mr. Swift heard me out politely, but they seemed to be taken aback by my strident diatribe. Swift responded with a question: "Admittedly, you have had considerable experience over here, but we have been briefed by others who have been here as long, or longer, than you. Why is it that these people—some of whom have much more experience in intelligence than you—have told us the opposite? We were briefed at CINCPAC headquarters in Hawaii and told that the South Vietnamese would make it. This very day we heard a briefing at the Embassy that concluded the same thing. How can you state that the ARVN could lose in ninety days?"

If Swift was trying to goad me into still greater bursts of candor, he succeeded. I conceded that my comments were probably a little rash and acknowledged that I could get into trouble for saying such things, but pointed out that I had answered their query honestly, as I felt obliged to do. Lest they think my pessimism was unique, I pointed out that there were other Americans in the DAO—mostly among the lower echelons—who agreed with me, but that they, too, felt stymied by the closed atmosphere of the U.S. Embassy. It was simply not healthy to run around espousing a view of reality that conflicted with the official version, and the official version was that the South Vietnamese were going to survive the dry season offensive after some initial setbacks. I argued that people who insisted with certainty that the ARVN would succeed either did not understand reality or were covering up the gravity of the current situation. Finally, I took a shot at Ambassador Martin for his reluctance to countenance negative reporting about the South Vietnamese. I pointed out that, until recently, I had read reports that described the morale of South Vietnamese pilots as high and ARVN morale as only a little lower. These reports gave only cursory attention to the economic difficulties of the Vietnamese military and invariably ended with the same conclusion—the ARVN would hack it, one way or another. This kind of reporting prevailed at a time when South Vietnamese military effectiveness was slipping alarmingly as our aid shrank and Hanoi's forces geared up for their attacks.

That final outburst put an end to our conversation. The

Ambassador thanked me for joining him, and I retreated with Larry Budow, already experiencing second thoughts about my emotional criticism of Ambassador Martin. Later, I took Larry to a party hosted by some of the analysts in the Intelligence Branch and introduced him to several others who shared my pessimism. Somehow, though, I had the feeling that I had opened my big mouth just a bit too wide with Ambassador King.

The King dinner took place on the evening of 3 March, just hours before the North Vietnamese initiated what became the final offensive of the war. General Dung's forces blitzed the unsuspecting city of Ban Me Thuot on 10 March and overran its outgunned defenders in a matter of hours. The defeat stunned President Thieu, whose recent encounter with the congressional delegations had convinced him that he could expect no more help from Washington. Under this assumption, the former general decided that he could not afford to feed his scarce main force units into a Communist meat grinder in the remote Central Highlands. Thieu thus issued the fateful order to withdraw from Pleiku and Kontum, an extremely difficult operation that quickly disintegrated into an uncontrolled rout in the hands of an inept commander. This debacle was followed by an abortive attempt to retrench ARVN defenses in Military Region I, an operation that commenced with a pullback from Quang Tri city and rapidly turned sour. The North Vietnamese soon seized the initiative everywhere in the northern provinces of South Vietnam as Thieu's troops fell back in disorganized droves on the coastal cities. By the last week of March, all that remained of the northern half of the country was a string of coastal enclaves. At Saigon's Joint General Staff Headquarters, the South Vietnamese high command ordered the establishment of a defensive perimeter around the port city of Danang, which was threatened by the advancing North Vietnamese. The future of South Vietnam depended upon these moves, for the ARVN had lost most of the 23rd Division at Ban Me Thuot and could not suffer the loss of the other forces in the north and still retain enough strength to contain the Communist juggernaut.

But one disaster begot another. After the withdrawal from Quang Tri, the situation in the Imperial City of Hue began to deteriorate as soldiers and civilians alike sensed the magnitude of the impending disaster. By the 25th of March, the once-proud ARVN 1st Division had evacuated the city in disarray. Since the Communists had cut Route 1 south of the city, the remnants of the shattered unit were attempting to withdraw to Danang on the beaches of the Vinh Loc peninsula. If the Danang enclave were to be successfully defended, these men and their equipment had to execute this movement in an orderly fashion.

It was at this critical juncture that I received my second invitation for dinner with Ambassador King. The Ambassador and his party had completed their work and were scheduled to depart for Washington on the day following our meeting. Once again, the evening found us at the Ambassador's quarters, where I learned that they had received an exit briefing on the military situation before leaving the Embassy.

According to Embassy briefers, the retreat from the Central Highlands had disintegrated into a rout because it had been precipitously executed. The ARVN, they told Ambassador King, remained an effective fighting force that had recovered from this setback. To support this contention, Embassy analysts cited the ongoing withdrawal from Hue. This operation, Ambassador King had been assured, was proceeding well as the ARVN executed an organized retrograde operation that made good strategic sense. The situation was under control as the marines and the 1st Division pulled back to Danang with most of their equipment, ready to fight another day. A new defensive perimeter would be established north of the Hai Van pass (north of Danang), where the ARVN and marines would stop the North Vietnamese advance.

I had prepared for this meeting by contacting friends in the Vietnamese Joint General Staff Headquarters. The picture they painted differed sharply from the Embassy's optimistic prognosis. Embassy analysts had provided the Ambassador with an accurate depiction of the ARVN plan, but, unfortunately, the execution of that plan was not going well. The withdrawal from Hue had degenerated into an undisciplined rout that had infected even the 1st Division as it struggled down the sand dunes of the Vinh Loc peninsula. After Communist forces overran one of the division's command posts, men had broken ranks and abandoned much of the vital equipment needed for the defense of Danang. It was every man for himself on the beaches as fleeing soldiers mobbed the helicopters and barges that were attempting to deliver bridging equipment to them to facilitate withdrawal. I told the Ambassador that the ARVN was now completely demoralized and that Saigon was rife with rumors that President Thieu and the Americans had sold out northern South Vietnam to the Communists. South Vietnamese soldiers in the northern enclaves were concerned only with saving themselves and their families. There would be no defense of Danang as pledged by President Thieu.

Ambassador King listened in silence, then reminded me of my earlier estimate that South Vietnam could fall in ninety days. Would I now care to revise this prognosis?

I took a deep breath before replying, conscious of the fact that my reply would be carried back to Washington on the following day. The North Vietnamese Army would quickly roll up the enclaves along the northern and central coast, I replied, and the ARVN would soon have its back up against the wall in Military Region III—the Saigon area. "It would not surprise me," I ventured, "if this country went down the drain in thirty days, especially if the North Vietnamese continue to do everything right, and the South Vietnamese continue to do everything wrong." Then I added a warning: The prospects for a severe anti-American reaction and a messy situation in Saigon were very real as ARVN fortunes declined and disillusioned soldiers began the quest for a scapegoat.

The King party departed for Washington on schedule the following day. Shortly thereafter, I learned that the team had interviewed dozens of Embassy employees and departed with an overall impression that conditions in the Saigon mission were not at all good. Personnel in the Consular Section were overworked to the point of exhaustion; morale among staffers was extremely low; and analysts felt constrained to follow the optimistic "party line" in all assessments of the military, political, and economic situation. Apparently, some staffers had taken the opportunity posed by their interviews to relate stories of former colleagues who had failed to abide by this unwritten rule and had been neatly "promoted" to better positions in faraway Third World countries as a reward for their independence.

Danang collapsed within three days of Ambassador King's departure, just as I had been told it would. South Vietnam's second largest city, 1.5 million people, and the better part of three irreplaceable ARVN divisions went down the tube together. Only the marine division managed to escape with any unit integrity, but it lost much of its equipment. On the overcrowded ships and barges that managed to escape from the city, violence and terror were the order of the day as the enraged marines vented their frustration. Within days of the loss of Danang, virtually all of the remaining coastal enclaves fell to the advancing North Vietnamese. In at least one case, Nha Trang, the ARVN gave up and evacuated well before enemy forces arrived in the area.

South Vietnam had been decapitated in less than three weeks. Of the seventeen provinces in Military Regions I and II, fifteen were now in enemy hands, while only a tenuous foothold remained in the other two—a presence that was short-lived. Approximately half of South Vietnam's thirteen divisions had ceased to exist as effective fighting forces. Scores of aircraft had been abandoned intact at Pleiku, Danang, Phu Cat, and Nha Trang. Intent upon saving their families, South Vietnamese Air Force personnel failed to destroy most of the abandoned aircraft, which were captured (and later used) by the Communists. The same was true of ammunition and fuel stocks. The retreating South Vietnamese managed to retrograde only a fraction of these precious stocks and failed to destroy much of what they left behind.

In the face of such bounteous and unanticipated successes, it was little wonder that the North Vietnamese altered their strategic plan. On 25 March, an elated General Dung received a cable from Hanoi. He was to concentrate his forces and mount an offensive to "liberate Saigon" by the end of the dry season in May. The current offensive had been intended to soften up the Saigon army for a still greater blow in 1976, but the unanticipated successes now convinced Hanoi's leaders that the time was ripe to strike. General Dung's recollection of the situation that had evolved by the end of March is accurate and to the point:

> Our armed forces matured in an outstanding manner during the fight. The number killed and wounded was very small in proportion to the victories won, and the expenditure in terms of weapons and ammunition was negligible. Meanwhile, we gained more experience in combat organization and command and seized vast amounts of weapons and ammunition. From the standpoint of strategic position and military and political forces, our strength overwhelmed the enemy.
>
> Our troops and people were fully able to take strategic initiatives while the enemy was in a passive, confused, and perplexed position, strategically and tactically deadlocked. Moreover, the United States had proven itself to be completely impotent. Even if it were to increase its aid, it would still be unable to save the puppets from imminent collapse—and by now total collapse had virtually become the inevitable fate of the enemy.[15]

Hanoi had won an unprecedented victory "on the cheap," leaving Nguyen van Thieu and what remained of his army to figure out how to salvage the situation—no small task for an ally that had shown little talent for fighting "a poor man's war."

Long lines appeared at the Defense Attaché Post Office as Americans, shocked by the headlines in *Stars and Stripes*, began to mail their possessions home. Nearby, in the DAO Conference Room, MG Homer Smith held his first and only officers' call. Smith, who had replaced General Murray, informed us in a solemn voice that he anticipated a difficult and trying period ahead, a period that he predicted would see the evacuation of all Americans from Vietnam. "I want you all to know," the general remarked, "that I regard you military men as the one group that I can really depend upon when the going gets tough —and things will get tough, sooner than we may think." Before adjourning the meeting, General Smith issued a series of directives to prepare for the trials that we all knew lay ahead. The most important task fell to Army LTC Dick Bean, who was

MG Homer D. Smith, the last Defense Attaché, Saigon.

made Chief of a Special Planning Group. Its mission: prepare for the total evacuation of the DAO. As we rose to depart, General Smith issued one final order: "I want this headquarters rigged for demolition. I'll be damned if I'm going to leave it for the bastards." We left the meeting full of apprehension as the meaning of those words sunk in.

That evening, three South Vietnamese rangers attacked an American civilian contractor within a block of my quarters. The hapless man was pulled out of his jeep at the traffic light by his assailants, who proved to be survivors of the disaster in the Central Highlands. Only the timely intervention of the Saigon police saved him from a beating. The three rangers, who had been drinking heavily, confessed that they had nothing personal against their victim, other than the fact that he was an American. General Dung's twenty divisions were not the only hostile forces that we might have to face in the days ahead.

"APRIL IS THE CRUELEST MONTH"

The retreat from the Central Highlands was in full swing when Mr. Doa Trong Ngo dropped by my office. Ngo was Colonel Madison's senior interpreter and special assistant. Like most of our interpreters, he was a native North Vietnamese, one of the almost one million northerners who had elected to migrate south after the 1954 Geneva Accords and the partition of his country. He was also easily one of the most articulate and intelligent men I had met during my long service in Vietnam. Unlike many of his Vietnamese peers, Ngo was normally direct and to the point in his dealings with his American supervisors. On this particular day, he was obviously deeply troubled.

"You know, Dai Uy," he began in a low voice, "we have regarded President Ford's request for $300 million of additional American aid as our last hope. We need a timely transfusion of American weapons and ammunition to give our combatants hope and to rebuild in time to defend what is left of our country. The congressional delegation's visit has almost completely killed our hopes for this aid. Now I feel so helpless that I don't know what to do. I don't believe Congress understands what it is really doing to us." Ngo paused and stared at the floor. Something was definitely on his mind beyond what he had already expressed. I probed.

"Now, Mr. Ngo, you can't lose hope. After all, our Army Chief of Staff, General Weyand, is upstairs at this very moment working on an assessment of your country's needs for President Ford. Surely the President will find a way to help. Right now, there is very little any of us can do except hope for the best."

"Well, Dai Uy," Ngo answered nervously, "I have written a letter to the Congress, but I don't know whether it will help or not. Would you read it and give me your reaction?" He handed me a neatly typed letter:

Saigon, 27 March 1975

Senators and Representatives
of the U.S. Congress

Dear Gentlemen,

While you are deliberating the Vietnam problem, I hope you will be objective-minded enough to read this letter. I know that you are all very busy, so I'll make it very brief; and as the temper of the time is short, I also hope that you will forgive my bluntness.

I'm not going to bewail and beseech you "please have pity on us poor, suffering Vietnamese and don't abandon us to our wretched fate." We are not beggars. If we were relying solely on the assistance and charity of others to survive, we would not still be here today. Our nation has survived to this day by fighting, not by begging.

I only wish to remind you of your responsibilities. You are responsible to yourselves if you want to remain a—if not the—big power; for big power comes in the same package with big responsibilities, and you will cease to be a big power if you refuse the big responsibilities. You are responsible to the world, for just as each effort makes the next effort easier, each failure makes the next failure easier; by failing to stand up to the challenge here you are actually paving the way for many other Vietnams to come until you are backed into another world war which will destroy it. You are responsible to our country, for you cannot consciously shove a partner into the sea in order to lighten your boat when the going gets tough any more than can a decent gentleman desert a girl he has made with child by his vows of constant love and fidelity.

If you plug the aid at this critical time and thus doom South Vietnam to certain defeat, all those heroes—both Vietnamese and Americans—will have died in vain. If Vietnam is to be reunified under the Communist regime, that should have been allowed to take place long ago—in 1956. Why intervene then with such confidence and promises and submit our nation to such agonies only to obtain the very same result? If you were drowning, would you thank the person who pulled you out of the water only to subject you to more sufferings, then drop you back to be drowned again? I regret having to say that you didn't seem to know what you were doing when you first got into Vietnam and now again you don't seem to know what you are doing when you try to get out of it.

I think you are big enough to take some strong, honest criticism. You had better stop your hypocrisy for a change. If things had gone your way and the Vietnam War had been easily won for you, it would not have been called a dirty war, nor would the American heroes fighting and dying during its duration have met with such a lack of appreciation, if not ingratitude, from their own people. That more aid to Vietnam means only more suffering to the Vietnamese serves only to cover American cowardice and lack of resolve and the guts to stick to it through all the ups and downs until final victory. Do as you wish, but don't lend truism to the Red Chinese saying that the U.S.A. is merely a paper tiger. That you don't want to continue to support a bunch of corrupt officials in Saigon fools no one but probably yourselves. You did everything you could to help set up a bad guy against the wish of the people and now you want to punish the people because the bad guy has proven to be really such a bad guy. Does it mean that your policy is always to support and deal with a small number of power seekers but never to really see and truly care for the entire people? If not, why make the innocent people suffer for the sins of leaders that are not of their own choice at that?

By showing your reluctance to aid Vietnam you have thrust your ally in the back and done the enemy a great service for which you can expect a medal from them. You are responsible for the current deterioration of the situation in Vietnam. It is already very late, but not too late yet if you decide now to call on the American heritage of courage and search in your conscience for an answer to the problem. I believe in the final triumph of the human ideals that we all cherish in our hearts, and for all that I have just said, I still believe in the great American people—or I would not have written this letter.

Yours sincerely,

Doa Trong Ngo
RVN Citizen
Saigon, Vietnam

I handed Mr. Ngo his letter, filled with a mixture of admiration, concern, and shame. It was a deeply moving piece of prose and clear to me that its anguished author had become progressively more angry and frustrated as he wrote. I doubted that his eloquent rebuke of Congress would make any difference in the ongoing aid debate but did feel that his words might find their way into the *Congressional Record* by the hand of some conservative legislator. This prospect was grounds for concern, for Ngo's bitter denunciation of President Thieu, so publicized, could easily have put him in a compromising situation. I cautioned Ngo not to send it unless he toned down the anti-Thieu rhetoric, but the distraught man was unreceptive. He would send the letter unrevised to Senator Kennedy and other anti-Vietnam legislators. "It is all I can do for my country, Dai Uy," he explained. "Maybe it will change somebody's mind."

April 1975 was to be the final month of South Vietnam's tortured existence. For those of us who lived in Saigon during this tragic and hectic month, life was an emotion-charged series of events, during which we were forced to make decisions that affected the lives of the people with whom we had lived and worked for months and, in some cases, years. After the loss of Ban Me Thuot, Saigon's normal midnight curfew had been gradually tightened—first to 10:00 P.M., then to 9:00 P.M. by early April, and, finally, to 8:00 P.M. Thus imprisoned in my quarters night after night, I began to commit a series of situation reports to audio cassettes and mail them to my parents in Florida. No one knew how we were all going to come through the mess that had ensnared us, and I wanted my family to understand it. On 2 April, I dictated a lengthy report explaining the events of March:

> The situation here in Saigon is tense. Last night, before I left the office, the word came that Nha Trang, the Military Region II Headquarters about 125 miles northeast of Saigon, has been overrun by the Communists. Of course, Military Region I is gone. The Communist flag flies over Hue and Danang. It is now only a matter of weeks—or perhaps days—until they attack in Military Region III, the Saigon area.
>
> This reversal all started with the decision to withdraw from the Central Highlands. We'll never know, but it is possible that if that move had been made in a more orderly way, the contagious fear and panic that now infects the population might have been avoided. As it was, the military simply packed up and left the Highlands with almost no planning, and the people became caught up in what looked like a bug-out—which I guess it was. Then came the voluntary withdrawal from Quang Tri city in the north next to the DMZ. That was the beginning of the

end, because when the Quang Tri population began to migrate south, everyone somehow came to the same conclusion: Thieu and the Americans have sold out to the Communists. People believe that Thieu has made a deal with the Communists, giving them the northern part of the country in exchange for some guarantee that they will leave Saigon and the Delta alone. There are numerous conspiracy theories going around now, all of which tell the average South Vietnamese soldier that to fight and die in such a rigged contest is stupid.

I just spent an evening with an old friend who served with me in Hau Nghia province. He left Danang on the last barge to escape, and he was still shaking from what he had seen. Danang was pure panic. They just barely got two hundred Americans out of there, and those who left were unable to live up to their commitments to their Vietnamese employees. They couldn't. There was no real plan to cope with a total breakdown of authority in the streets.

Two or three days later, it was Nha Trang. We had a more orderly evacuation of the Americans, but once again, many Vietnamese employees were left behind—an ugly commentary on our planning and performance.

Gen. Fred Weyand is here now, representing the President. He is preparing a report that will no doubt summarize what the South Vietnamese need to pull them through this crisis. The consensus is that they don't stand a chance of getting any of it from the Congress other than that which remains under the current appropriation. That equipment is being flown in here daily now.

The plans to evacuate us are going ahead full pace, but it's clear that the Embassy does not have the capability to oversee such an operation. There are at least six thousand Americans in Saigon, and they were barely able to get two hundred out of Danang. Consequently, I think we will see the intrusion of major American military forces into this country to get us out.

The danger is not so much from the North Vietnamese as it is from the irate and increasingly ill-disciplined ARVN, who are really bitter. That is the lesson of Danang. They think we have sold them out; they are not capable of looking to themselves for a fair share of the blame. The only thing that the South Vietnamese soldier can see is the better-armed North Vietnamese, and for that, they blame us. Of course, many blame President Thieu, and there is open talk that people wish that he be assassinated or leave the country.

Now Hanoi is moving its six strategic reserve divisions into South Vietnam. Indications are that the victory in the Central Highlands took them by surprise and gave ammunition to the "hawks" in the Hanoi government to prevail in their argument that it was time to "go for broke" in the south. I just read a dispatch from a diplomat in Hanoi who recently completed an automobile journey to North Vietnam. He reported that the main road from Hanoi to the DMZ was totally clogged up with bumper-to-bumper convoys—all heading south. We will have fifteen to twenty North Vietnamese divisions around Saigon within a week. To oppose them, the South Vietnamese can muster six divisions—and that includes three in the Delta. In other words, the fighter is on the ropes, and his opponent hasn't swung the big punch yet.

As the North Vietnamese forces moved inexorably closer to Saigon, preparations for the evacuation proceeded smoothly at the Defense Attaché Office. Outside our window, technicians installed the large white dish antenna of a U.S. Army satellite communications transceiver that had been flown in to compensate for the loss of our outlying communications facilities to the onrushing North Vietnamese. Down the hall in the former MACV Command Center, an Evacuation Control Center (ECC) commenced a twenty-four-hour operation. Colonel Bean's task force worked tirelessly to finalize plans for moving all DAO personnel to the security of the headquarters in the event evacuation were ordered. Creating a self-sufficient emergency holding area that could accommodate more than five thousand people for up to a week was a challenging mission, but the Bean group was able to work miracles. Here is Major General Smith's recollection of what was accomplished:

This small group did a magnificent job within a matter of days. Almost overnight food was moved in and stored. C rations were requisitioned and received, lister bags were positioned within the compound, a bulldozer and other heavy equipment were parked within the compound on a nightly basis for use if required, auxiliary generators were placed for use in case the main power source was rendered inactive, equipment for outside latrines was built and positioned, additional bunkering materials were put in place, chemicals to convert the water in the swimming pool to potable condition were secured and put in place, the gymnasium was surveyed and materials were stored to configure it into a processing center with necessary medical facilities, additional telephone lines were installed in critical spots, and many other things were done to provide for a quick transition into a viable posture for assisting the mass evacuation of DAO and other mission personnel. The planning also included a survey as to the number of U.S. personnel necessary to secure adequately the DAO complex if required. At this point in time, I had grave doubts that my local hire national guards would be able to provide the requisite security if pressed by RVNAF (South Vietnamese) elements. A message asking for two USMC-reinforced companies on a standby basis was dispatched on 2 April.[16]

In the wake of the emotional shock wave that followed the fall of Nha Trang, Mr. Ngo sought me out and acted as spokesman for our twenty-seven Vietnamese employees. Ugly stories about Americans fleeing Danang and Nha Trang without regard for the fate of their Vietnamese employees were circulating in the corridors of the DAO. Since our Vietnamese secretaries and interpreters were known to our Communist adversaries, it was not surprising that they were frightened of such a fate. Many of them had come to believe that we might evacuate and leave them in the grips of the Communists, but, in typical Vietnamese fashion, they were reluctant to approach Colonel Madison and surface these fears. Not so the pragmatic Mr. Ngo, who bluntly told me that morale in the office had sunk to new depths as his co-workers contemplated their fate under a Communist regime. I counseled patience and reassured Ngo that Colonel Madison would never be guilty of the mistakes made in Nha Trang. He should put out the word that we would take care of our people, one way or another.

The loss of the northern half of the country also alarmed many Americans who had married Vietnamese but had not yet gotten their spouses out of the country. As the military outlook bleakened, our phones became busy with calls from these men, most of whom were servicemen stationed elsewhere and who could not come to Vietnam. The callers implored us to locate their families and put them on the next plane out of the country. But this was easier said than done, for most of their wives did not have the required documentation to leave the country. Without a passport and an exit visa, such people could not depart, and the Vietnamese Ministry of Interior had refused to streamline its time-consuming bureaucratic procedures. Only a healthy bribe could cut the red tape, and even this could not insure success. If we were to reunify these divided families, it would have to be done by outwitting the Vietnamese authorities.

During early April, "Operation Babylift" provided us with an opportunity to do this. Our official mission was to assist in the evacuation of some twenty thousand Vietnamese orphans to the United States. This we were able to do—and more. For several days, those of us assigned to "Babylift" employed every imaginable ruse to fool the alert South Vietnamese Customs and Security Police. One American Air Force sergeant called us from Clark Air Force Base in the Philippines. His Vietnamese wife was an American citizen, trapped in Saigon because she had overstayed her entry visa. Could we get her out?

The following day, several of us escorted a busload of forty-five Catholic nuns to the Tan Son Nhut flight line. One of the "nuns" was the wife of the sergeant. Under the watchful eyes of the police, the sisters carried the orphans aboard a waiting Air Force C-141 transport. The infants, cradled in cardboard boxes from the commissary, were strapped into the seats by the nuns, who then returned to their bus. During the confusion of the loading, we implemented our plan. While we kept the nearest police officer busy, the plane's crew hustled the sergeant's wife up the steps to the flight deck of the aircraft and hid her there. On the ramp, another customs officer attempted to count the nuns as they returned to the bus, but the roar of the engines and general pandemonium on the flight line worked to our advantage. The confused officer paused in his count, poked his head into the aircraft for a final check, and shrugged his shoulders in resignation. A few minutes later, the C-141 took off for the Philippines, where an anxious husband awaited its arrival.

During the next few days, we executed countless variations of this theme as word spread at Clark and elsewhere that a "Can

Do" team was operating in Saigon. Calls for help came from as far away as the United States. No challenge was insurmountable for our ad hoc underground railroad. We directed the buses over circuitous routes to the flight line to pick up prepositioned human cargo and outfoxed the Vietnamese security police with every conceivable ruse and diversion. Some passengers on the buses hid under the skirts of others during the head count. In other cases, the buses passed through the checkpoint and then doubled back through a parking lot for a quick pickup on the far side of the terminal, out of sight of the guards. In this way, we managed to exfiltrate many people to Clark, with never a thought of the consequences at that end of the railroad. Eventually, our well-intentioned acts caused a problem. The Philippine government protested to the American Ambassador about the growing numbers of undocumented Vietnamese who were arriving in the country. We hadn't meant to cause an international incident, but it was difficult to say no to all of the needy cases that came to our attention, and every case seemed equally compelling.

It was a time of high emotions for many Americans in Saigon. Tony Lawson is a good example—the same Tony Lawson who had prepared the revealing report on the economic conditions of the Vietnamese military in mid-1974. On 4 April, Tony went to the press with a letter that he had written to President Ford, a letter than contained a ringing denunciation of the performance of our State Department personnel during the evacuations of Danang and Nha Trang. "Your mission here has performed poorly," Tony wrote the President, "and, in spite of the glowing reports you may hear, both planning and personal performances have fallen short, with every indication that they will continue to do so. The Consulate Staffs in both Danang and Nha Trang panicked and lost control. From all indications, Saigon is no better prepared."[17]* Tony was firmly convinced that State

---

*Major General Smith believes that the Lawson indictment of MR-1 Consul General Al Francis was unfair. As I was writing this book, the general reminded me (correctly) that Francis "did everything possible to get as many folks out as he could. He didn't lose control—the Vietnamese public authorities did."

Department personnel in Saigon were not competent to handle evacuation planning. Many of us agreed with him, for an evacuation of the scale required was fundamentally a military operation, beyond the training and capabilities of Ambassador Martin's staff. To his controversial letter, Tony attached his own version of an evacuation plan for Saigon. When the press broke his story, Tony's popularity in official Saigon sank to an all-time low. Here is his recollection of what followed:

Most of my guys [Americans] were the last ones out of Pleiku, Danang, and Nha Trang. So it was clear to me that the Ambassador was making positive assumptions about all this and that we were headed for disaster. So, during the Weyand visit, I got in touch with Ken Quinn, of the National Security Council [NSC], who was accompanying Weyand. I sat down with Ken and a colonel from the NSC who was accompanying him, and I explained what I thought was wrong and what I thought should be done. They were impressed, commenting that it was the best thinking they had seen on the subject and that the "right people" should see it. So, I thought that it could make some impact and do some good if it went to the White House. Since Ken was on the White House Staff, I wrote a letter to the President, essentially telling him that his mission was not performing well and making suggestions (via an attached plan) of how we could do better. I sent the original to the White House with Ken, who promised to see to it that it got into the "right in-box." The second copy I gave to David Kennerly, the White House photographer who had close ties to the Ford family. I showed the third copy to UPI, but not with the plan and its sensitive details.

As soon as it hit *Stars and Stripes*, the feedback I got was that most of the people at the Embassy liked it and agreed, but Ambassador Martin and his inner circle were displeased. Al Francis, the Consul General who barely got out of Danang, called me into his office for a personal interview and began to shout. I explained to him that great heroism often flows from disasters— that is, very often in history someone is a hero because someone else fouled up and created a disaster from which others emerged as heroes. I was certain that individuals in Danang had performed heroically, but that this did not change the fact that there had been no plan and that was the reason for the need to become exposed to danger. Anyway, nothing came of it. I wasn't fired, even though I know that there were a few people who would have liked to see me go. I stayed until the 22nd of April.[18]

But Tony Lawson wasn't the only person who was distressed by the human cost of American policy as the situation grew more critical. Many of Saigon's American population reacted emotionally as they began to realize the finality of our evacuation preparations. Pete Galpin, one of the medics who supported our small DAO clinic, unsuccessfully tried to resign his American citizenship to Embassy officials before departing the country in disgust. Another DAO official, Ron Radda, was too busy exfiltrating "sensitive" Vietnamese to reflect on events, until he had a sobering encounter. Almost eight years later, Ron described what happened. As he talked, his voice and gestures told me that time had not healed this wound:

Shortly before Saigon fell, I sought out an old friend, a former boss whom I had seen only infrequently for several years. Even though we met only rarely, our relationship during the war had been close, and some bonds continue without the need for reinforcement.

He lived in a typical Saigon flat above one of the many shops on Cach Mang Street near the entrance to Tan Son Nhut Air Base. Noisy and dusty from the busy street below, the apartment was not what one would expect of a retired officer of his grade. But he offered no apologies. The apartment was in the home of a Vietnamese officer he had known since the Diem days, and one sensed from his composure that he felt at home here among friends. He struggled to balance his beer as a pair of dark-eyed Vietnamese children tried to clamber onto his lap, and he explained to a ubiquitous old aunt that I would drink my quinine out of the bottle.

A tall, quiet man who had been respected for his firm leadership, he had developed an affection for the Vietnamese that had compelled him to remain in Saigon after his retirement. On this particular occasion, he was in an unusually talkative mood. As the representative of a private firm, he lived in Vietnam on a temporary visa, making occasional excursions out of country to renew it. Business was tough. After the cease-fire, Japanese companies had been anxious to do business with the South Vietnamese, but the Vietnamese had preferred to do business with the Americans. He commented bitterly that he believed the American Embassy was subtly discouraging American business ties and investment with the desperate South Vietnamese, while maintaining a public face of support.

But why, he asked, had I appeared unannounced and for the first time at his home? I explained that my role in the evacuation preparations was to insure that at least some of our good friends and former counterparts might survive. I said that I knew he was not one to ask for personal favors, but that I wanted to offer a way out to him and anyone he wished to bring along. My first Vietnamese counterpart was no longer working with any Americans and would therefore be out of luck without my help. Surely he and his Vietnamese friends were similarly handicapped, and I was in a position to help.

At first, he didn't answer at all. When he finally spoke, he struggled for the right words. He had been one of the last Americans to leave China in 1949 when the Nationalists abandoned the mainland to the Communists—and he was still ashamed of that departure. He had left behind broken promises, commitments, and close friends—and he could never repeat that performance. Not understanding the depth of his feelings, I argued with him. Surely he knew that the other side would not believe an American like him had really retired to a personal life. Didn't he understand that he was branded by the Communists and could not expect them to allow him to live in peace? I pleaded with him to reconsider and accept my offer to leave with some of his Vietnamese friends. But my persistence angered him.

He could, he insisted, live quite well on rice and vegetables in a Communist Vietnam. As for me, he rebuked, I could play God by picking and choosing a few Vietnamese to leave with me—but he had obeyed such "orders" once in China and would never repeat that act. His words I understood; his feelings, not yet. I knew he was serious, but promised that I would recontact him later in case he changed his mind.

I failed to keep this promise and never saw him again. Memories and promises were tenuous during those hectic final days as we worked through the nights on our exfiltration project. Late on the last afternoon, I shuttled past the Cach Mang apartment several times, but I never thought of him. At dusk, when General

Smith forbid any more rescue forays into the city, I finally had my first chance to sit down and decide whether or not to leave myself.

Suddenly I knew and understood too late what my former boss had tried to describe. I would leave as ordered, but there would be neither peace nor honor in what I did. Like my friend, I would be forced to live with the knowledge that I had left a part of myself behind with my Vietnamese friends—and, like my friend, I could never do it again.

A year or so later, I read in the newspaper that the body of my good friend, Tucker Gugelman, was being returned by the Vietnamese Communists to the United States. I don't know any details of what happened to him—official or other, but I do know that Tucker regained his honor as he martyred himself for his conscience.

While Saigon's American community agonized over events, President Thieu and his government tried desperately to hold Washington to its commitment to replace South Vietnam's lost weapons and equipment on a one-for-one basis as permitted by the Paris Agreement. During General Weyand's visit, fresh government banners around the city proclaimed in English, "The people and the army of South Vietnam are not lacking in combat spirit, but only need the means for combat." To further hammer home the message to Washington, President Thieu delivered a televised report to his people on the events in the northern provinces. "In the past two weeks," Thieu explained, "we have been fighting under conditions resulting from weak American military assistance. Therefore our army could not defend Pleiku and Kontum and the other areas from Quang Tri and Hue to the coast and even to III and IV Corps."[19] Saigon's official government radio station went a step further than the President, laying the blame for the military reversals in the north at the feet of both Hanoi and Washington:

Obviously, the Americans have a moral duty to insure the implementation of this agreement [the Paris Agreement] and to prevent the Communist side from violating its provisions. However, recent events prove undeniable realities—Hanoi's determination to push ahead with its aggression, and U.S. sluggishness in helping the South Vietnamese armed forces and people protect themselves. The United States, which calls itself a fortress of freedom and justice, must shoulder its responsibility and take resolute action.[20]

One day in early April, after the fall of Danang, my Vietnamese press assistant stalked into my office and slapped a copy of the *Saigon Post* on my desk. She went by the American name of Terry, but Nguyen thi Bich Loc was a native North Vietnamese who had mastered English better than many Americans. Fiercely independent and proud, Terry rivaled the intellectual Mr. Ngo for the spiritual leadership of our Vietnamese employees. I never knew what to expect from her, so I didn't react when she glared at me like I was Ho Chi Minh incarnate and directed me to read an editorial in the paper. As I began to read, I noticed that she had annotated it with a large "Amen!" in the margin. The editorial turned out to be a letter written by a former South Vietnamese legislator and addressed to "Pope Paul IV and the Freedom-Loving Nations of the World." I read it as Terry glared at me triumphantly. A few lines of her discovery reveal something of the atmosphere that had begun to permeate Saigon at the time:

> Cry, LaFayette! Cry, Holy Father! Yes, cry LaFayette, cry Washington. Cry heroic settlers of the thirteen states who rose against an unjust law. . . . Your sacrifices have been in vain for the U.S. Congress has profaned them. . . . Cry, France, who built the Statue of Liberty at the New York gate. The Statue does not say anything more to the world. Cry, Asia, Africa, Europe, Australia, for the sacrifice of your children now becomes useless as the infinite sacrifice of the Vietnamese people. They cry Vengeance in the face of the moral resignation of the U.S.A.[21]

No single day of South Vietnam's final agony looms larger in my memory than Friday, 4 April. A C5A "Galaxy" cargo aircraft had arrived in Saigon with the first large shipment of war materiel for the desperate South Vietnamese military. Since it would have been foolish to allow the mammoth transport to depart empty, the idea was conceived to use it for evacuating Vietnamese orphans under "Operation Babylift." To accelerate the drawdown of "nonessential" Americans from Saigon, some forty women who worked in the DAO were directed to accompany the infants as escorts. It was a perfect cover for our first major move to evacuate Americans from the sprawling headquarters.

Throughout the morning of 4 April, supervisors in the DAO struggled with the problem of identifying nonessential employees and then convincing them to leave on short notice. Many of the women selected resisted the "offer," but they were declared "nonessential" and ordered to leave. With only a few hours to pack a bag and report to the flight line, more than a few of the thirty-seven DAO women who finally boarded the huge aircraft were upset at what they perceived to be summary treatment. Some didn't want to leave because they feared that no one would look out for their Vietnamese employees in their absence. Others resented leaving their furniture and other personal possessions behind. Barbara Kavulia, our secretary in the Negotiations Division, was among those who resisted. Her husband was a contractor employee working in Saigon, and she didn't want to leave him. In spite of this, we prevailed on her to take advantage of the free ride to the States. The flight was a good opportunity, and Colonel Summers even lamented the fact that he had just paid a stiff fare to fly his wife and son to the States on a commercial carrier. Bill Bell, one of our noncommissioned officers, put his wife and two children on the plane, grateful for the timely free service. Altogether, more than three hundred people boarded the mammoth transport before it took off. Some 250 of the passengers were orphans, most of whom were infants in soapbox cradles. Of the forty-four DAO employees on board, thirty-seven were women, comprising a significant number of our total female work force.

The C5 departed at 4:15 P.M., and disaster struck soon after. As it climbed to 23,000 feet off the coast of Vung Tau, an explosive decompression suddenly blew off the rear cargo doors and seriously damaged the aircraft's tail. The pilot, Capt. Dennis

Traynor, managed to maintain control of the stricken bird and reverse its course, radioing ahead to Tan Son Nhut that he would be making an emergency landing. But the damage to the aircraft's controls was severe, and Traynor's best efforts were not quite enough. The crippled bird was losing altitude rapidly as he wrestled with the controls, and the young officer was forced to attempt a landing in a field near the Saigon River. The heavily laden aircraft plummeted into an earthen dike, jumped the river, and then broke up in a marsh on the opposite side.

Several of us in the DAO Operations Center had been following Traynor's attempt to land at Tan Son Nhut. When the plane went down, we rushed to the nearby flight line as a column of black smoke billowed skyward to the east of the runway. Within minutes, a helicopter had flown us to the crash site. The silver and white plane had broken up into several parts; its massive main fuselage lay twisted and burning in the mud. Rescue helicopters were already shuttling in and out of the area, and we joined others as they searched for survivors. The field was actually a marsh, and mud-covered infants were strewn everywhere —some of them ashen-faced and quiet, others screaming in pain or fright. Crowds of curious Vietnamese soldiers and civilians began to appear; some picked through the debris for valuables; others lent a hand as we evacuated the dead and wounded. I struggled through the mud with an Army medic, and we approached the burning main fuselage, struggling to find a way inside. But it was hopeless; the flames were intense and licking along the wings, where we feared the fuel was stored. The plane's belly was completely crushed from the impact of the crash, and it was evident that none of the unlucky passengers still in there could have survived.

Luggage, clothing, and wreckage were strewn everywhere. One of the medics recognized Bill Bell's daughter sitting on a paddy dike, quietly sobbing, her blond hair streaked with mud. We couldn't find any trace of her mother or little brother. Someone scooped her up gently and thrust her into a helicopter. Minutes later we came upon the body of one of our DAO secretaries, then another. I recoiled as I recognized the torn remains of one girl, an old friend I had first met during 1971 in Hau

Nghia. Wearing the uniform of a "Donut Dolly" then, she had helicoptered out to our remote advisory team to provide us with a badly needed boost in morale. We put her shattered body on a stretcher and stumbled through the waist-high muck to high ground and a waiting helicopter.

As we returned to the wreckage, we found the body of one crew member, a sergeant. The man lay unmarked in his flight suit, his ashen face the only hint that he was dead. Then we found a survivor—one of the DAO secretaries—breathing faintly, but definitely alive. We rushed her onto a helicopter, and I accompanied her on the short flight to the waiting ambulances, all the while rubbing her wrists and holding her hand. Then I returned to the wreckage, learning only later that she died before arriving at the hospital.

Back at the crash site, I searched in vain for Barbara Kavulia and Bill Bell's family, moving from one group of gaping Vietnamese to another. Then I sprang aboard a Vietnamese Air Force helicopter that was bound for nearby Cong Hoa Hospital, Saigon's largest military medical facility. At the Cong Hoa chopper pad, ambulances were attempting to keep up with the flow of casualties. Nearby, a crowd of curious civilians stared silently at the growing collection of bodies. I recognized several close friends among the dead, but not Barbara or Bill Bell's family.* A search of the emergency ward also yielded no results, so I hitched a ride back to the DAO in an ARVN jeep.

Just inside the DAO main entrance, I encountered General Smith and told him that we had lost almost all of our people in the crash. Bill Bell came around the corner, an anxious, strained look on his face. When I told him that his daughter was alive at Cong Hoa Hospital, he bolted for the door. Then I told a stunned Colonel Madison and Colonel Summers that I had been unable to find any sign of Barbara. In the office, all of our Vietnamese secretaries were in tears as they joined the rest of the DAO in mourning. Exhausted and overwhelmed with grief, I retreated to my quarters to change my mud-soaked uniform and recover.

*Captain Traynor and some of his crew survived the crash. There is no doubt that the young pilot's skilled recovery of control of the stricken aircraft saved the lives of all of those fortunate enough to survive the crash.

Only days earlier, I had attended a rooftop Easter dinner hosted by Becky Martin, one of the women who worked in the Intelligence Branch. Of the eight DAO women at that dinner, seven perished in the crash of the C5A; only Becky had survived. The morale of the remaining DAO personnel plummeted, never to recover fully. Colonel Summers became despondent because he too had prevailed on Barbara to leave, and he blamed himself for her loss.

Many Americans were incensed at the stories of the local populace looting the wreckage, and it required some time for tempers to subside. One of the lucky DAO women who had not gone on the flight was so outraged at the "chauvinist practice" of evacuating women and children first that it required all of my powers of persuasion to restrain her from protesting to General Smith that her friends had been "railroaded to their deaths." It was a deeply distressing time for everyone. April was only four days old, but we had already witnessed the fall of Nha Trang and the loss of many close friends. Thus far, the month had certainly lived up to T. S. Eliot's description—it had indeed been "the cruelest month" for all of us.

Part VI

EVACUATION LOOMS

"DESPERATE MICE BITE CATS"

The Communists reacted quickly to "Operation Babylift" and our thinly veiled commencement of evacuation operations. Press spokesman Colonel Vo Dong Giang used the Saturday morning press conference to condemn the Ford administration and the "Thieu clique" for "forcing people to evacuate and for kidnapping and transporting Vietnamese children to the United States." The Communists' Liberation Radio claimed that "tens of thousands of children have been herded together with their parents into detention and concentration camps" by the Americans and their South Vietnamese henchmen. In contrast to these brutalities, the Communist radio claimed, life in the "newly liberated zones" had already settled down to a peaceful norm. There, the radio boasted, "children have started a peaceful and joyful life and can study in peace, independence, and freedom." Radio Hanoi attacked the United States for "propagandizing noisily in monk's clothing about the humanity in its cruel plan to evacuate children with a view to diverting U.S. and world opinion and continuing its involvement in South Vietnam and its aid to the Thieu puppet clique."[1]

In the corridors of the DAO, the issue most hotly debated was whether or not the North Vietnamese steamroller would continue its drive southward. Some argued that this was not possible—that Hanoi would be forced to pause in its drive in order to

regroup and digest its sudden gains. But this was wishful thinking, for the evidence suggested that Hanoi had decided to exploit
its gains without giving Saigon the opportunity to recover. One
morning, for example, my in-box turned up this ominous passage that had been read over the Communist radio:

> The southern revolution is presently at a stage where it is devel-
> oping in leaps and bounds, making as much progress in one day
> as it did in twenty years. In order to fully exploit this one-in-a-
> thousand-years opportunity, all of our armed forces and people
> must concentrate all their moral strength and force to achieve
> total victory for the revolutionary cause of the liberation of the
> south and to bring to a glorious conclusion our people's thirty-
> year fight for independence and freedom. . . . We must attack in
> a way that does not give the enemy time to react.[2]

Equally ominous were the words of National Liberation Front
Chairman Nguyen Huu Tho. When asked by a reporter if the
recent developments in the military situation portended heightened offensive operations, Tho answered cryptically, "Desperate mice bite cats."[3]

I believed that Hanoi had decided to go for broke and that
Saigon could not be defended by the crippled South Vietnamese
Army, even if we were to somehow miraculously rearm the
stragglers from the disasters in the north. Supported by Colonel
Summers, I began serious planning to evacuate our Vietnamese
employees, lest we fall victim to events as had already happened
in Danang and Nha Trang. The abandonment of Vietnamese
employees and the narrow escape of the Americans themselves
told us that the Embassy's appreciation of the problems involved in evacuating people under hostile conditions left something to be desired. Tony Lawson insisted that the Embassy's
evacuation plan began and ended with the phrase, "Everyone
should go to Tan Son Nhut and get on a plane." I soon learned
that Tony was wrong—but not by much.

By early April, I had been designated as "Resident Warden"
of my billet on Hoang Dieu Street. In this capacity, I attended a
meeting at the Embassy for a briefing on "the plan."

Embassy planners had designated twenty-nine American billets in Saigon as "safe areas" for staging. Embassy Security Chief Marv Garrett explained: When the decision was made by the Ambassador to evacuate, the American radio would broadcast a signal to alert all Americans and selected "Third Country Nationals" (Allied personnel, such as South Koreans, Filipinos) to gather at these staging areas. The signal would be the playing of Bing Crosby's "White Christmas," followed by the announcement that "the temperature in Saigon is 105 degrees and rising." Garrett then instructed us that our job as resident wardens would then be to "select some strong men, man the gates of our safe sites, and admit only Americans, Third Country Nationals, and Vietnamese employees with families," in that order. Once everyone was safely assembled in the staging areas, we would be bused to Tan Son Nhut and flown out of the country.

Garrett's plan did not go over well with his audience. Haunted by the specter of Danang, a chorus of voices pointed out the obvious difficulties of such a scheme, not the least of which was the likelihood of civil disorder and panic. Garrett responded by assurances that his planners understood this and that weapons (shotguns!) would be issued if necessary. He then made a note for himself to "check and see how many bullhorns we have available for crowd control." Looking around at my fellow resident wardens, I could just imagine that group of mild-mannered government civilians taming panicky crowds of Saigonese by brandishing shotguns and shouting commands over bullhorns in English. The Embassy's plan was an accident waiting to happen—a sure prescription for failure.

Deputy Chief of Mission Wolfgang Lehmann spoke briefly. Clearly concerned that we not be anxious, he insisted to our incredulous group that "no evacuation of the U.S. mission is under way." In fact, he continued, "militarily, the North Vietnamese do not have the capability to launch an offensive against Saigon." I bit my tongue and remained silent. Surely he knew better than this? Or did he? I could appreciate the Ambassador's determined refusal to acknowledge that an American evacuation was under way—the delicate military-political situation forced him into this stance. But the naive, ostrichlike approach to evacuation planning and Mr. Lehmann's attempts to reassure us were disturbing.

Immediately after the meeting adjourned, I returned to the office and drafted a memo to Colonel Madison. Its subject was "Responsibility for U.S. Delegation Local National Employees."

1. While the time frame for total evacuation of the U.S. mission is unclear, it is nonetheless evident that evacuation/withdrawal will take place.

2. In this event, the U.S. delegation must accept responsibility for our Vietnamese employees, many of whom have been exposed to the Communists during their service in the delegation.

3. While there are countless versions of how the entire U.S. mission intends to approach this problem, I am convinced that, at this time, there is no firm decision on the key questions: "Who goes, who stays?" "What about the families of Vietnamese employees?" "What means of assembly-exfiltration, etc.?" In fact, since plans for evacuation of U.S. nationals remain in flux, it is not surprising that the sticky question of our Vietnamese employees remains unanswered.

In the next two paragraphs, I described the performances of Marv Garrett and Mr. Lehmann at the Embassy meeting, then turned to the final business that had been conducted there:

6. Mr. Boudreau, Counselor for Administrative Affairs, dealt with the question of our obligations to the Vietnamese employees of the U.S. mission. He addressed the question after it was pointed out that Ambassador Martin had personally committed the Embassy to "do its best" to evacuate "key Vietnamese personnel" of one U.S. business firm in Saigon. Mr. Boudreau pointed out that "we could be talking about two hundred thousand people" and that the problem increases when one considers the task of gathering and moving such a crowd (with perhaps two hundred thousand additional hangers-on). Mr. Boudreau informed our group that twenty-one Vietnamese employees of the Embassy wrote a letter to Ambassador Martin asking what the U.S. intended to do about mission Vietnamese employees and families.

Ambassador Martin personally interviewed the drafter of the letter and assured him, "When the airplane taking you out leaves, I will personally be there to see you off." Thus, Mr. Boudreau pointed out, a commitment has been made. . . .

8. The foregoing paragraphs demonstrate that:

Our commitment is undeniable. It has been verbalized by Ambassador Martin himself.

The problem now has the planners (at the American Embassy, anyway) at bay. I am convinced that if evacuation were ordered in the near future, the U.S. mission would fail miserably in its obligation to Vietnamese employees.

9. In view of the above, and keeping in mind that there is a chance that the U.S. delegation could depart Vietnam prior to any general evacuation, it is essential that steps be taken now to insure we do not fail in our obligations to our employees. (If the U.S. delegation should depart early, who will look after our people?) Furthermore, according to Embassy spokesmen, the criteria for evacuation include persons in sensitive positions (intelligence, and presumably, our organization) and those persons whose talents/training would be essential upon reestablishment of a U.S. mission in the evacuated country. The mission of the U.S. delegation does not depend upon the political-military outcome in South Vietnam. Negotiations on the MIA issue will clearly continue, if not in Saigon, then elsewhere. The U.S. delegation's trained and experienced Vietnamese personnel are essential to our operation. For this reason, and the obvious moral imperative involved, I strongly recommend that you take immediate steps to insure that under no circumstances will the U.S. delegation abandon its Vietnamese personnel. The U.S. government has committed itself to Filipinos, Chinese, and West Germans—to name a few—not to mention "key Vietnamese" of at least one U.S. business firm. The U.S. delegation must take the initiative on behalf of our Vietnamese coworkers—we cannot afford to entrust this mission to any outside plan, person, or organization.

Colonel Madison was receptive to the idea of taking unilateral action to evacuate our employees, particularly after he heard my horror story about the meeting in the Embassy. He agreed with the conclusion in my memo and instructed me to reassure our employees that they were not to be abandoned. I complied, but my words of comfort had little effect. The recent American failures in Danang and Nha Trang loomed as ugly precedents, and, as Mr. Ngo reminded me, good intentions were the basis of our presence in Vietnam from the beginning. Our employees were looking for action, and action to them meant a plan to take care of them and their families. Thus, with Colonel Madison's permission, I instructed them to prepare to flee their country and to regard seven persons per family as a planning figure for the evacuation. Since the average Vietnamese family group numbered ten persons, the effect of this guidance was devastating. Morale in the office sunk even lower.

Each day saw new sources of tension as the North Vietnamese offensive ground on. The population of the mountain resort of Dalat streamed into the city, a particularly distressing thing for the Saigonese, who held a special affection for the picturesque mountain retreat. The price of vegetables at the central market promptly doubled—truck farming was Dalat's major contribution to the local economy. Tensions escalated still further when an air force defector bombed the Presidential Palace on 8 April. The bombs themselves caused little damage, but the bold act symbolized the Thieu government's precarious position. When the sleek aircraft made its first pass on the palace, we didn't know whether we were witnessing a coup d'etat or an enemy attack—doubts that were symptomatic of President Thieu's weakened position.

But "Liberation Radio" soon cleared up the mystery of the bold attack for us. The pilot was Lieutenant Nguyen Thanh Trung, a South Vietnamese officer who (according to the Communists) had long been a secret Vietcong cadre. After bombing the palace, Trung had flown his American-built F5 fighter to a hero's welcome at an enemy-held airfield. Behind him he left a city that had moved one step closer to the psychological brink as a result of his parting gesture. Nguyen Thanh Trung thus became an overnight hero of the revolution. Thereafter, an almost daily feature of the Communist radio was an appeal to South Vietnamese Air Force personnel, calling on them to emulate Trung—or else. The appeal is worth noting:

The South Vietnam People's Liberation Armed Forces Command urgently calls on the troops, NCOs, technicians and officers in the air force of the Nguyen van Thieu puppet administration to clearly realize the situation, to follow the example set by the patriotic 1st Lieutenant Nguyen Thanh Trung, and to urgently seek an opportunity to act to their greatest benefit and to that of the nation. Hesitation means committing crimes against the fatherland and courting disaster. Let you, brothers, refuse to set out to bomb, strafe, and kill the people and oppose the Liberation Armed Forces. Take antiwar action. Achieve merits and fly your aircraft to the liberated zone. Use aircraft, bombs, and munitions to smash the den of the Nguyen van Thieu clique . . . Those who deliberately continue to oppose the people and the Liberation Armed Forces will certainly be punished.[4]

But there were no more takers of this offer, in spite of the fact that Hanoi's troops were closing the ring around Saigon, and it must have been clear to the officers and men of the Vietnamese armed forces that their situation was desperate. Instead, the air force launched a series of devastating air raids against the massed North Vietnamese forces that were openly ringing the city of Xuan Loc on the eastern approaches to Saigon. Eventually, many South Vietnamese pilots did heed the Communist plea to fly their aircraft out of the war zone, but only after their government had surrendered—and their destination was either Thailand or the ships of the Seventh Fleet, not the "Liberated Zones."

By April 11, 1975, Saigon was all but surrounded by six of Hanoi's divisions; ten more divisions were rushing south to join in the final battle. Americans in Cambodia were preparing to evacuate Phnom Penh within hours, and our delegation had established an "alternate command post" in Thailand in anticipation of the need to evacuate Saigon. Under these circumstances, it seemed somehow inappropriate to fly to Hanoi with a "business as usual" attitude, but we had been ordered by the Embassy to conduct the flight. I boarded the C-130 full of dread at the prospect of facing our smug adversaries.

Saigon was tense; Hanoi, the opposite. The usually quiet

North Vietnamese capital was crowded with people, both military and civilians. As our bus plied its way through the busy
streets, I read the brightly colored propaganda banners and
flags that hung from trees and lamp posts. Red and gold banners
extolled the "Giant Victories" in the south and touted the "fra-
ternal brotherhood" of the Hanoi government and its southern
faction. As we neared the hotel, I noticed a long banner that
proclaimed, "Hearty Congratulations to the Soldiers and People
of the South on Their General Uprising and Gigantic Victories!"
As we disembarked to enter the Hoa Binh Hotel for lunch,
smiling children reached out to touch the hand of a grim-faced
American Air Force officer. The North Vietnamese had already
begun to celebrate their impending victory.

Our visit got off to a somber beginning when I informed our
escort officer (Major Huyen, as usual) of the deaths of our people in the C5A crash. Huyen received the news in silence, which
he maintained until our bus approached the Doumer Bridge.
Then the usually easygoing officer began to talk. "Our Foreign
Ministry has denounced the American scheme of a refugee-
orphan airlift as a crime similar to those committed during the
Hitler era."

I was in no mood for this kind of polemic. "Major," I fired
back, "I have always believed you to be an educated and intelligent person. Therefore, I refuse to believe that you really believe
what you have just said."

Huyen glared at me but made no reply. It would be a cold
visit. The heavy silence continued until we had begun our lunch
at the hotel. When one of the South Vietnamese officers attempted to lighten the atmosphere by asking our hosts when
they would visit Dalat, we suddenly found ourselves in the midst
of a bitter debate, unlike anything we had ever experienced in
Hanoi. Our North Vietnamese hosts gloated over their successes
on the battlefield, and the South Vietnamese, stung by the sarcasm and insults, lashed back. No one at the table could avoid
the flak during the long and acrimonious exchange. While I
argued with Major Huyen over the merits of socialism versus
democracy, Mr. Ngo fended off three North Vietnamese at once.
The supercilious Mr. Quang had attempted to browbeat the

feisty interpreter by ridiculing the ARVN. "We scared the hell
out of your soldiers so that all they did was run, run, and run,"
Quang crowed.

The quick-witted Ngo responded without hesitation: "That
they ran fast proves how they feared your 'liberation.' They ran
away because they thought the rug was being pulled from under
their feet because of rumors of a secret agreement to let you
have the land above Nha Trang and Dalat. So, fear gave them
wings, not the fear of being killed in combat, but the fear of not
being quick enough and having to live under your regime."

Ngo's impudence drew an immediate response from Major
Huyen. "Mr. Ngo, I don't think you know what the words 'communism' or 'socialism' mean."

Ngo ignored the major's angry tone of voice and replied
calmly: "I admit that many of us who are anti-Communist don't
understand what Communism is, but I can see clearly that you
who are against us don't understand one bit what freedom is
either. Posterity may judge that we were both foolish."

Major Huyen could not accept this remark. "History will be
on our side. Hasn't history shown you that more and more
people representing the progressive majority of mankind are
embracing socialism as the best political system? You cannot go
against the force of history."

"You claim the force of history is on your side," Ngo responded, "and I claim that it is on our side. Since that can only be
settled in the future, let's wait for a few hundred more years to
see who is right, and let no one assert now that he is completely
right if he really wants national reconciliation and concord."

Later, as our bus moved back to the airport, Major Huyen
abruptly changed the tenor of discussion by insisting that he
"could see no obstacle to good relations between the United
States and Vietnam." As if unaware that this was our final
meeting, the major volunteered that he admired and respected
me and that, in regard to the Vietnam situation, he "knew what
was in my heart." I responded that I desired peace for the Vietnamese people, but, on the basis of our lunchtime debate, I seriously doubted that he knew what was in my heart.

At the terminal, I suggested to Major Huyen that, instead of condemning our evacuation efforts, his government should be grateful to Washington. After all, was not every anti-Communist Vietnamese who fled to the United States one less opponent for the new regime to worry about? As we shook hands for the last time, I reiterated this point and suggested that Hanoi should let us take our Vietnamese friends and depart Saigon in peace.

The major responded with a half-smile. "We have been trying to get you to leave our country for twenty years, Dai Uy. You may therefore rest assured that, when you are finally ready to go, we will not stand in your way."

As the C-130 winged its way back to Saigon, Mr. Ngo became embroiled in a debate with the officers of the South Vietnamese delegation. The subject was President Thieu. Later, Ngo wrote of the exchange in his trip report:

> With regards to President Thieu, I told them that if I were he, I would resign so that all the national efforts could be united against the enemy because he had become so unpopular as to do more harm than good to the nation in his present position. However, I would request to continue to serve the country as commander of a special division, and I would go to where the enemy threat was the worst and set the fighting example myself. If he did that and proved to be as good as his words, he would become a national hero, and, come the next election, he would win the presidency again in a landslide. Major Thinh and Captain Loc nodded concurrence with me but Lieutenant Lap disagreed, saying hotly, "If he steps down, who can lead the country? That would be playing into the hands of the enemy." Only then did I suddenly remember I should watch out what I say in his presence as he is from the security service. I thought wryly to myself that my tongue would get me into trouble yet. I'll watch my tongue carefully but I have no fear.

We approached Tan Son Nhut at 12,000 feet and then executed a dizzying corkscrew descent to the runway. During the stomach-churning approach, an airman sat in the open door of the C-130 with a flare pistol and scanned the sky for the telltale track of heat-seeking antiaircraft missiles. The air force had learned that a timely shot from a flare pistol could cause a missile guidance system to lock onto the flare. As our wheels touched the concrete runway, I noticed that my palms were clammy with sweat. Landing in Saigon had become a riskier ordeal than landing in Hanoi.

"TO THE LAST BULLET AND THE LAST GRAIN OF RICE"

General Smith's staff developed an evacuation plan based on a worst-case situation such as had overtaken Americans in Danang. Its essence was the use of helicopters as a backup to the Embassy's busing scheme. In the event civil disorder precluded movement by bus from the assembly points to the DAO, the plan called for a helicopter shuttle from predesignated pickup points around Saigon to the DAO compound on Tan Son Nhut Air Base. Once safely on Tan Son Nhut, evacuees would be ferried by heavy-lift helicopters to the carriers of the Seventh Fleet.

By the middle of April, planners had surveyed Saigon's tallest American-leased buildings and selected thirteen locations to be used as helicopter pickup points. Since my billet was one of the chosen locations, I acquired still another title—marshalling area control officer. If the busing scheme broke down—and many of us felt certain that it would—I would supervise a helicopter landing zone on the flat roof of my billet.

At the same time, the Embassy's planning effort continued apace. At yet another planning session for all resident wardens, we were exposed once again to evidence that Embassy planners did not appreciate the task at hand. One amendment to the plan for surface movement affected my duties. Since the street outside the gate of our billet was too narrow for a bus to negotiate, I would now have to assemble my evacuees and march them some three hundred meters down the street to a neighboring American building, where we would link up with the buses. How I was to control such an exodus in an environment that might require shotguns and bullhorns wasn't quite clear. When I pointed out my reservations, the mission warden briefer expressed his hope that the Thieu government would cooperate and declare a twenty-four-hour curfew to cover our escape.

Once again, such hopes and assumptions seemed out of place. It was difficult to imagine such an easy escape, aided and abetted by the government we were abandoning—particularly since it had become public knowledge that the United States was considering the evacuation of as many as two hundred thousand Vietnamese. My fellow resident wardens and I left this meeting filled with renewed skepticism about "the plan."

Once again, I reported to Colonel Madison that Embassy planners did not seem to appreciate the magnitude of the task at hand. I also informed him that covert, "black" flights were already under way to evacuate sensitive intelligence personnel. Because our delegation was not a part of the intelligence community, we technically did not qualify for inclusion in this project, although our Vietnamese personnel were clearly threatened in the event of a Communist takeover.

Colonel Madison acted promptly. On 18 April, he dispatched a message directly to Dr. Roger Shields, the Deputy Assistant Secretary of Defense who had cognizance over POW/MIA affairs. His message was blunt and to the point:

It looks like if we don't take care of our own people, nothing will be done. Conversations with intel community—whose people are no more vulnerable than ours—indicate they have been taking unilateral action to successfully get their people out. From what we know of the official "plan," extraction of U.S. personnel appears workable. However, unannounced extraction of U.S. personnel probably during curfew hours will negate any chance for subsequent Vietnamese extraction. These facts necessitate independent U.S. delegation action. Imperative that we get our people out now. Aside from the moral aspects, from a political standpoint these people might later be useful to the U.S. government if negotiations resume and would certainly be valuable to the other side if they fell into their hands. Have not raised issue with American Embassy here because of their stated views on exfiltration. Need you to convince Secretary of State that our people are in special category and should be ordered out now and have him so direct Embassy here . . . Cannot overstate urgency of situation. Immediate action is critical. In meantime, we are continuing to work within system here, but are not optimistic that their "plan" will work.

All of us breathed a little easier after the colonel dispatched
this message, which we didn't fail to notice involved a fearless
end-run around the Embassy. For the moment, there was little
more we could do except pray that Dr. Shields would be able to
move things at his end. Meanwhile, we endured the daily en-
counters with our distraught employees. The collective moodi-
ness and air of resignation in the office told it all—most of our
people expected to wake up one day soon and find that we had
left without them.

Between 18 and 21 April, I made my final entries into the cas-
sette machine that had by now become my electronic diary.
Even though I had intended to continue the project until the
evacuation, the pace of events did not permit this. The final
entries are lengthy, but merit inclusion here, for they convey
some idea of the atmosphere that prevailed as Saigon lived its
final days as a free city:

Saigon, 18 April 1975: Hanging over everyone's head here is the
fact that it's clear that we are about to evacuate. I am now living
out of one suitcase in my apartment. The rest of the place is full
of smoke grenades, radios, panel markers, and the other gear
one associates with sudden departure. I am supposed to establish
a helicopter pad on the roof of the billet, for which I have a can
of luminous paint to paint a large "H," a wind sock to erect, and
strobe blinkers to signal the helicopters at night. I have also been
given a basic load of emergency rations, flashlights, and first-aid
equipment.

It would appear that we are going to implement the plan—
such as it is—sometime soon. We received the word today that
we are supposed to send four thousand of the five thousand
Americans remaining in Saigon out of here in the next five days
on Air Force transports. This is the proverbial "easier said than
done" task, since many of the Americans here have Vietnamese
families or other interests that make them resist forced evacuation.

Sixty of these Americans live in my billet, and it is my job to
get them and probably several hundred Vietnamese safely out of
here when the balloon goes up. The gate to the billet must be
secured, any panicky mobs must be kept out, and the evacuees
spirited off the roof in helicopters if necessary.

Ambassador Martin is faced with a simple dilemma. If he orders evacuation and we commence the operation because we are afraid that further delay may make evacuation impossible, the very order itself and the initiation of even a limited evacuation risks triggering the conditions we are afraid of in the first place. But if we wait until things have gotten to where it is essential to evacuate, we may not be able to get away—as Danang and Nha Trang dramatically illustrated.

President Thieu has declared that all is not lost and that the ARVN must fight on "to the last bullet and the last grain of rice." Thieu knows that the minute he agrees to allow a mass exodus of Americans, his people and the military will interpret this as a sign of final abandonment. That is exactly what just happened in Cambodia, which fell to the Communists four days after the Americans left. So, until now, there are no signs of cooperation between the Vietnamese government and the U.S. mission as we attempt to expedite the departure of Americans.

I have begun to receive phone calls and Vietnamese visitors like never before. A Mr. Khai contacted me yesterday. He was an interpreter for the advisors in Hau Nghia province when I was assigned there in 1972. He needed a letter from me verifying that he once worked for the Americans. When I came home today, there was a letter at the guard post from Lieutenant Tuan, who commanded the intelligence platoon in Hau Nghia. The note read, "Dear Captain, If you are able to help my family and me, please come to Bien Hoa. You know the house. If you can't help us, we are dead for certain." Tuan is a North Vietnamese Catholic.

It's the 18th of April, and we canceled the Hanoi flight today. We were suspicious because last week the North Vietnamese captain who accompanied me to Hanoi failed to show up at the airport for the return flight—claiming by phone that he had a flat tire. A quick check has revealed that the North Vietnamese have been sending more men to Hanoi than have returned ever since January, so that their thirty-four-man delegation is now down to about twenty men. Today, the chief of their delegation, Colonel Tu, was supposed to fly to Hanoi, giving rise to suspicions that he too might "safe-haven." We informed the Embassy and received authorization to cancel the flight, which we did when the C-130 aircraft developed "mechanical difficulties."

I have never been a part of anything as fouled up as this situation. Here's a good example: Recently, it was decided to use eleven pickup points around the city during the evacuation. Someone printed seven thousand copies of a map of Saigon that shows these eleven sites. The idea was to give the maps to Americans. Someone down at the Embassy slipped up and put these maps out on the counter of the Consular Section, where they were passed out to Vietnamese. Before anyone caught the mistake, six thousand copies of the map had been distributed to the Saigon citizenry. So, if they give the order to evacuate, you can imagine what's going to happen at my billet and the other sites on that map.

General Smith has closed up the DAO theater and turned it into a processing center. I thought at first that there had been a breakthrough in relations with the Vietnam government, for they even have representatives of the Ministry of Interior in the theater. Then I learned that these officials did not have the authority to sign exit visas—that still has to be done downtown. Consequently, the entire operation is bottlenecked at the end because all paperwork must be couriered downtown for final approval. The result is a sight to behold. There are literally hundreds of people ready to depart for the States camped all over the real estate outside the theater. Everyone is awaiting the return of their paperwork from the Ministry of the Interior, and patience has worn out long ago. There is a sea of family groups sitting on their luggage and grumbling that the U.S. government should be able to do better.

Meanwhile, there is strong evidence that the Vietnamese are not at all ready to cooperate. Today at 12:30 they told the couriers who carry the paperwork down there that the Ministry was closing for a lunch break. Two hours later, the couriers found the building locked up—closed for the weekend. So the situation outside the theater becomes more and more tense, while out on the nearby flight line, C-141 jet transports are departing nearly empty. And all the while, the North Vietnamese Army gets closer and closer.

I just hope there are a lot of marines on the fleet, because we will need them. Rumors persist of an imminent departure, but nothing is definite. The official community who are in the know are more nervous than ever now that it is clear that Hanoi is rushing its divisions into positions around the city. Evacuation planning remains so ad hoc and hurried that I think it's foolish to count on anything. Tomorrow I will go to the office with my ear to the ground. If I am able to confirm that there is an evacuation planned for tomorrow night—that's rumor #100—I'll quietly notify our employees and my friends and hope that they can somehow stay on the base—which would be ideal. If they go home to get their families, then how do we get them all past the security guards at the gate?

I am still worried about one final breach of faith here. The idea of Americans first and then we will do our best to get out as many Vietnamese as possible scares me. I'm afraid that if I get all my Americans on the helicopter, someone will say, "That's it. Get the landing zone controller on the next bird." I don't know how I would react if that were to happen and my people were on the ground.

On 20 April, we received the first good news in some time when Dr. Shields replied to Colonel Madison's request for help. Our "clout" in the Pentagon came through handsomely with a commitment for a dedicated aircraft to evacuate our employees and their families to Guam. We quickly spread the good news to our people and cautioned them to keep their special treatment confidential. None of the other divisions in the DAO could command a dedicated aircraft, and we dared not flaunt our good fortune. Then Colonel Madison unveiled still another encouraging development. He had arranged to place all of our Vietnamese employees on temporary duty for sixty days. They would thus depart their country not as refugees but as employees of the U.S. government—on the payroll.

But the news was not all good, for each family group still had to be limited to seven persons if we were to be able to accomplish the evacuation in the single precious aircraft allotted. Almost every family thus faced the cruel decision of determining who would remain behind to live under Communism, a decision that was a major trauma to the family-oriented Vietnamese. To make matters worse, there was almost no time to deliberate. Our evacuation flight would depart within seventy-two hours.

"YOU MUST WIN; OTHERWISE, DO NOT RETURN"

We needed marines to get us out of Saigon, but would we get them? Frustrated at the grant of power assumed by Presidents

Johnson and Nixon in their conduct of the war, Congress had enacted severe restrictions on the use of American military forces in Southeast Asia. As a result, we were uncertain until the very end whether the law permitted the insertion of marines to rescue us from the embittered South Vietnamese and the victorious North Vietnamese Army. We knew that President Ford had requested this authority at the same time he requisitioned emergency military aid for the Saigon government on 9 April and that the President had asked Congress for a decision within ten days because of the urgent situation. But Congress demurred. By the 28th of April, North Vietnamese tanks and artillery completely encircled Saigon, enemy gunners had launched rocket attacks against the city itself, and we had been bombed by Communist-piloted jet aircraft as we struggled to evacuate as many Vietnamese as possible. Saigon had less than thirty-six hours to live, but the U.S. House of Representatives had not yet found time to consider the President's request to use marines to evacuate us (no doubt because the administration had tied the request to the supplemental aid request, which had few supporters). We read in the *Saigon Post* that the House would act on the bill on Tuesday, April 29. By that time, we would be evacuating under enemy fire under the direct orders of President Ford. It was hardly a reassuring performance by our elected representatives.

But our anxieties were nothing compared to the mind-boggling moral dilemmas faced by our Vietnamese employees. With a limit of seven persons per family group permitted on the evacuation flight, they faced the question, "Who goes, and who stays?" One secretary begged for an exception in her case. Could she please bring her husband's parents and his seven sisters? Her husband was an only son, and he was refusing to leave unless his parents could accompany him. The parents, in turn, steadfastly refused to leave without their seven daughters. How could I explain to her that an exception in her case would force me to make exceptions for others? And that such exceptions were impossible due to the capacity of the aircraft? Mr. Ngo intervened. He would give up the places for himself and his family to make room for the distressed woman's family. Confronted with this kind of solidarity, I caved in. And so it went. On the day prior to the flight, one of the interpreters sheepishly requested guidance on how to list both of his wives on the manifest. Like many Vietnamese men, he had a *vo lon* (literally, "big wife," his first wife) and a *vo nho* ("small wife," his mistress). I told him that I would forget he had asked such a question and would expect to see his wife and his "sister" on the list.

In Washington, Congress was still considering President Ford's request for $722 million in emergency aid, but few of us in Saigon held out any hope for passage of the bill (nor did anyone in the know believe by mid-April that more aid could have altered the outcome of the war). Yet many Vietnamese clung desperately to the hope that, somehow, the United States would once again bail them out of impending disaster. Downtown, a new set of English-language banners proclaimed: "In driving back the Communist massive attack on Xuan Loc and Long An, the ARVN have proven their will to defend their countrymen and their capability to defeat Communist aggressors." And on the front page of the *Saigon Post*, the government placed a daily message clearly directed at the U.S. Congress: "Military aid will hasten the end of the present conflict. It will boost the position of South Vietnam to reach a political settlement with the other side."[5] But in Washington, the prevailing sentiment in Congress was exactly the opposite. More aid would only prolong the inevitable. By April 1975, this was a correct conclusion.

Within days of the fall of Cambodia, both the *Saigon Post* and the *Stars and Stripes* reported that the Khmer Rouge were beheading their political opponents. A shudder swept through Saigon. The South Vietnamese had not forgotten the brutal massacre of several thousand people during the brief Communist occupation of Hue in 1968. Horror stories circulated about executions in the "liberated zones"— accounts that were readily believed by the frightened Saigonese. "Liberation Radio" protested in vain that "realities in the newly liberated areas have completely exploded the myth about the 'massacres' and 'bloodbath' cooked up by the U.S. and its henchmen." The Communists denounced American warnings about a bloodbath as "an odious slander to cover up the forcible evacuation of the South

Vietnamese population and the abduction of Vietnamese children." Radio Hanoi benignly reassured those who had cooper-
ated with the Americans that "they [would] be kindly treated in
the spirit of national reconciliation and concord, free from all
hostilities and suspicions."[6] But many nervous Saigonese ignored these assurances and preferred to rely instead on the
advice of the scarlet banner that hung on Le Loi Boulevard:
"Don't listen to a thing that the Communists say, but watch
very closely everything that the Communists do!"

By 20 April, near panic had gripped the Saigonese and the
countless refugees who had sought refuge in the capital—people
who brought with them their own fright stories of the North
Vietnamese offensive. Runs on the banks to withdraw precious
savings escalated, while the black-market rate for the dollar
shot up to 3,000 piasters (the official rate was 750 to 1). It was
commonly understood that bribes for exit visas or seats on aircraft had a better chance of success when offered in hard currency. A headline in the *Stars and Stripes* announced "Embassy
Burns Files—U.S. Accelerates Evacuation," while AP and UPI
dispatches reported that the majority and minority leaders of
the Senate had come out against additional aid for South Vietnam. My press assistant, Terry, tossed these reports into my
in-box and then broke into tears. "I hate you Americans for
what you have done to my country," she sobbed. "Why don't
you just kill us all quickly and be done with it? I won't go and
live in your country—I couldn't stand it. I'd rather stay here
and die." I tried clumsily to comfort her, but she would have
none of it. Until the day of the flight to Guam, I feared that she
would make good her threat. Terry had a fiancé in Washington,
and I couldn't leave her to whatever fate the Communists had
reserved for an outspoken anti-Communist who had traveled to
Hanoi in the employ of the U.S. government. At the time, I was
so concerned for her fate that I even considered drugging her if
necessary and evacuating her to Guam against her will.

On 21 April, the courageous stand of the South Vietnamese
18th Division at Xuan Loc ended in defeat. The superior North
Vietnamese forces simply flanked the stubborn South Vietnamese unit and drove toward Bien Hoa, thus making Xuan Loc

untenable. The road to Saigon was now open. As the 18th Division's survivors struggled to extricate themselves, Nguyen van Thieu finally accepted reality and resigned as president of the country. A consummate politician to the end, Thieu delivered a ninety-minute farewell soliloquy over national television during prime time. In an angry and tearful performance, the former army general and leader of his country for almost a decade laid the blame for the demise of his country at the feet of the United States:

> The big brothers of the aggressors have helped them become increasingly stronger. Despite this, the United States has not made any moves vis-à-vis the Soviet Union or Red China—nor has the United States dared to touch the hair on the legs of the North Vietnamese Communists and the Communists in the south. . . .
>
> I have therefore told them: You have asked us to do something that you failed to do with half a million powerful troops and skilled commanders and with nearly $300 billion in expenditures over six long years. If I do not say that you were defeated by the Communists in Vietnam, I must modestly say that you did not win either. But you found an honorable way out. And at present, when our Army lacks weapons, ammunition, helicopters, aircraft, and B-52s, you ask us to do an impossible thing like filling up the ocean with stones. This is like the case in which you give me only three dollars and urge me to go by plane, first-class, to rent a room in the hotel for thirty dollars per day, to eat four or five slices of beefsteak and to drink seven or eight glasses of wine per day. This is an impossible, absurd thing.
>
> Likewise, you have let our combatants die under the hail of shells. This is an inhumane act by an inhumane ally; refusing to aid an ally and abandoning it is an inhumane act. . . .
>
> This is not a fight against the North alone. North Vietnam can do nothing better than South Vietnam, because it can produce no bullets, weapons, rockets, or tanks. So, this small Republic of Vietnam is fighting against the Soviet Union and Red China while its ally fails to protect and aid it.

Toward the end of his speech, Thieu turned his wrath on his American critics:

Some U.S. people and some U.S. congressmen hold that so long as Mr. Thieu remains in power, there cannot be negotiations; Mr. Thieu is not the man to agree to negotiate. Mr. Thieu is bellicose and refuses to implement the Paris Agreement. So long as Mr. Thieu remains in power, U.S. aid cannot be given in full because so long as he receives U.S. aid, he will continue to fight and will not agree to negotiate.

This is the U.S. scheme to stop providing us with aid and to wash their hands of us. This is a scheme of people who have completely lost their conscience and humanity, or this may be the opinion of people who misunderstand me. Therefore, I resign today.

We'll see whether or not negotiations will be satisfactorily conducted with the agreement of the Communists when Mr. Thieu is no longer in power. In the affirmative, it is something that our people and the world would gladly welcome. If, with Mr. Thieu's departure, abundant U.S. aid will be provided immediately to help the RVN armed forces conduct the fight, this is something very lucky for us, and my departure is just like a grain of sand in the desert.

Finally, in a tearful conclusion, Nguyen van Thieu made his last pledge to the Vietnamese people:

I am resigning but not deserting. From this moment, I place myself at the services of the President, the people, and the Army. . . . I will stand shoulder-to-shoulder with the compatriots and combatants to defend the country.[7]

Four days later, Thieu fled to Taiwan aboard a U.S. Air Force C-118. The following day, one of the officers on the South Vietnamese delegation explained to me that it would have been impossible for the ex-president to take command of a combat division and fight in the defense of the capital. "He would have been killed almost instantly," my friend quipped, "and not by a Communist bullet."

Nguyen van Thieu's escape to Taiwan revealed something of his sincerity, but the theme of his swan song was compelling to the many South Vietnamese who believed that the Americans had made some sort of agreement with Peking and Moscow and sold out South Vietnam on the altar of détente. Only among the educated and the officer corps did one find a more balanced view. One colonel told me openly that Thieu's speech had been correct—as far as it went—but that the president had only addressed half the reason for the national disaster. What Thieu could not acknowledge was his own role in South Vietnam's demise. There was no mention in his speech of any personal responsibility for the corruption of his government, yet it was the corruption issue that had hastened congressional disenchantment with South Vietnam's cause and led to the end of American military aid.

We evacuated our Vietnamese employees and their families on 23 April. Since none of them had passports and exit visas, it was necessary to sneak them out of their own country. To accomplish this, we used a closed freezer truck borrowed from some of my enterprising friends in the intelligence community. The precious vehicle had already been used for more than a week in a series of "black" exfiltrations, and I was able to borrow it with the proviso that I return it within three hours—three hours to move nearly two hundred people. We were forced to plan carefully to meet this demanding schedule, for our vehicle could only accommodate fifty people at a time, even if we squeezed them in standing up with only a minimum of baggage. MSG Bill Herron and I made the clandestine pickups at a prearranged safe-house near the air base while Colonels Madison and Summers insured that the aircraft was identified and ready to receive its human cargo.

The first two pickups went smoothly. We locked fifty frightened and tense people in the cargo space and drove past the South Vietnamese security police without incident. Inside the truck, mothers muzzled their frightened children to prevent them from crying out as we passed the guards. It was as we loaded our third and final group that we encountered a problem. Someone had reported to the police that suspicious activity was taking place at the villa, and a messenger arrived at the gate with orders for the home's owner to report immediately to the local police station. The owner, a friend of Bill Herron's, hesitated momentarily, shrugged his shoulders in resignation, and climbed into the back of the truck with the other Guam-bound passengers. He had not planned to flee the country, but the summons to report for questioning had changed his mind. Within a few hours, he too was on his way out of Vietnam into permanent exile. Our operation had gone well. In the space of two hours, we had lived up to our commitments and eliminated a problem that had been plaguing us ever since the first disaster in the Central Highlands.

Before returning the borrowed truck, I had a personal mission to accomplish. At a house in Saigon's Dakao section, I made a rendezvous with twenty-seven more passengers. This group included several of my closest friends, former counterparts during my tour of duty in Hau Nghia province. Major Sang and his family were among them, as were other intelligence officers of the once-proud Military Security Service. In a cruel irony, I was aiding in the desertion of men whose mission it had been to combat desertion in their army. One officer handed me his pistol as he climbed into the dark recesses of the truck, telling me in a subdued voice that he would not need it in Guam or America. I swallowed hard, both ashamed and a bit frightened at what I was doing. We were expressly forbidden to exfiltrate military men, and I had decided on this step only after a diffi-cult inner struggle. Other covert exfiltrations had been under way for several days, and I had finally decided not to risk losing these friends by further delay. I slammed the heavy doors of the truck and padlocked them. By late that day, this group too would be safe on Guam—rid at last of the trials of nearly thirty years of war. Surely this was a wrong that was right, I consoled myself as I headed for the airport.

In the midst of the confusion of that final week, Col. Harry Summers drew the honors to make what would certainly be our terminal flight to Hanoi. It was a bizarre and memorable expe-rience that the colonel remembers vividly to this day—for the Hanoi connection provided by our weekly flight was virtually the only communication that then existed between ourselves and the North Vietnamese, not to mention between the South Vietnamese and their adversaries. Thus it was that the liaison flight of 25 April 1975 was anything but routine.

The normal Friday morning departure was delayed by a confrontation on the flight line when a South Vietnamese general officer appeared and announced that he was going to fly to Hanoi to seek a negotiated settlement of the war. The officer, Brig. Gen. Phan Hoa Hiep, was the Chief of the South Vietnamese delegation to the Joint Military Commission and had only recently been appointed Minister of the Interior in the reshuffled government. With the new government's blessing, Hiep was to convey a peace feeler to the North Vietnamese.

But the time for talking was clearly over, a reality that was driven home by the North Vietnamese, who brusquely informed Colonel Summers on the flight line that General Hiep would not be received if he insisted on flying to Hanoi. Hanoi's leaders had argued that a political settlement of the war would only be possible if President Thieu resigned. Now that Thieu was gone, they had characteristically upped the ante once again. Radio Hanoi denounced the new government as "a new political scheme, a Nguyen van Thieu regime without Nguyen van Thieu, with a cabinet of Thieu's henchmen. . . ."[8] Hiep would not be received because Saigon had nothing left to negotiate.

But as Colonel Summers winged his way to Hanoi, he had no way of knowing that Hanoi had already decided to reject any form of political settlement. By that time, any sentiments that may have existed for negotiations among the Hanoi leadership had taken a backseat to the decision to drive for "total liberation" of the south by the People's Army. Politburo member Le Duc Tho, the co-architect of the cease-fire agreement, had taken a leading role in explaining the attack strategy to Hanoi's senior commanders on 14 April, long before Colonel Summers' Hanoi trip. At a North Vietnamese forward command post north of Saigon, Tho addressed the impending battle:

We will attack Saigon when the enemy is disintegrating and in a weak position. However, since that city is his last stronghold, he will strike back because he has no escape route. The enemy has five divisions against our fifteen, excluding the strategic reserve forces. Thus, we cannot fail to win victory.[9]

To impress upon the assembled commanders the determination of Hanoi's leaders to complete the liberation of the south in 1975, Tho revealed that his colleagues in the Politburo had told him: "You must win; otherwise, do not return."[10]

In Hanoi, Colonel Summers met with Major Huyen, who had reassumed the role of the conciliatory host. The major explained apologetically that the usual tour and luncheon was canceled because Hanoi had thought the flight had been postponed. Colonel Summers sensed that his counterpart had serious business to conduct and listened attentively over tea served in the airport waiting room as the Communist officer made his pitch. The colonel recalls that Major Huyen made several points during their historic conversation:

a. The U.S. delegation, Four-Party Joint Military Team *must* stay in Vietnam to accomplish its humanitarian tasks. He asked me directly if I would return to Hanoi to settle the question of the dead and the missing if I were asked to. When I replied that I would do what I was ordered to do, he said, "You *will* be asked." As usual, he linked Article 8(b) (the dead and the missing issue) to Article 21 (reparation aid). In general conversation, he mentioned several times the success of the Marshall Plan—to which I replied that while it was a great success with advanced industrial countries with developed economic infrastructures and a skilled work force, it could not be expected to work in poor underdeveloped societies . . . On several occasions Major Huyen told me, "You have done more than enough . . . more than enough for the RVN and you have no reason to feel badly."

b. The DAO *must* go. In a rather circumspect approach, Major Huyen began by saying, in an excited voice, "Why are all you Americans leaving? You know that we have told you that we mean you no harm. It is only the military advisors that must go." I replied that, in all honesty, in my ten months in Vietnam I knew for a fact that there were never more than fifty

U.S. military in country. He acknowledged this but said that the civilians who worked for the military were just as bad as the military. I told him that he must be aware that these people were leaving—not because of the DRV or the PRG but because they had been ordered to leave by the President under congressional pressure. . . .

c. The Embassy must work out its future with the new government. Major Huyen went to great pains to make the point that there was no reason friendly relations could not be quickly established between the U.S. and the DRV. He reminded us that even though Hanoi had been bombed, the people never showed us any discourtesy and were always friendly when we toured the city. Even the POWs had been well treated (I took exception to that statement but acknowledged that what the DRV considered "good" treatment might be seen as barbaric by Americans). To this general line I replied that much depended on how the war ended. If there was great loss of life, great atrocities, it might take the U.S. as long as it took with China to establish relations. If the U.S. was not humiliated and made to feel guilty, then I saw no reason why normal relations could not be established some time in the future.

d. There will be no "reprisals." Major Huyen asked if I really believed the "bloodbath" stories. I replied that it didn't really matter what I believed . . . that the people in Saigon believed it, and their beliefs were reinforced by what was happening in Cambodia—that if they were not true, the Khmer Rouge was doing the DRV no favor. Major Huyen said, "I tell you honestly, there will be no reprisals—we need these people to rebuild Vietnam." I replied that I had no reason to doubt Major Huyen's sincerity—but he was a lawyer sitting in Hanoi, a North Vietnamese. I could even believe that the DRV would not permit mass executions. But I found it hard to believe that the PRG would not extract blood debts, and said that I had heard many horror stories about events in Danang and Hue. He said that just was not true. Captured RVN generals had made radio broadcasts and press statements about their good treatment. I replied that no one in Saigon believed such broadcasts. He said that a group of Western observers would shortly tour the "liberated areas" and they would report the truth. I told him that I certainly hoped that such a group represented a broad strata of public opinion, since the

Americans that had visited Hanoi had no credibility what-
soever with me. I considered them traitors and would not
believe them if they told me the sun would rise in the east.
"Take Jane Fonda, for example," I said, "a great actress, but
with the political sensitivities of a three-year-old." He laughed
and said, "But, she's a beautiful woman . . ." I said, "Yes, we
can agree that she is a beautiful woman and a great actress,
but she is still politically immature—and not only on Vietnam." My final words on the "reprisal" issue were that it
didn't matter what the DRV said, or what the press or radio
said. The people in Saigon were convinced there would be a
bloodbath. The only way the DRV could convince them otherwise was by their actions. If there was some kind of interim
government, then the people could see for themselves what
the policies of the DRV were.[11]

During the return flight to Saigon, Colonel Tu, the Chief of
the Hanoi delegation, sought out Colonel Summers and reiterated Major Huyen's main points. By the time the C-130 landed
in Saigon, Hanoi had made its point quite clearly. Colonel Summers relayed the main themes of Major Huyen's conversation in
his trip report and observed that the discussions in Hanoi
seemed to indicate clearly that the North Vietnamese were
ready for a negotiated settlement of the war.

Since fifteen NVA divisions were scrambling into jump-off
positions for the assault on Saigon at this time, Colonel Summers' experience in Hanoi poses an intriguing question. Were
Major Huyen and Colonel Tu unaware of the Politburo's decision to attack Saigon, or were the North Vietnamese using us as
another conduit in an elaborate deception to mislead the Americans about their military decision?

At the time of Colonel Summers' trip, Saigon was filled with
rumors about the chances for a political settlement. There was
open speculation that if retired Gen. Duong Van ("Big") Minh
became president, the Communists might forestall an attack
against the capital in favor of a negotiated settlement. General
Minh himself apparently believed this speculation, since he was
promoting his own candidacy. The subsequent attack on Saigon
demonstrated that such hopes had been in vain. Minh became

president, but the Communist answer was hardly the offering of an olive branch. One had to wonder at Minh's motives. Why would a man desire to assume the helm of a clearly sinking ship of state? Former Chairman of the Joint General Staff, Gen. Cao Van Vien, believes he has the answer to this question. General Vien recalls that he met Minh in late April, shortly before he became president. Vien recalls:

[Minh] boasted he used to keep in constant touch with the other side by radio communication. It was a fact he said he could not disclose before for fear of arrest, but it was all right to tell me now. So it was his firm belief that a government with him at the head would be acceptable to the Communists and that they were willing to negotiate with him for a political solution to end the war in South Vietnam . . . As it turned out, North Vietnam had changed its mind. I understand that by late March, the U.S. Embassy in Saigon had received reports from one of its agents who had succeeded in penetrating COSVN* that North Vietnam was inclined toward a military victory rather than a political arrangement.

General Minh waited in vain for a favorable word from the other side, but nothing came. The response of the Communists was ominous; they bombed Tan Son Nhut Air Base the moment he was sworn in and shelled Saigon barely twelve hours later . . . General Minh personally admitted that he had been duped by the Communists. He had advised his closest aide and his son-in-law, Colonel Nguyen Hong Dai, to leave Vietnam. But the tragic fact was that General Minh was not the only one to be duped. Several other credulous Vietnamese had also been duped, and they became stranded in Saigon, unable to leave because it was too late by the time they realized what had happened.[12]

While Colonel Summers debated with Major Huyen in the Hanoi air terminal, Bill Herron and I were immersed in still another smuggling operation. General Smith had secured permission for the DAO to begin evacuating the families of our

*Central Office for South Vietnam: the Communist control headquarters in South Vietnam.

military counterparts. The plan was to safe-haven our counterparts' wives, in-laws, and children in Guam. The husbands,
soldiers like us, would remain and do their duty. If and when
we left as a part of a general evacuation, we would bring the
men with us to rejoin their families. For us, this meant the evacuation of the dependents of the South Vietnamese delegation to
the Joint Military Commission—a staggering total of some
1,500 people. It was a considerable undertaking, but one that
we could not shirk. Flushed with our success in spiriting our
employees off to Guam, Bill and I attacked our new mission
enthusiastically. It was impossible for us to sneak this many
people onto the air base, even if we had been able to use the
freezer truck—which we were not. We thus decided on a different approach. While Bill set out to commandeer a bus somewhere, I explained to Colonel Nghia (Colonel Madison's counterpart) that he and his staff would have to somehow get his
people onto Tan Son Nhut Air Base to an assembly area in the
dependent housing village. Bill and I would then shuttle the
evacuees to the American-run staging area near the flight line.
To this day, we don't know how Colonel Nghia and his men
managed, but, in four days, they succeeded in either smuggling
or bribing more than 1,000 of their dependents onto the base.
Bill Herron managed to expropriate a black bus with Embassy
license plates, which we used to ferry our groups to the flight
line, where aircraft somehow procured by Colonels Madison
and Summers were waiting to take them to safety. Our operation went well because we were better organized than the com-
petition. With the aid of our counterparts, we were able to move
our groups to the flight line and onto aircraft as fast as we could
assemble them. Other organizations were not quite so lucky.
The makeshift processing center and holding area around the
DAO gym and swimming pool soon became jammed with literally hundreds of people, all camped with their luggage, patiently
awaiting the signal to board shuttle buses for the flight line.

On 27 April, I visited Colonel Nghia in his office with good
news. Colonel Madison had arranged for two more precious
C-141 aircraft, which would enable us to move four hundred
more of his people that afternoon. As we made our plans for this

load, the phone rang. From Colonel Nghia's end of the conversation, I could tell that the caller was either a general or a high-ranking civilian.

"No, sir, I'm sorry. I can't do it."

"Yes, I know, sir, but it just isn't possible."

"I'm really sorry, sir, but I don't dare. It's too tightly controlled."

"Yes, sir; good-bye, sir."

Colonel Nghia hung up the phone, his eyes reflecting the heavy sadness in his voice. "The phone has been ringing like this for days, Dai Uy. That was Ky. He wants me to take some people out on our flights. One day he gives a speech condemning traitors and cowards who leave the country. The next day he is begging me to help evacuate people. He was even crying."

I told the discouraged colonel that other organizations were responsible for people like Air Marshal (and former Vice-President) Nguyen Cao Ky, and I reassured him that the most difficult course was the right one in handling access to the scarce evacuation flights. We had already evacuated more than six hundred of Colonel Nghia's people, but his own family had yet to depart. The colonel wrung his hands nervously.

"You know, Dai Uy, I couldn't do this if I didn't know deep down that, in the end, the United States will intervene and save us. Somehow, I just feel that we didn't come this far together for it to end like this. I just can't believe that the American Congress will allow Communist troops to march into Saigon."

I was silent for a moment, not wanting to tell him that he had more faith than I, yet determined not to mouth false hopes. In the end, I steered the conversation back to the coordination of the next flight.

During the next twenty-four hours, we succeeded in evacuating two more planeloads, which brought our total to almost 1,100 souls. Colonel Nghia's family was on the last flight. (We learned later that, in the confusion of the final hours, only a handful of the officers and men of the South Vietnamese delegation managed to escape and join their families on Guam. The trusting Colonel Nghia was not among them. He was trapped in Saigon and captured by the North Vietnamese.)

"TWO KIAs AT POST 4!"

On 27 April, the North Vietnamese forces that ringed Saigon fired four 122-millimeter rockets into the center of the capital, killing seven civilians and wounding twenty-four others. These "political rockets" carried a clear message: The Americans should cease their attempts to evacuate thousands of Vietnamese and go home. By now, enemy radio broadcasts beamed into Saigon called for a "total disbanding of the puppet armed forces"—Communist jargon for unconditional surrender.

In a small coffee shop near Tan Son Nhut Air Base, several alert ARVN airborne troops noticed an unfamiliar officer wearing their unit insignia. The stranger had a northern accent, which in itself was not unusual, for many of the airborne officers were natives of the north. But what did seem strange was the new lieutenant's odd unfamiliarity with local prices and customs. The suspicious troopers summoned the military police, who quickly determined that the officer's papers were bogus. When interrogated, the imposter confessed that he was a North Vietnamese artillery forward observer. His orders were to infiltrate the Joint General Staff compound, steal a radio, and establish contact with his unit. The hour of the North Vietnamese assault on Saigon was drawing near if the enemy was positioning his artillery spotters.

Outside the gates of Tan Son Nhut, large crowds had become a daily routine. As soon as President Thieu resigned, the Saigon press had begun to report openly on the ongoing American airlift, and the Saigonese had been drawn into the air base as if by magnetism. Everyone in the growing crowd of anxious people camped at the gate clutched some form of written proof that they had once worked for the Americans or that they had relatives in the United States. For the unscrupulous, these desperate people posed an opportunity to make some easy money. They would—and did—pay well for a ride past the checkpoint.

Each night after curfew, I made a room-by-room check of my billet. If no one responded to my knock, I used a set of master keys to gain entrance to each apartment. I soon learned not to be surprised at anything I might uncover during these nocturnal rounds. In the four apartments where victims of the C5A crash had lived, furniture and personal effects lay untouched. Three weeks after the tragic wreck, no one had bothered to ship their possessions to the States. During one check, I found only four-teen Americans in the sixty apartments—the rest had either been declared "nonessential" and flown home, or were sleeping in their offices, fearful that they would be trapped in the city if the order to evacuate were issued at night. That same evening, I counted more than sixty Vietnamese camped in the compound —some in vacant apartments, others in the laundry room. Most of them were either our guards and their families, or other employees of the housing office. I didn't have the heart to eject them. In one vacant apartment, I found an attractive Vietna-mese woman and her three young sons. I recognized her as the former occupant's live-in "maid." When I asked why she had not gone home, she showed me a pass given to her by her Ameri-can boss, whom she referred to as her "fiancé." "He told me to wait here and he would pick us up and take us to the United States, Dai Uy," she explained. Only then did I notice their suit-cases on the floor near the door. I winced. I had seen her "fi-ancé" that very afternoon as he prepared to board an evacua-tion flight. He clearly had no intention of bringing her and her sons with him. In fact, he had a wife in the States. (The next day, I smuggled her and the children onto Tan Son Nhut Air Base on the floor of my pickup truck and turned them loose near the flight line. I later learned that the resourceful woman had man-aged to link up with one of her unfaithful "fiancé's" co-workers. The disgusted man had sent her off to the States armed with his colleague's address and phone number in California.)

To simplify the security task, General Smith had earlier directed the evacuation processing center to move from the DAO theater to the gymnasium–swimming pool area of the for-mer MACV Annex. American marines appeared to assist with crowd control, summoned from the fleet at the general's re-quest. Thereafter, we staged our groups of evacuees by the gym and then bused them to the flight line when directed by dis-patchers who were in contact with the Evacuation Control Cen-ter. It was an effective system that enabled thousands to depart in an orderly fashion in an environment that could easily have gotten out of control.

On the afternoon of 28 April, I was escorting a group of two hundred evacuees when I noticed something odd. As my Vietnamese counterpart read the manifested names, the evacuees were supposed to line up in order. But when he read the name, "Sergeant Chung," a family of six stood up to get in line—and, as the four children's names were read, it was evident from their confused reactions that they didn't know what their names were supposed to be. Something was clearly wrong. If the six people were indeed the Chung family, then why had all four children moved at once when they heard the first name?

A pair of pointed questions solved the mystery. "Sergeant Chung" was really a Saigon surgeon who had paid five million piasters (about $2,500 at the going rate of exchange) to an officer in the South Vietnamese delegation for the six places on the flight.

"What about Sergeant Chung and his family?" I asked angrily.

"I don't know, Dai Uy," my counterpart answered lamely. "Maybe they just don't want to go."

I was furious. At that moment, an American civilian drove by in a pickup truck on his way to the main gate. In a fit of temper, I stopped the truck and ordered the frightened doctor and his family to climb aboard. When they complied, I instructed the driver to "take them out the gate and leave them there."

"That kind of funny business is one of the main reasons we are here right now," I snapped at my counterpart. The doctor and his family gave me a futile, pleading look as the truck pulled away. Within minutes, I regretted my hasty decision, but it was too late. Now I had extra seats on the next flight. Then I spotted a young Vietnamese couple hovering on the fringe of my group. The woman carried an infant in one arm, a travel case in the other.

"What are you doing here?" I asked the husband, who wore the longish hair and bell-bottomed pants of a student.

"We were supposed to meet a friend who would let us go with his group, Dai Uy," he replied, "but we were late and they have already left. I am a law student and cannot live under the Communists."

"OK, if you want to go, write your names on this list and get in line. But quickly, the buses are about to leave."

As the surprised young student hastily scrawled their names on the manifest, his wife blinked back tears and then spoke in near-perfect English, "Thank you, Captain. You have saved our lives and the life of our son. We will always think of you as our guardian angel, and we will remember you in our prayers each year at Tet."

We were just loading this group on buses when someone shouted a warning. Four A-37 jet fighters flashed overhead on a low pass and dropped a stick of bombs, which exploded with a sharp crash on the nearby flight line. We were on the receiving end of the first Communist air strike of the Vietnam War. The sharp explosions rocked the ground, and huge columns of black smoke welled up from the aircraft parking area. Panic began to sweep through the crowd of almost three thousand evacuees gathered at the gymnasium. Using a battery-powered bullhorn, I directed the crowd to take cover under the swimming pool, explaining reassuringly that the attacks were most certainly a *dao chanh* (coup d'etat). Within minutes, friendly troops opened fire with machine guns and anything else that would shoot, but by then the intruders were out of range.

We later learned that the raid had been led by Lieutenant Nguyen Thanh Trung, the South Vietnamese pilot who had defected and bombed President Thieu's palace three weeks earlier. The North Vietnamese had promoted him to captain, or so we were told by the supercilious Mr. Quang in Hanoi, and had nicknamed him "the invisible star of the Milky Way," a poetic reference to his alleged long years of covert service to the revolution before his dramatic defection. Trung had trained several North Vietnamese pilots to fly the relatively simple A-37 "Dragonfly" jets.* The surprise attack destroyed at least ten mothballed aircraft on the ground and heavily damaged the base operations building.

*The whole story is related in General Dung's memoirs.

This attack signaled the beginning of the end of the use of the Tan Son Nhut runways by air force cargo planes. Within hours of learning of the attack, Washington ordered an end to the use of the base for C-141 operations. Our lifeline was becoming thinner and thinner.

Shortly after midnight on the 29th of April, I flopped down on the couch in Colonel Madison's office to catch a few hours of sleep. The pace had been hectic, and because of the curfew, I couldn't drive to my quarters. Exhausted, I took off my boots and lay down, placing my small radio transceiver on the table next to my ear. At 4:00 A.M., a tremendous explosion shook the building, followed by yet another louder one that caused the flags behind Colonel Madison's desk to jump out of their stands. I was frantically lacing my boots when yet another loud explosion rocked the building. The loud "whoosh" that preceded the explosions meant that we were under a rocket attack. Within minutes, at least four rounds had impacted directly on the DAO compound within a short distance of where I stood. The voice of an unidentified American came over the radio, "My God, they've hit the gymnasium!" Just outside the door there was a row of concrete shelters. A squad of marines who had been sleeping in the building was holed up in the nearest bunker.

"Are any of you guys medics?" I shouted over the crash of continued detonations. "Yes, sir, right here," replied a voice in the dark.

"Good. How about hot-footing it over to the gym? They've got casualties over there." The marine responded instantly.

More unpleasant news came over the radio. "We've got two marines kilo-india-alfa (killed-in-action) at Post #4," a tense voice reported. "Request an ambulance to evacuate the bodies."

I hurried to Post #4, arriving as Mission Warden ambulance attendants were loading the remains of the two unfortunate marines who had manned the post. A marine sergeant stood guard beside a smoking crater in the parking lot where, minutes before, Marine Corporals Judge and McMahon had stood guard. The twisted motor of a 122-millimeter rocket lay in the center of the charred hole. A few meters away, a pile of twisted and smoking motorcycles and other vehicles gave mute testimony to the force of the explosion that had killed the two men. Bits of uniform and flesh hung from the chain-link fence.

The marine introduced himself. "I'm the squad leader, sir. Judge and McMahon were my men." His name was Sgt. Ken Maloney, and he seemed awfully young to me to be a combat leader who had just lost two men to an enemy rocket. A deafening roar overhead terminated in an explosion directly across the street, in front of the Tan Son Nhut passenger terminal. Maloney and I dove into the ditch, where I shouted some advice to him above the freight-train roar of incoming North Vietnamese artillery fire. If he insisted on manning his lost men's post, he should do it in the prone position from the cover of this ditch. As Maloney nodded his agreement, a fierce barrage of artillery rounds impacted across the street, the rounds walking their way in the direction of the flight line. The rustle of the incoming fire was unnerving, and the short rounds caused shrapnel to plink against the fence and nearby vehicles. I decided to stay in the ditch and help Maloney man his post for a while.

My small radio crackled. Casualties at the gym had been remarkably light. The rocket that had slammed into the processing center had exploded in the unoccupied handball courts. Over at the Command Mess, several rockets had also impacted, and Colonels Madison and Summers were waking up the heavy sleepers in their trailers. A loud explosion rocked the flight line across the street, followed by a ball of fire that lighted up the control tower. Over the air came the voice of an American who was even more exposed than we were. He reported hearing small arms fire on the far side of the runways. Maloney and I exchanged worried glances. Were the North Vietnamese knocking at the door? The unknown American also reported that the fireball had been an American C-130 that had sustained a direct hit and exploded. My heart sank at the thought of an American crew and a planeload of refugees.

At my side in the ditch, Maloney suddenly stiffened. Two figures moved stealthily across the open area to our front. We strained to identify them in the intermittent flashes of light provided by the fires on the runway, but all we could see was that one of them carried something that looked like a radio with a long antenna. I recalled the captured North Vietnamese forward observer, and how neatly the last artillery rounds had walked their way toward the flight line. The path of the two men would take them within twenty meters of our position, and Maloney clicked off the safety of his M-16 as I drew my .45 automatic. Without a signal, Maloney sprang out of the ditch and accosted the two men with a loud and threatening shout. The men had no time to react; they threw up their arms and began to shout in Vietnamese. Both were deeply frightened and began to talk excitedly when they recognized me. Maloney had apprehended two of our Vietnamese guards who had been posted across the street near the flight line when the attack commenced. *"Ho ban chinh xac lam, Dai Uy oi!"* ("They're firing very accurately, Captain!") one of them prattled. *"Nguy hiem lam!"* ("Really dangerous!") Once again I thought of the captured North Vietnamese forward observer. No doubt his comrades who hadn't been caught were on top of the water towers.

By now, daylight was approaching. Maloney called for another ambulance to complete the job of evacuating the remains of his fallen men. Then we searched the area. Fifty meters from the guard post, we stumbled on the barrel and receiver group of a shattered M-16 rifle, then a torn and bloody flak jacket, and, finally, a combat boot that still contained the foot of one of the unlucky men. I reported to the command center, where I turned in the M-16 to a marine colonel and informed him that we had evacuated the two bodies to the nearby Adventist Hospital. (Later, in a sad but understandable oversight, the marines left the two bodies behind in their haste to evacuate.)

By the time I linked up with Colonels Madison and Summers, new orders had come down for our small group. Washington had decided that our delegation should remain in Saigon following the evacuation. Colonel Madison was to assemble his team, gather up whatever equipment we needed to remain in Saigon, and proceed to the Embassy. There we would receive further orders, but it appeared that we were to remain in Saigon as the representatives of the U.S. government after the surrender of South Vietnam. Whether or not the Ambassador would remain was not clear to us. What was clear was that we faced a delicate and potentially risky mission. American military men in Saigon on the heels of a surrender to the Communists would not win a popularity contest with either side.

As we collected radios, medical supplies, and emergency rations, the rockets and artillery shells continued to rain down on the base, causing fires that blackened the sky overhead. In the Operations Center, the debate centered on the declaration of "Option IV," the helicopter extraction of the remaining Americans and Vietnamese from Saigon. Certainly it was no longer practical to use C-130 transports—one of them was already burning on the flight line.

I was surprised that we were directed to remain in Saigon, even though we had been preparing for such a contingency ever since Major Huyen had suggested it to Colonel Summers in Hanoi three days earlier. Since the Communists had clearly linked progress on the MIA issue to American economic aid to rebuild postwar Vietnam, Hanoi could easily interpret our continued presence in Saigon as a sign that the United States was amenable to this idea—that the provisions of the Paris Agreement remained valid in spite of Hanoi's military conquest of the south. This was a position that I did not believe Washington would adopt. However, Colonel Madison had already outlined the impact of the various options to Dr. Shields after the Summers mission to Hanoi, and we were prepared to remain in Saigon, if ordered. The emergency rations, radios, medical supplies, and other gear that we were now loading into our small fleet of vehicles had been collected for this contingency. We had even broken out a supply of Joint Military Team flags, bright orange banners with a black "4" in the center. The flags were supposed to guarantee our diplomatic immunity, although privately I doubted that anything would protect us from the defeated South Vietnamese except the arrival of the North Vietnamese Army. As we lined up our vehicles to make the dash to the Embassy, I found myself silently pulling for the North Vietnamese, then rebuking myself for such heresy.

By late morning, we were ready to make our move to the Embassy. Our party now numbered only six—the three officers, MSG Bill Herron, Marine Gunnery Sgt. Ernie Pace, and Specialist 7 Bill Bell, who had taken his daughter back to the States after she survived the C5A crash, then returned to assist in the evacuation. Our four black vehicles were crammed with equipment and judiciously bedecked with orange flags. When the rocketing let up, we pulled out of the gate, past the place where the two marines had died.

It was around 11:30 A.M. and the main gate of the base was already besieged by crowds of Vietnamese trying to gain admission. The exit lane was blocked by a crowd of people surging around a stalled vehicle. As I accelerated and forced my Land Rover into the ditch to bypass this obstacle, I breathed a prayer that Colonel Madison's sedan would not bog down when he attempted to follow. The colonel pulled it off, and we sped the remaining four miles to the Embassy down streets that were already beginning to fill up with crowds of confused and frightened people. Most of them seemed to be heading in the direction of Tan Son Nhut. The stage was set for the final act of the tragedy.

CRA compound, 29 April (noon). Note pool in rear and Embassy parking lot in foreground.

American Embassy, 29 April, 3 P.M. Ambassador Martin's tamarind tree being taken from parking lot.

Helicopters set down in a parking lot during evacuation exercises in Operation Frequent Wind, 29 April 1975. (USMC photo by Sgt. D. L. Shearer)

People begin to materialize, 29 April, 3:30 P.M.

A Maine CH-53 helicopter sets down on a blacktopped baseball field during Operation Frequent Wind. (USMC photo by Sergeant Shearer)

Coming through the gates.

Prayer before liftoff at U.S. Embassy, 29 April.

DAO tennis courts with fences removed for helicopter landings.

211

Helicopter alights on Embassy roof.

Loading for takeoff.

Author waiting at Embassy, 0230 hours, 30 April 1975.

USS *Okinawa*'s chopper fleet after Operation Frequent Wind.

Colonels Summers and Madison with author on *Okinawa*, 30 April 1975.

Marine Sgt. Ken Maloney and Colonel Madison, USS *Okinawa*.

Part VII

THE FINAL ACT: WHY?

"A PRESIDENTIAL ORDER"

A grim-faced marine security guard admitted our small convoy to the Embassy compound. Word of the two dead marines at Tan Son Nhut had reached the Embassy, and the nervous security guards were in a no-nonsense mood as most of them faced the prospect of hostilities for the first time in their careers. Outside the gate, a small group of Vietnamese had already gathered, seeking a way out of their stricken country. As we parked our vehicles on the grass, the drone of a chain saw pierced the air. The marines were felling a large tamarind tree that stood on an island in the center of the main parking lot. Someone was obviously contemplating use of the lot as a helicopter landing zone. Inside the Embassy, tight-lipped American civilians were preparing to depart. Many of them walked around in a daze, their faces registering disbelief at what was happening. In the Political-Military Affairs Office, Colonel Madison received new orders. The "highest authority" had decreed that all Americans must evacuate, including our team and the Ambassador himself. There would be no official American presence at the conclusion of "Operation Frequent Wind," the code name for the impending total evacuation.

We also learned that Washington had finally directed the implementation of "Option IV," the code name for a helicopter

evacuation of the remaining Americans and selected others—all
of whom would be ferried to ships waiting off the South Vietnamese coast in international waters. Ambassador Martin had
resisted this step throughout the morning. Deeply conscious of
his personal commitment to the thousands of Vietnamese who
desired to flee the Communists, he knew that continued flights
by the air force C-130s were the best way to move large numbers of people. Once we abandoned the fixed-wing evacuation,
helicopters would be the only way out, and many were likely to
be left behind. But by now, the runways at Tan Son Nhut were
unsafe for the C-130s. General Smith had recommended Option
IV when he learned that the airfield's runways were cluttered
with jettisoned bombs and other debris, but Ambassador Martin
was stubborn. Only after satisfying himself by a risky personnel
inspection under fire that Tan Son Nhut was too dangerous for
continued fixed-wing operations did he cave in and accept
General Smith's recommendation.

Relieved of the burden of planning for a "last redoubt," we
conducted a reconnaissance of the Embassy compound. What
we saw convinced us that we faced a complex and dangerous
situation. To begin with, both the Embassy and the adjacent
Combined Recreation Association (CRA) compound were already packed with humanity. Looting was in progress in the
restaurant, where employees had surrendered to the mob. Hungry American civilians had pulled slabs of beef out of the locker
and were hacking off pieces to cook over the kitchen burners.
Even more disturbing was the problem of the club's abundant
stock of unsecured liquor. The drinks were on the house, and
the crowd was taking full advantage of the situation. Colonel
Summers and I exchanged glances. The last thing we needed
was a mob of frightened drunks on our hands. We located the
padlocks on a nearby shelf and ignored the hostile looks that
were directed at us as we locked up the liquor cabinets.

Silver Huey helicopters began landing on the Embassy roof,
disgorging Vietnamese and Americans who had been picked up
at various points throughout the city. At the sound of these
choppers, curious crowds of people emerged from the buildings
in the CRA compound and gathered in the courtyard by the

swimming pool, their eyes on the rooftop pad. Only then did we realize the magnitude of our problem. At least one thousand persons were camped within the walls of the small compound, and the figure was growing hourly. The crowd was a mixture of Americans, Vietnamese, Korean diplomats, and other "Third Country Nationals" who were counting on the United States to snatch them out of the jaws of the advancing Communists. All of them had one thing in common—they were afraid. When they saw the first helicopters, the smarter ones began to stake out their claims to places near the gate that led to the parking lot where the marines were preparing a landing zone. Two American civilians voluntarily surrendered their pistols to me, which was not a bad idea. Weapons would be forbidden on the helicopters and navy ships. We located a cardboard box and circulated through the crowd, quickly filling it with a variety of handguns.

In the Embassy chancery, tensions had escalated. Phones were ringing off the hook as Americans and Vietnamese alike called to report that they had assembled at their assigned pick-up points. All wanted to know where the promised transportation was to take them to Tan Son Nhut. Several buses had been prepositioned at the Embassy for this purpose. Now, however, no one could locate the drivers. After a vain search, the call went out for volunteers who could drive a bus and who would dare to brave the streets of downtown Saigon.

In the Political-Military Affairs Office, a bitter telephone exchange was under way between one agency chief and a frightened employee in a downtown safe site. The employee had reported as ordered to a villa, along with dozens of Vietnamese who worked for the agency. Now he was demanding to be picked up. "You'll have to make your way to the Embassy, that's all I can tell you!" his boss shouted in frustration before hanging up. Moments later, after a frantic and unsuccessful search for a way to have his people picked up, the man solved his dilemma by boarding a helicopter flight to the safety of the fleet. The haunting phone calls from Embassy employees stranded throughout the city continued all day, long past the point when it was possible to send anyone to pick up the callers.

Embassy planners had thought that it would be possible to move most of the Embassy staff to Tan Son Nhut by bus, where they could be shuttled by helicopter to the fleet. Only key American staffers were supposed to depart by helicopter directly from the Embassy roof. Overall, the plan envisioned that no more than three hundred persons would require evacuation from the Embassy. No one anticipated that the Embassy would be occupied by more than two thousand persons demanding evacuation. But the tall, modern building just down the street from the Presidential Palace had become the symbol of our presence in Vietnam, and as conditions deteriorated, people seeking safety were drawn to it.

The Embassy thus became the focal point for a major, unplanned military operation, for which its civilian staffers were ill-prepared. Radio transmissions from the volunteer bus drivers who were attempting to make the rounds of the pickup points revealed a deteriorating situation. One terrified voice reported that mobs of desperate and angry Saigonese were beating on the doors of his stranded bus. It was clear that the "surface movement plan" was breaking down from the beginning and that the transfer of the crowds in the courtyard to Tan Son Nhut was impractical. The only way remaining to evacuate the growing crowd in the courtyard was with the heavy-lift helicopters on the carriers floating off the Vung Tau coast. Colonel Madison volunteered the services of our small team to Deputy Chief of Mission Wolfgang Lehmann. Lehmann seized on the colonel's offer and asked him to take charge of the evacuation. A division of responsibility was quickly determined. The senior marine officer in the compound, Major Kean, would control his security guards and direct the landing of the helicopters. Colonel Madison and his men would organize and marshal the evacuees and load them on the helicopters.

It was a formidable task. By late afternoon, the crowd had grown to well over two thousand, and people were still arriving. During the day, eight busloads of evacuees abandoned attempts to reach the DAO after encountering impassable conditions near Tan Son Nhut. The entire city of Saigon appeared to be disintegrating into anarchy. The buses finally made their way to the Embassy and deposited their desperate human cargo with us after a long and traumatic ride, and three hundred more souls became our responsibility. Until early afternoon, the silver Huey helicopters continued to shuttle passengers to the Embassy, all of whom would ultimately require transportation to the fleet. Throughout the day, a steady flow of Americans, Allied diplomats, and Vietnamese desiring evacuation converged on the Embassy gates. Some carried luggage, others children; some even clung to pets. The Vietnamese among them clung to the familiar clutch of papers that proved their right to evacuate. The overwhelmed marines did their best to admit the Americans, but they admitted very few Vietnamese. As the day drew on, the guards became less and less patient, and there were numerous instances of rough treatment as people were either hoisted over the wall or forced off.

The marine guards were under strict orders to secure the landing zone. This meant above all that they had to prevent the Embassy from being overrun by panicky mobs, a condition that would have forced the shutdown of the landing zone. Our worst fear was that the Embassy evacuation might deteriorate into a repeat of the Danang or Nha Trang debacles, for the potential for such a loss of control was ever-present during those last hours. In their efforts to comply with these orders, our young and frightened marines resorted to the use of force to secure the walls, as several historic photographs graphically testify. This was regrettable, but the marines' determined performance of duty prevented the Embassy landing zone from being overrun by panicky Saigonese. Had this happened, no one would have escaped.

By late afternoon, when we finally received three platoons of reinforcements from the fleet, an undetermined number of wall-jumpers had managed to join the anxious crowd in the compound. After the arrival of these reinforcements, the walls were secure. We were then able to concentrate on preparing the landing zone, reassuring the restless crowd, and marshaling them into groups for loading when the helicopter flow commenced.

The chain-link fence between the CRA compound and the parking lot enabled us to control access to the makeshift landing zone, but it also posed problems. Isolated by the fence and adjacent firehouse, the tense crowd could not see that we had removed trees, parked sedans around the perimeter (their head-lights would illuminate the landing zone), and painted a large "H" on the asphalt to mark the touchdown spot—all in prepa-ration for their evacuation. But what they could see were the continuous arrivals and departures of the silver helicopters at the rooftop pad, and this sight produced mounting fear. Rumors swept the crowd that the Ambassador and his staff were leaving and that the remaining evacuees were being abandoned. By mid-afternoon, conditions in the compound had begun to deteri-orate as our impatient charges smarted under the prospect of being left behind. The marines experienced growing difficulties with the unruly crowd, many of whom were American con-tractor employees with their Vietnamese families, demanding their "right" to evacuation. Colonel Summers observed the increasingly volatile situation and entered the compound.

Assisted by Rev. Tom Stebbins, a local missionary who spoke Vietnamese, the colonel circulated among the crowd in an effort to arrest the growing fear. His message was that everyone would be evacuated and that the order of priority was Americans and their dependents first, followed by Third Country Nationals and Vietnamese. These assurances from an authoritative source alleviated the unrest; the tension remained, but it was manage-able. The problem of crowd unrest was to haunt us throughout the evacuation operation. Each time there was a delay in the arrival of the helicopters, the crowd's reaction was the same. Rumors would begin that the remaining Americans were leav-ing, and angry pushing and shoving would follow. Each delay in the arrival of a helicopter seemed interminable as the Evacu-ation Control Center struggled to control what was a most com-plex operation. This difficulty was not shared by our comrades at the DAO, where almost five thousand persons were evacuated in a smoothly executed extraction from the landing zones that General Smith's planners had prepared during the month. The first big marine chopper had landed at the DAO at 3:00 P.M., and the evacuation had proceeded like a "piece of cake," to use General Smith's words.[1] Prior planning had paid off. This was not so at the Embassy, where the entire heavy-lift helicopter evacuation was a product of improvisation, and where many of the two thousand evacuees had narrowly escaped the chaos in the streets on their way downtown.

Most of the early lifts that did land in the Embassy were CH-46 helicopters, into which we could only cram fifty persons, and then only if they abandoned their luggage. Thus the going was slow at the beginning. When a pair of marine "Cobra" helicopter gunships and several navy fighters appeared overhead, a cheer went up from the crowd. In the "on-deck circle," some evacuees knelt and prayed as they awaited their turn to depart.

When the frequency of the arriving birds increased, we decided to speed up the departures by operating two landing zones simultaneously. The Embassy engineer warned that the rooftop pad was not designed to accommodate heavy-lift helicopters, but we had to take this risk. There were simply too many people for the single, tight landing zone in the parking lot.

Colonel Madison directed us to escort a large number of persons from the CRA holding area into the Embassy chancery, where they filled the six-story stairwell to the roof. As the CH-46 helicopters alighted on the rooftop pad, these people were funneled up the final flight of stairs to the roof and evacuated. At the same time, other helicopters shuttled in and out of the landing zone in the parking lot below. We were stretched to the limit of our manpower to orchestrate this operation, but it was an efficient system, marred only by the frustrating delays between aircraft. Just when we would think that the controllers at the DAO had mastered the problem, the skies overhead would empty and our nervous charges would once again begin to doubt their future. Then, suddenly, we would be swamped with aircraft, all arriving at the same time.

Darkness approached, and with it came rumors from the fleet that the evacuation might be discontinued until the following morning. A light rain began to fall, and flying conditions deteriorated, but someone made the courageous and wise decision to keep on flying in spite of the heightened risk. It would have been difficult, if not impossible, to control our frightened charges in the face of an all-night delay. American ingenuity triumphed when an alert Embassy staffer produced a 35-millimeter slide projector and mounted it on the roof overlooking the parking lot. As the lumbering helicopters began their harrowing vertical descents, a marine turned the projector on and bathed the landing zone in a rectangle of white light.

Some of the marine pilots had experienced difficulties locating the Embassy during the day. To guide them, Major Kean and his men had been forced to pop colored smoke grenades on several occasions. Since Kean and his small command group had a radio, we assumed he was in contact with the pilots. Only after nightfall did we learn that this assumption was false. Kean had neither the frequency nor the call signs to communicate with the pilots. Using a tactical radio that we had brought with us that morning, I established contact with the DAO Evacuation Control Center to find out the reason for the sporadic flow of evacuation flights. A voice at the other end explained. At the DAO, a massive evacuation from several landing zones was under way. Some five thousand people had gathered there for pickup, and this operation had first priority for the precious helicopters. The voice told me that the DAO operation would be complete by midnight, after which the Embassy would receive priority for the large helicopters. In the meantime, we could only sit tight and be ready to fill those aircraft that were diverted our way. The voice advised me to insure that all evacuees abandoned their luggage. The helicopters would only take people from then on—no suitcases.

Conditions outside the Embassy wall settled down considerably as darkness descended on the city. Apart from sporadic gunshots in the distance (no doubt from undisciplined ARVN troops), downtown Saigon was quiet. We were not besieged by thousands of panic-stricken Saigonese, as some journalistic accounts have suggested, nor were we under hostile fire. The North Vietnamese armored thrust that ended at the Presidential Palace a few blocks away did not commence until midnight. Nonetheless, in the minds of those controlling the evacuation, the impression had taken hold that we did not have control of the situation. Ultimately, this erroneous impression would contribute to a tragic development.

We began to encounter serious difficulties around midnight. For almost an hour, no aircraft arrived. The fleet of helicopters was refueling at sea after emptying out the DAO. More than one thousand people were still penned up behind the chain-link fence. Interpreting the long lull as proof that they were being abandoned, the crowd began to panic. Pressure mounted against the frail chain-link fence. At the gate, two young marines held their own, but tempers were getting short. If the gate gave, controlled admission of the evacuees to the landing zone would have been impossible. The tense marine guards began fending off the desperate people with their rifle butts, which didn't help a bit. Rumors again swept through the apprehensive crowd. "The North Vietnamese have given us until midnight to get out, then they are going to start shooting at the evacuation helicopters." Hence the panic. Everyone tried to be among the first fifty through the tiny, four-foot gate.

"Open the gate and let me in," I ordered one of the marines.

"Sir, you can't go in there," he replied, still fending off the people who were pushing at the overloaded gate.

"Just open the gate. We've got to get them under control or no one else will get out."

The marine cracked the gate and cursed at the panicky crowd to back off. With a battery-powered bullhorn, I forced my way into the crowd.

"*Xin quy vi, im lang lai! Im lang lai di!*" ("Ladies and gentlemen, please be quiet! Be quiet!") I repeated these words over and over, urging them to "*Xep hang hai di*" ("Form a double line"). No response. No one wanted anything to do with it.

"*Dung lo!* ("Don't worry!") You will all be evacuated. I'm in here with you, and I'll be on the last helicopter. They will not leave me behind. No one is abandoning you. In a little while, the helicopters will begin arriving again. But you must cooperate. Throw away all suitcases and form a double line. You people right here, back away from the gate so we can open it!"

No one listened. More shoving and maneuvering toward the gate. Those in front began to use their suitcases as battering rams. I could feel the panic spreading, and the sinking sensation swept over me that we were about to see a replay of Danang. A

few meters away, an American with a Vietnamese wife collapsed of a heart attack. Someone carried him to the main compound for departure on the next lift—whenever that would be. I
tried again.

"Ladies and gentlemen, please be quiet! If you don't listen to
me, no one will go, including me. You must listen! All of you
will get to go. Please! Form a double line, and throw away your
suitcases. Line up in family groups. The helicopters will take
only people—not suitcases. *Khong ai se bi bo lai!*" ("No one will
be left behind!")

Still no results. Everyone wanted the real estate next to the
gate. A diminutive Vietnamese in a white shirt tugged on my
arm.

"Excuse me, sir, I am interpreter here in the Embassy. The
Vietnamese all want to cooperate, but these people (he gestured
toward the crowd closest to the gate) are Koreans and have
pushed our people out of the way. I will try to help you with our
people, but you must do something about the Koreans."

Sheepishly, I realized he was right. The sidewalk next to the
gate was "held" by a phalanx of taller, flat-faced Koreans.
"God! Almost four years over here and they still all look alike!"
I tried English.

"Is there a Korean officer here please?"

In a moment, a Korean naval officer shoved his way to the
front.

"Look, sir, you've got to discipline your people. No shoving!
Back off from the gate and get them in a double line! Please!
They don't understand me. You may use the bullhorn if you
wish. Tell them that I'm in here and wouldn't be here if the
evacuation were really over. No one will leave *me* behind! But
they must cooperate."

The Korean nodded. "Our people have disciplined themselves, but the Vietnamese began pushing. We will cooperate
with you now." He rejected the offer of the bullhorn and faded
away.

Reinforcements finally arrived. Colonel Summers and Bill
Herron, observing my plight, waded into the crowd and bailed
me out. We linked arms at the gate and physically assaulted the

closest people into retreating. Then, magically, the Koreans formed a double line on the left, followed promptly by the Vietnamese on the right. My arms were weary and my legs ached from being battered by suitcases, but the crowd had quieted down and the situation was once again under control. Without delay, we moved everyone through the gate into the main compound, herding them up a flight of stairs to the roof of the firehouse. From there they could see the ongoing departures and be reassured that no one was abandoning them—if only we could get some helicopters. We also got an accurate count; Reverend Stebbins revealed that we had pushed eighteen hundred people onto helicopters by midnight, and that eleven hundred had just come through the gate.

When the last family had come through the gate, I prepared to lock it, but hesitated when I spotted several people picking through the debris on the far side of the pool.

"*Di khong?*" ("Are you going?")

"*Da khong. O lai.*" ("No, sir, we're staying.") One family. Tempted by the chance to loot the mountain of abandoned suitcases? Or more frightened of leaving Vietnam than of the advancing Communists? No time for discussion. We sealed the gate, thereby reducing the size of the remaining American-held real estate in Vietnam by 50 percent. Now the marines had only the Embassy wall proper to guard. It was almost 2:00 A.M., 30 April.

Once inside the Embassy compound, the evacuees became cooperative, almost docile. They willingly discarded their suitcases when we explained the reason why, tucking family papers, money, and pictures into their clothing. We continued to reassure them that we would leave last and that Ambassador Martin himself had stated his intention to remain until the last Vietnamese employees were safely on the fleet.

The chopper flow resumed. Several groups moved into the Embassy stairwell and departed on CH-46 "Sea Knight" helicopters from the rooftop pad. In the parking lot, other groups boarded the larger CH-53s. We soon learned that we could stuff ninety Vietnamese men, women, and children into a CH-53, as long as they brought no luggage. We held our breath each time one of the lumbering giants strained its way through the one hundred–foot vertical lift required for it to maneuver out of the walled compound.

By 3:00 A.M., we were deluged by arriving helicopters. We worked frantically to hustle the evacuees onto birds that had begun to arrive almost on top of one another. Their motors screamed as they lifted off and peeled right in a sharp bank to avoid an antenna, then headed for the ships of "Task Force 75" off the coast near Vung Tau.

A Vietnamese-speaking German priest joined the Embassy firemen in volunteering to remain until the last lift. "I'll go when you go," he insisted as he circulated among the refugees, repeating our assurances that no one would be left behind. The firemen asked to remain until the end so that they could per-form emergency duties in the event of an accident. At their request, I saw to it that their families were evacuated together on one lift.

Six lifts cleared out all but 420 of our charges. No more Americans remained.

Ambassador Martin appeared in the parking lot, accompa-nied by his marine bodyguard. The angular, stoop-shouldered man looked completely exhausted as he moved about, surveying our situation. Before disappearing into the Embassy, he directed Colonel Madison to assemble all remaining evacuees in the parking lot and obtain an accurate head count.

At 4:15 A.M. Colonel Madison informed Mr. Lehmann that only six more helicopters were required to complete the evacu-ation. Lehmann shook his head. There would be no more heli-copters. The evacuation was over. The next helicopters that arrived were to take only the remaining Americans. Colonel Madison shook his head, reminding Lehmann of our commit-ment to the remaining Vietnamese. Then he firmly told the dip-lomat that he and his men would only leave on the final lift after all evacuees under our care had been safely evacuated. Leh-mann relented. The birds would be provided. Colonel Madison relayed the word to us, and we once again reassured the Vietna-mese in the parking lot that we would all depart together. A few minutes later, we received further reassurances from Ambassador Martin's Special Assistant, Brunson McKinley, who came out of the Embassy to tell Colonel Summers that the required helicopter lifts would be provided.

But it was not to be. Within minutes, Major Kean appeared and informed Colonel Madison that no additional helicopters would be available except for those required to extract us and his marines. Nearby, the 420 remaining evacuees sat in eight disciplined groups, their eyes searching the sky for the helicopters that we had promised them over and over. Colonel Madison reacted angrily. "We were promised the six lifts to get these people out. I'll take this up with the Ambassador or his deputy."

Pointing to a CH-46 that had just lifted off the Embassy roof, the marine replied, "You can't, sir, they just left."

Colonel Madison set his jaw and calmly announced our intention to remain until everyone was evacuated as promised. The marine countered: The President had personally ordered the cancellation of all further lifts, and he, Major Kean, would not "risk the safety of his men any longer."

With this announcement, we realized that we were finished. A quick conference followed. No one wanted to abandon the remaining Vietnamese, but a Presidential order? Perhaps things were happening that we didn't know about. Maybe the North Vietnamese have entered the city, or perhaps they have begun to shoot at the evacuation helicopters. One thing was certain. No marines, no more helicopters. No American helicopter would land on an unsecured landing zone, which is what the Embassy was about to become when Kean and his marines departed on the next helicopter. Colonel Madison then made the most painful decision of his career. We must leave, in spite of our repeated assurances to the people in the parking lot that we would depart only after they were safe.

The colonel ordered me to remain with the refugees while the others made discreet preparations to transfer our gear to the roof. I sat on the trunk of a sedan, manning the radio and glancing skyward, sick inside at the impending betrayal. I contemplated staying, then rejected this course as fruitless. ("You won't get them out anyway, and you'll be branded as a defector, or at least as one who disobeyed a presidential order.")

Minutes that seemed like hours passed as I struggled with my conscience. Then a CH-46 alighted on the roof and quickly departed. I wondered whether or not I was supposed to be on board. The refugees squatting closest to me glanced anxiously at the departing bird. I reassured them that a "big helicopter" was on its way to pick them up. Then I gazed skyward, pretending to look for helicopters that I knew would never come. Minutes later, I excused myself to go to the bathroom and slipped into the back door of the Embassy.

In the foyer, my glance fell on the bronze plaque dedicated to the marines and military policemen who had died defending the Embassy during the 1968 Tet Offensive. Earlier in the day, I had obtained permission to take it with us rather than leave it for the Communists or the looters. I had even removed it from the wall with a crowbar. Now, the heavy plaque lay on the floor, almost obscured by a carpet of rubble. Books, Vietnamese piaster notes, abandoned pistol belts, canteens, holsters, attaché cases, mountains of shredded documents—the debris of evacuation was strewn everywhere, all materialized in the brief twenty-four hours since Communist rockets and artillery had set the final drama in motion. Disgusted at what I was about to do, I canceled my plans to rescue the plaque. ("Those guys would roll over in their graves if they could see what's happening now!")

I made a quick dash up the stairs and glanced into the Political-Military Affairs Office, confirming that the others were already gone. The Embassy was still and empty. On my way to the roof, I stumbled on the litter in the stairwell up which hundreds had just fled to freedom. A helicopter had just landed, and I encountered two of our sergeants at the head of the stairs. The others had all left on the previous lift. We were it. Gunny Pace boarded the helicopter, followed by Bill Bell. Bell was so exhausted from fighting the crowds that he crawled up the ramp of the helicopter. I scrambled aboard, and the aircraft lifted off a minute later carrying only the three of us and one stray marine guard.

As the chopper banked, I caught a final glimpse of the illuminated parking lot, where the remaining refugees were still squatting in disciplined groups. The Embassy firemen were easy to identify by their yellow coats and helmets. I winced, thinking of their families, waiting for them on one of the carriers. Although I couldn't see him, I knew that the German priest was down there too, probably continuing to relay our assurances to the trusting evacuees. Also seated among the unlucky group were more than a dozen diplomats of the South Korean Embassy. It had not yet dawned on the pathetic group huddled below that they were the victims of the final betrayal. It was 5:30 A.M., 30 April, and outside the Embassy walls, the streets of Saigon were quiet and empty as South Vietnam awaited the arrival of the revolution.

We sat silently. The helicopter's turbines were deafening with the ramp partly open, but it was a blessing. If I had tried to talk, I would have cried. I know of no words in any language that are adequate to describe the sense of shame that swept over me during that flight.

"A BOTTOMLESS PIT"

Aboard the U.S.S. *Okinawa*, an irate Colonel Madison sought out the helicopter squadron commander to learn why the evacuation had ended prematurely. The marine officer, LTC Jim Bolton, confessed that he and his fellow aviators had been unaware that six more missions would have completed the Embassy evacuation. Bolton explained apologetically that the heavy-lift commanders had believed that they were dealing with "a bottomless pit" at the Embassy. Because of this, they had generated pressure to terminate the evacuation. Bolton explained that some of the marine aviators had already flown more than eighteen hours without a break. The impression had spread throughout the fleet that the headstrong Ambassador Martin was trying to evacuate the entire population of Saigon through the Embassy conduit. Heartsick at the news of the abandoned Vietnamese, Colonel Bolton told Colonel Madison that he and the other commanders would never have pressured for termination if they had known the true situation. The news that they had failed to make a clean sweep of the Embassy was not well received by the aviators, who had performed heroically only to be robbed of complete success by a communications breakdown.

Much later, at Subic Bay, Marine Brig. Gen. Richard Carey explained to me that he, too, had believed that the Embassy situation was out of control. Carey, the commander of the marine ground security force, recalled that when the decision to recommend termination was made, he believed that "we had to shut off that flow or we'd probably still be there." He, too, had been deeply disappointed when he learned how close we had come to a flawless extraction from the Embassy.

Air Force LTCs Art Laehr and Jack Hilgenberg manned the Evacuation Control Center at the DAO. From their account of the Embassy situation, one can reconstruct at least part of President Ford's reason for ordering the untimely halt to the evacuation:

> One of the things that kept the Evacuation Control Center busy was the situation at the Embassy. There were approximately one thousand persons at the Embassy on the morning of the 29th. During the day, an additional one thousand plus would come aboard. It was ironic that no matter how many people the helicopters hauled out of the Embassy, the estimate of evacuees was always two thousand. How long that would have continued is anyone's guess. The Commander in Chief, Pacific and (the headquarters at) Nakhon Phanom kept calling for updates on the Embassy situation, and it was always the same—two thousand to go. This caused considerable concern with the evacuation control personnel outside the country, but the Defense Attaché Office had no way to verify the figure. At 19:30 that evening, the U.S. Embassy was still reporting two thousand to go. Everyone in the Evacuation Control Center believed that if the evacuation had continued for days, the estimate would have remained two thousand.[2]

On board the *Okinawa*, our reunited team was understandably bitter at what we had just been forced to do. Near the end of our emotional and physical endurance, we blamed Ambassador Martin, Minister Lehmann, President Ford, and several other actors in the drama for the unconscionable breach of faith in the Embassy courtyard. In the heat of the moment, it was small comfort that we had successfully evacuated more than two thousand persons as North Vietnamese tanks were entering Saigon. We could not—and still cannot—fully understand why accurate reporting of conditions in the Embassy parking lot did not make it out of the Embassy. Both the Ambassador and Minister Lehmann had toured the landing zone as late as 4:00 A.M. and observed the empty staging areas, as well as the remaining refugees whom we had marshaled in the parking lot. In fact, Ambassador Martin made his surprise appearance in the parking lot at that time because of his sincere concern that no one be left behind. It was he who directed us to assemble the remaining evacuees in the parking lot and obtain a firm head count. In retrospect, I have little doubt that the Ambassador strained himself to the breaking point in his efforts to fulfill his personal commitment to his Vietnamese employees. Why then did he suddenly depart and leave us with no choice but to abandon our unfortunate charges? The answer lies in the presidential order that directed him to board the helicopter "Lady Ace 09" and depart the Embassy. That order, issued in Washington, was based on an inaccurate impression of the situation on the ground in the Embassy—the apparent result of vague and confused reporting by persons inside the Embassy building during the actual helilift operations. Once Ambassador Martin had departed the Embassy, no one else remained who shared his firm commitment to a complete evacuation of everyone in the compound. No one, that is, except Colonel Madison and the rest of our small group, and we had no way to communicate with the fleet. Furthermore, even if we had been able to communicate, it is doubtful whether anyone would have believed our situation report. We had been victimized by a tragic breakdown in communications, the cost of which was the fate of 420 human beings.

WHO LOST VIETNAM?

Americans tend to be poor losers, and this American is no exception. Several years elapsed before I could look objectively at the events described in these chapters. During that time, I wasted considerable emotional energy in a pointless vendetta to fix the blame for what we had done as instruments of our government. It was impossible to purge my mind of that final betrayal in the Embassy courtyard. We had given our word to those people with the same good intentions that had motivated our country's original pledge to assist their government. Like our government, we had failed to keep a solemn commitment. I had spent almost four years of my life in an endeavor that ended in the shabbiest of political sellouts, and I needed someone to hold responsible for my frustration. Chief among the targets of my wrath was Henry Kissinger. After all, had he not negotiated the Paris Agreement that led me to the roof of the Embassy and resulted in South Vietnam's unconditional surrender and subjugation? Next came the U.S. Congress, particularly the coalition of liberal "doves" whose hands had thrust the fiscal dagger into South Vietnam's back. President Thieu appeared high on my list for his failure to institute domestic reforms that might have made his government more acceptable to the Vietnamese and to the American people. Finally, I held Ambassador Graham Martin responsible for what I perceived to be his contributions to the alienation of both the press and Congress, and his rigid control over reporting from the U.S. mission in Saigon. Ironically, I seemed to blame almost everyone except the most obvious villains, the North Vietnamese themselves.

As time passed, I began to realize that nothing could be gained from emotional finger-pointing, and I embarked on a reassessment of the entire drama. Not surprisingly, the main actors did not emerge from this inquiry as either clear-cut heroes or villains. Dr. Kissinger, for example, grappled with the difficult art of the possible when he negotiated the Paris Agreement. The flawed results of his efforts reflected our eternal dilemma in Vietnam—if the Communists didn't lose, they won. One can argue ad infinitum whether Dr. Kissinger was guilty of naivete or cynicism in Paris, but he did accomplish what President Nixon and the American people demanded of him. I personally do not believe that he extracted the best possible agreement from a Hanoi government whose army had just been shattered in the south, even considering the political restraints of 1972.

But, if it is true that the terms of the Paris Agreement were advantageous to Hanoi, it is equally true that the newly elected U.S. Congress seemed to be fully prepared to vote for a unilateral end to American involvement in Vietnam in 1973. It was frustrating to live in Saigon and observe the gradual undoing of the South Vietnamese under the aegis of the stillborn cease-fire, but the congressional alternative was a unilateral American withdrawal with no cease-fire—a guaranteed prescription for a South Vietnamese defeat. Dr. Kissinger's dilemma in Paris was how to reach a settlement with Hanoi that involved some North Vietnamese concessions before Congress served up South Vietnam for free on a silver platter. At least the Paris Agreement offered a slim possibility for the survival of our ally.

Dr. Kissinger himself defends the signing of the Paris Agreement as well as President Nixon's promises to the South Vietnamese that the U.S. military would react and punish Hanoi for any major violations of the accords. "We did not intend to sign a surrender," he argues in his memoirs. "We considered that we had a right to enforce a solemn agreement signed by Hanoi and confirmed at an international conference . . ."[3] Replying to frequently voiced accusations that the Paris peace was a cynical escape for the United States at South Vietnam's expense, Kissinger contends that the Watergate scandal undermined what would otherwise have been a workable arrangement:

> We had no illusions about Hanoi's long-term goals. Nor did we go through the agony of four years of searing negotiations simply to achieve a "decent interval" for our withdrawal. We were determined to do our utmost to enable Saigon to grow in security and prosperity so that it could prevail in any political struggle. We sought not an interval before collapse, but lasting peace with honor. But for the collapse of executive authority as a result of Watergate, I believe we would have succeeded.[4]

I would like to believe that our intentions were this honorable, but this is a judgment that will have to be made by historians armed with more than the limited information and perspective available at this writing. (Other contradictory views of the mood at the time have already surfaced. Presidential Assistant John Erlichman, for example, contends that when he asked Kissinger in January 1973 how long he felt the South Vietnamese could survive under the Paris terms, Kissinger replied, "I think that if they're lucky they can hold out for a year and a half.")[5]

It is considerably more difficult to rationalize the congressional role in the loss of Vietnam. As life in cease-fire Saigon amply demonstrated, the reductions in American military assistance dealt a devastating blow to South Vietnamese morale, eroded the Saigon army's self-defense capability, and contributed to President Thieu's political bankruptcy. Not only that, but overt congressional hostility to South Vietnam most certainly encouraged Hanoi to pursue final victory with greater confidence. As one commentator aptly observed, "For all its political defects, South Vietnam will not be overcome by political means. If North Vietnam wins in the end, it will be thanks to its military strength and, above all, the constancy of its foreign backers."[6]

Still, one wonders what would have happened if Congress had continued to underwrite the South Vietnamese cause. Even if the Saigon government had been blessed with adequate aid, how much longer could it have withstood Hanoi's relentless attacks? My feeling is that North Vietnam had the capability to outlast Washington and its South Vietnamese ally just as it had outlasted the French before us. Hence, as shameful as the abandonment of our ally was, I believe that, by 1975, continued aid at the levels Congress might underwrite would have been matched or exceeded by Hanoi's allies, which would have delayed the inevitable at a great cost in human lives. Both militarily and politically, Saigon was on the short end of a losing equation. Militarily, the war-weary ARVN had to defend South Vietnam's vast territory and its long lines of communication against an enemy that could achieve local superiority at virtually any place of his choosing. Politically, the leaders in Hanoi had undisputed control of a population that believed in a nationalistic cause, for which they enjoyed backing by faithful allies. The Thieu government, on the other hand, suffered from internal contradictions and was cursed with an ally that had exhibited little patience for the long-term sacrifices of a protracted war far from its shores. This latter fact was, in my view, the single major cause of the demise of the Republic of South Vietnam. Our attempt to "rescue" the South Vietnamese from the Communists simply turned out to be an elusive mission that dragged on and on until the disillusioned American electorate tired of it all and began to look for a reason to put the whole affair behind it. The reason, in this case, turned out to be the belated conclusion that the South Vietnamese did not deserve to be rescued.

President Thieu unquestionably failed his people by his failure to move forcefully against corruption, for his government's unsavory image earned him no friends where he needed them the most—on the floor of the U.S. Congress. Thieu must also be held responsible for his ill-timed decision to evacuate the Central Highlands under North Vietnamese military pressure. Curiously enough, this latter failure caused most South Vietnamese military men to turn against Thieu. Corruption was one thing; strategic incompetence and meddling was something else. As one officer explained to me, "The idea of redeploying our army had merit, but only if it had been done on our own initiative, not as a reaction to a Communist offensive. President Thieu's poor timing communicated the wrong message to many of our soldiers and thereby contributed to the panic." Another former Vietnamese officer's comments testify to the bitterness that has survived the passage of time:

> You have asked me about Mr. Thieu. At this time, four and a half years after the fall of South Vietnam, we would be wise to forget him. Moreover, I am not really qualified to answer this question. The only thought the Vietnamese had in mind all their life was that Mr. Thieu had been an efficient and obedient collaborator of the U.S. government; he had done a good job for the U.S. and a very poor one for his country. He used all the means, good and bad, to maintain his throne, with the total support of the U.S. government, so as a President, he should recognize his responsibility in the loss of South Vietnam and should not blame it on anyone; the American "imperialists"? His collaborators? His soldiers and countrymen? He should remember what happened under his reign, be aware of the misery and humiliation

that his countrymen, soldiers, comrades, and collaborators are suffering under the Communist regime; and if he is a man of honor and conscience, having the dignity of a General and Chief of State, he should commit suicide or at least become mad. The Vietnamese people don't have any means to remind him about that, and I hope that these lines, written by one of his soldiers, will be printed in your book so that by chance, he can have the opportunity to read them.[7]

I am no apologist for President Thieu's performance as the leader of his people, but I believe that he was treated shabbily by the United States during and after the Paris negotiations, that we most certainly made promises to him that we did not fulfill, and that we overreacted to the corruption and the authoritarian character of his government. It is still difficult for me to accept the fact that we condemned Nguyen van Thieu and the South Vietnamese government for crimes of which other American allies were guilty. In some cases, dramatically confirmed by Watergate and subsequent revelations, the hand that pointed the accusing finger was not clean. I can still vividly recall a front-page editorial in one of Saigon's sixteen daily newspapers during mid-1974. The writer attacked President Thieu, calling him a dictator and accusing him of denying freedom of the press. The story was not unusual but was one of a series of vitriolic attacks against Thieu, a part of a hard-hitting public debate that simply could not have taken place had Thieu been the full-blown dictator that his detractors claimed. Political life in Saigon may not have been as open as life in Washington and London, but it was certainly preferable to Hanoi-style Communism. Col. Harry Summers has said it better than anyone: "If the American people insisted that South Vietnam be a liberal democracy as a precondition for aid, then what we should have done was declare a Vietnamese Magna Charta and wait 750 years. That's how long it took us." Regrettably, the American people are not known for their sense of history, nor for their understanding and tolerance. Hence, in its search for reasons to end American involvement in an unpopular war, Congress demanded of the South Vietnamese something that the United States had been unable to accomplish. South Vietnam thus suffered what one commentator has called "death by a thousand cuts."[8]

In the eight years since the Communists seized power in South Vietnam, I have interviewed dozens of the "boat people" who have fled the "Socialist Republic of Vietnam." Regardless of their political persuasion at the time of the takeover, they unanimously paint an Orwellian picture of life in their country. The citizens of Ho Chi Minh City now read only a single, government-controlled newspaper; Chi Hoa prison is filled with political prisoners; thousands of former South Vietnamese officers have disappeared into reeducation camps; corrupt Communist cadre demand up to three thousand dollars in gold for an exit visa from Vietnamese who desire to join their relatives overseas; and eighteen-year-old southern boys are being drafted by the North Vietnamese–dominated government to serve in a Vietnamese army of occupation in Kampuchea. At the same time, disillusioned former North and South Vietnamese Communist cadre are now fleeing their homeland to join a burgeoning overseas resistance movement. South Vietnam under the Communists is a country devoid of human rights, a country that now truly needs the liberation that Hanoi promised but did not deliver. Ho Chi Minh City would be fertile hunting ground for the Ramsey Clarks, the Jane Fondas, and the Bella Abzugs. One wonders at their present indifference to the fate of a people for whom they once professed great concern.

Finally, it is difficult to imagine any time in the history of our country when an American Ambassador faced difficulties of the magnitude inherited by the unfortunate Graham Martin in Saigon. His was a classic "mission impossible," doomed to failure. Tasked to oversee the completion of his country's extrication from Vietnam with dignity without jeopardizing South Vietnam's security, Ambassador Martin did not have the means to accomplish what was expected of him. Instead, he confronted an increasingly hostile Congress, a largely cynical press corps, and a disintegrating South Vietnamese economy. The South Vietnamese military faced a determined North Vietnamese Army that had been given a badly needed breather and the strategic advantage by the imperfect Paris Agreement. Under these circumstances, Ambassador Martin's influence on the outcome could only have been marginal at best. His strident exchanges with Congress and the press probably did little to help South Vietnam's cause, but Congress and the media would probably have seen things no differently had he taken a less dogmatic stance.

The tight control over public relations exercised by the Martin Embassy and its sensitivity to any reporting that conflicted with the "official" version of events must be seen in the context of the struggle for continued military assistance for the South Vietnamese. Support for our efforts in Vietnam was so shaky in Washington that the Embassy lived in daily fear of providing the opposition (Congress and the liberal press, not the North Vietnamese) with any ammunition that might be used against its cause. The Embassy thus preferred to forward or release a single, "authoritative" version of the situation in the belief that multiple interpretations of events could only work to Saigon's disadvantage by creating confusion in Washington. I recall one occasion when the Consul General in Military Region IV severely criticized the DAO Weekly Wrap-Up report because it had predicted hostilities in an area where the Embassy's official assessment had forecast no activity. The thrust of the Consul General's objection was that such conflicting reporting only created confusion. His suggestion to resolve the problem was that all future DAO predictions should be cleared with him to insure accuracy. This solution would have eliminated the problem of conflicting assessments, but it would have subjected the conclusions of a trained intelligence analyst to the veto of a foreign service officer. It was not implemented, and DAO intelligence reporting remained independent and uncensored throughout the cease-fire.

Although the single-minded approach of the Martin Embassy caused some bitterness and controversy, I do not believe a different atmosphere would have altered the outcome of the war. A more disturbing matter, it seems to me, was the political impasse in Washington and the defensive mentality in the Saigon Embassy that resulted from this impasse. When an American Ambassador charged with executing his country's policy finds himself caught in a cross fire between the President and Congress, and Congress holds the trump card in the form of appropriations, then the policy process has broken down. One could argue convincingly that South Vietnam was the victim of a constitutional battle between a resurgent Congress and the "Imperial Presidency."

My experiences during the war in Hau Nghia province and as a member of the U.S. mission in Saigon convinced me that we never did well in understanding what military men label "the friendly situation." During the period of the cease-fire and collapse, our understanding of North Vietnamese capabilities and intentions far exceeded our grasp of the South Vietnamese capacity to sustain the battle. Consider, for example, the state of the South Vietnamese body politic by the spring of 1975, as described by South Vietnamese General Cao Van Vien:

> Finally, after many years of continuous war, South Vietnam had edged toward political and economic bankruptcy. National unity no longer existed. No one was able to rally the people behind the national cause, which, because of bad and self-serving leadership, became increasingly dubious. Riddled by corruption, and sometimes ineptitude and dereliction, the government hardly responded to the needs of a public who had gradually lost confidence in it. Despite rosy plans and projects, the national economy continued its course downward and appeared doomed short of a miracle. Under these conditions, the South Vietnamese social fabric gradually disintegrated, influenced in part by mistrust, divisiveness, uncertainty, and defeatism until the whole nation appeared to some to resemble a rotten fruit ready to fall at the first passing breeze.[9]

General Vien's blunt assessment of South Vietnamese society differs substantially from the overly optimistic views held by key members of the U.S. mission during 1974 and 1975. Long after defeatism had infected the ranks of the war-weary South Vietnamese, our senior analysts failed to recognize its symptoms. This was one of the major reasons for the widespread surprise at the "sudden disintegration" of the South Vietnamese military in 1975. *

During the crucial turning point in 1974, the members of the U.S. mission most sensitive to South Vietnamese vulnerabilities tended to be those relatively few people who spoke Vietnamese and who had served as advisors during the war. Of more than sixty American military officers in Saigon, very few spoke any Vietnamese; almost no one was fluent in the language. And the situation in the Embassy was not much better. We had trained thousands of Vietnamese linguists during a decade of involvement in Vietnam, many of whom had served as advisors in the countryside during the war, yet our personnel systems failed to staff the U.S. mission with genuine expertise. Many members of the mission were actually serving their first tour in Vietnam, but they became "experts" by virtue of their positions. Among my acquaintances in Saigon were German linguists, Latin American experts, Indonesian and Arabic specialists, and Chinese linguists. Few members of our mission had the background and qualifications to enable them to understand Vietnam in the way required to serve effectively. (Ambassador Martin himself had never served in Vietnam; Minister Lehmann was likewise a newcomer who had spent much of his career in Europe.) When I conducted a study aimed at reorganizing the DAO intelligence apparatus for General Smith, one of the senior civilians in the intelligence branch admitted that none of his civilian collectors and analysts spoke Vietnamese fluently. "They don't need it," he argued. "We have excellent interpreters." Little wonder that we consistently underestimated the enemy's determination and failed to understand South Vietnamese society as it sought to cope with the corrosive internal effects of the insurgency, the assaults of the North Vietnamese Army, and the damages caused by the "invasion" of a well-intentioned but clumsy American military. We were blinded by a near terminal case of linguistic-cultural myopia that contributed significantly to our difficulties in grasping the nuances of either the friendly or the enemy

---

*In fact, even though the Communists' assessment of South Vietnam society was frequently off the mark, it was more accurate than our own by 1974.

situation. Not surprisingly, the operational concept that flowed from such a blurred perception was no better than its assumptions. In the words of one unidentified pundit, "It was easy to see the light at the end of the tunnel when we were backing into it."

In spite of our many blunders and inadequacies, the insurgency in the south had been crippled by 1972. One of the lessons of Vietnam should be that insurgencies can be defeated, but this truth has been overshadowed by the victory of the North Vietnamese Army in 1975. In fact, even though the Thieu government failed to eliminate many of the grievances that the Vietcong had exploited for years, the pacification program was remarkably effective in restoring security to much of the countryside by the time of the American withdrawal. Ultimately, Hanoi was forced to mount two massive conventional invasions of the south to support the faltering insurgents. Convincing evidence of Vietcong weakness by 1975 was the need to establish North Vietnamese "Military Management Committees" to impose martial law on "liberated" South Vietnam. "Provisional Revolutionary Government" cadre were simply too few in number to manage the government bureaucracy. Hanoi was even forced to call upon former civil servants of the Thieu regime to keep the wheels of government turning. *

Unfortunately for the South Vietnamese, crippling the insurgency did not equate to winning the war—a truth that has been lost on many an armchair strategist. For this reason, it has become fashionable to argue that the war was all but won by 1972. After all, had we not decimated the insurgency in the south, and was not Hanoi on its knees from fierce and effective strategic bombing? Proponents of this theory argue that the United States proceeded to throw away its victory at the confer-

---

*If our Vietnam experience proved that insurgencies can be defeated, it also demonstrated that one does not have the luxury of wasting several years in search of the correct combination for victory. For it is true that the elusive nature of the insurgency denied us the quick victory that the American people require of their military. Since the protracted conflict that resulted ultimately led to our withdrawal and the defeat of the South Vietnamese, my North Vietnamese Communist friends would no doubt argue that the insurgency served its function quite effectively.

ence table in Paris. It is a compelling argument, almost as compelling as the theory that we could have won the war by 1967 if the United States military had been allowed to pursue a strategy of total victory (usually defined as unrestrained bombing, denial of sanctuaries, and an Inchon-like invasion of North Vietnam) unfettered by the politicians. "If only the politicians hadn't meddled!" is the watchword of those who advance this thesis.

Both theories appeal to our national inclination to assume that American ingenuity can handle any task, given sufficient resources and the time to force reality to conform to our notions. Few people doubt that an unrestrained American military could have easily defeated Hanoi, but neither theory addresses how such a military defeat would have somehow convinced the North Vietnamese Communists to abandon their protracted military-political struggle to end foreign influence in Vietnam and reunite its two parts. If we had followed this prescription for victory (even assuming that the Chinese would have stood idly by and permitted us to occupy North Vietnam), what would have been our strategy after establishing a headquarters in Hanoi? How long could the United States have maintained a garrison army on the ground in Indochina? Presumably, we would have made some attempt to create a united, non-Communist Vietnam, but what of the deposed Communists? History suggests that our efforts to establish a viable, free Vietnam would have been inept, and that the Communists would have reacted by repeating the cycle that led to Dien Bien Phu in 1954. Operating initially from sanctuaries in Laos and China, then expanding into the mountains of the Tay Bac region, the insurgency would have renewed its campaign to seize power. Armed with the legacy of Ho Chi Minh, backed by faithful allies, and blessed with favorable terrain, would the Communists have allowed a temporary military defeat to force abandonment of Ho's dream? And, if confronted with a renewed protracted conflict, could the United States have avoided the same kind of domestic discontent that had confronted Mendes France, Lyndon Johnson, and Richard Nixon?

If we have learned anything from our Vietnam experience, we should understand that the application of military power unsupported by adequate political consensus and resolve is insufficient to insure victory. Our military forces cannot operate in a political vacuum, for we are a consensus-oriented society, served rather than dominated by its defense establishment. The violation of this principle can only lead to the worst form of pyrrhic victory—when an army wins virtually every battle only to lose the highly political act that we call war. Thus, when reminded that his army had not defeated the U.S. Army on the battlefield, a North Vietnamese officer aptly replied, "That may be so, but it is also irrelevant." [10]

Notes

PART II

1. Van Tien Dung, "Great Spring Victory," FBIS-APA-76-110, 7 June 1977, Vol. IV, No. 110, Supplement 38, p. 15.
2. Letter dated 19 November 1973. Author's personal papers.
3. Frank Snepp, *Decent Interval* (New York: Random House, 1977), p. 131.

PART III

1. "Restoring Peace in Vietnam," Basic Documents on Ending the War and Restoring Peace in Vietnam, U.S. Information Service, 1975, p. 64.
2. Tom Wolfe, *Mauve Gloves & Madmen, Clutter & Vine* (New York: Farrar Straus and Giroux, 1976), p. 21.
3. *Thong Nhat*, Hanoi, Vietnam, Number 237, 23 March 1974, p. 5.
4. *Ibid.*
5. *Ibid.*
6. *Ibid.*

PART IV

1. Charles J. Timmes, MG, "Vietnam Summary: Military Operations After the Cease-Fire Agreement," *Military Review*, Vol. LVI, No. 8, August 1976, p. 68.

244

2. Dung, pp. 1–2.

3. *Ibid*, p. 5.

4. *Ibid*.

5. Anthony B. Lawson, "Survey of the Economic Situation of RVNAF Personnel, Phase III," report by the DAO Special Studies Section, pp. 2–17.

6. *Ibid*.

7. *Ibid*, p. 7.

8. Dung, p. 3.

9. *Ibid*, p. 7.

10. *Ibid*.

11. *Ibid*.

12. *Ibid*, p. 6.

13. *Ibid*, p. 5.

14. Henry Kissinger, *White House Years* (Boston, Toronto: Little, Brown & Company, 1979), p. 1462. It is also worthy of note that the Nixon promise was reiterated in writing by President Ford shortly after the Nixon resignation.

15. Dung, p. 5.

16. *Ibid*, p. 3.

17. *Ibid*.

18. Lawson, p. 17.

19. Quoted in "Vietnam: From Cease-Fire to Capitulation," by Col. William E. LeGro, U.S. Government Printing Office, 1981, p. 128.

20. *New York Times*, August 9, 1974, p. 26.

21. Quoted from a letter dated October 18, 1979, from MG Murray to author.

22. *Chicago Daily News*, August 9, 1974, p. 26.

23. Dung, p. 3.

PART V

1. LeGro, p. 207.

2. Cao Van Vien, "The Final Collapse," unpublished manuscript to

be published by the U.S. Army Center for Military History, p. 68. Quoted with permission.

3. "History, U.S. Delegation, Four-Party Joint Military Team: 31 March 1973 to 30 April 1975," p. 17.

4. Much of the account of the congressional delegation's encounter with the Communists is taken from a report submitted by the author to the Embassy on 4 March 1975.

5. "South Vietnam, The Struggle," March 17, 1975, p. 6.

6. Vien, p. 88.

7. *Ibid*, p. 89.

8. LeGro, p. 222.

9. *Ibid*.

10. *Ibid*, p. 224.

11. Dung, p. 10.

12. LeGro, p. 217.

13. *Ibid*, p. 224.

14. *Ibid*.

15. Dung, pp. 62–63.

16. MG Homer D. Smith, "The Final Forty-Five Days of Vietnam," an unpublished paper, p. 10. Used with MG Smith's permission.

17. *Stars and Stripes*, 4 April 1975, p. 1.

18. Interview (telephonic) between author and Mr. Lawson, 14 January 1980.

19. *Saigon Post*, March 22, 1975, p. 1.

20. FBIS, 200424Z, April 1975, p. 3.

21. *Saigon Post*, April 3, 1975, p. 3.

PART VI

1. FBIS, 200825Z, April 1975, pp. 1–3.

2. *Ibid*, 191546Z, April 1975, p. 2.

3. *Ibid*, 190936Z, April 1975, p. 2.

4. *Ibid*, 210414Z, April 1975, p. 2.

5. *Saigon Post*, April 21, 1975, p. 1.

6. FBIS, 031400Z, April 1975, p. 3.

7. *Ibid*, 211220Z, April 1975, p. 3.

8. *Ibid*, 211400Z, April 1975, p. 1.

9. Dung, Vol. II, p. 76.

10. *Ibid*, p. 77.

11. Four-Party Joint Military Team, Memorandum for Record, 27 April 1975, "Saigon-Hanoi Liaison Flight, 25 April 1975," pp. 2–4.

12. Vien, p. 200.

PART VII

1. Letter from MG Smith to author, dated 21 January 1980.

2. "Last Flight from Saigon," LTCs Thomas G. Tobin, Arthur E. Laehr, and John F. Hilgenberg, USAF, USAF Southeast Asia Monograph Series, Vol. IV, Monograph 6, p. 106.

3. Kissinger, pp. 1412–13.

4. *Ibid*, p. 1470.

5. John Erlichman, *Witness to Power* (New York: Simon & Schuster), p. 316.

6. "The Economist," December 28, 1975, p. 11.

7. From a letter to the author from a former South Vietnamese lieutenant colonel who prefers to remain anonymous.

8. "The Economist," p. 11.

9. Vien, p. 205.

10. Harry G. Summers, Jr., *On Strategy: A Critical Analysis of the Vietnam War* (Novato, CA: Presidio Press, 1982).

Index